The

Coupon Mom's Guide

to Cutting Your

Grocery Bills in Half

The
Coupon Mom's Guide
to Cutting Your
Grocery Bills in Half

*The Strategic Shopping Method Proven
to Slash Food and Drugstore Costs*

STEPHANIE NELSON

Founder, CouponMom.com

AVERY
a member of Penguin Group (USA) Inc.
New York

Published by the Penguin Group
Penguin Group (USA) Inc., 375 Hudson Street, New York,
New York 10014, USA • Penguin Group (Canada), 90 Eglinton Avenue East, Suite 700,
Toronto, Ontario M4P 2Y3, Canada (a division of Pearson Penguin Canada Inc.) •
Penguin Books Ltd, 80 Strand, London WC2R 0RL, England • Penguin Ireland,
25 St Stephen's Green, Dublin 2, Ireland (a division of Penguin Books Ltd) •
Penguin Group (Australia), 250 Camberwell Road, Camberwell, Victoria 3124,
Australia (a division of Pearson Australia Group Pty Ltd) • Penguin Books India Pvt Ltd,
11 Community Centre, Panchsheel Park, New Delhi–110 017, India •
Penguin Group (NZ), 67 Apollo Drive, Rosedale, North Shore 0632, New Zealand
(a division of Pearson New Zealand Ltd) • Penguin Books (South Africa) (Pty) Ltd,
24 Sturdee Avenue, Rosebank, Johannesburg 2196, South Africa •

Penguin Books Ltd, Registered Offices: 80 Strand, London WC2R 0RL, England

Most Avery books are available at special quantity discounts for bulk purchase for sales promotions,
premiums, fund-raising, and educational needs. Special books or book excerpts also can be created to fit
specific needs. For details, write Penguin Group (USA) Inc. Special Markets, 375 Hudson Street,
New York, NY 10014.

Library of Congress Cataloging-in-Publication Data

Nelson, Stephanie, date.
The coupon mom's guide to cutting your grocery bills in half : the strategic shopping method proven to
slash food and drugstore costs / Stephanie Nelson.
p.   cm.
Includes index.
ISBN 978-1-58333-368-6
1. Grocery shopping.   I. Title.
TX356.N44   2009   2009040687
640.73—dc22

Printed in the United States of America
3   5   7   9   10   8   6   4   2

BOOK DESIGN BY AMANDA DEWEY

The recipes contained in this book are intended to be a helpful resource and we hope you like them. The author and publisher are not responsible for your specific health or allergy needs that may require medical supervision. The author and publisher are not responsible for any adverse reactions to the recipes contained in this book.

This publication is designed to provide accurate and authoritative information in regard to the subject matter covered. It is sold with the understanding that the publisher is not engaged in rendering legal, accounting, or other professional services. If you require legal advice or other expert assistance, you should seek the services of a competent professional.

While the author has made every effort to provide accurate telephone numbers and Internet addresses at the time of publication, neither the publisher nor the author assumes any responsibility for errors, or for changes that occur after publication. Further, the publisher does not have any control over and does not assume any responsibility for author or third-party websites or their content.

To my mother, for her constant encouragement, and to my father,
for giving me the frugality gene in the first place

Contents

Introduction

I never meant to become the Coupon Mom. I certainly never dreamed I'd have a website with two million members.

My intention was to feed my family for less money, and to help families less fortunate than ours.

After graduating from college with a major in finance, I worked for ten years in sales and marketing for Procter & Gamble and the Marriott hotel chain. In 1995, my husband and I made the decision to downsize our lifestyle so that I could stay home with our boys, a two-year-old and a new baby. My quitting the corporate world meant our income would be cut in half, so I knew I was actually taking on two new roles: stay-at-home mom and CEO of our family budget. To get by on one income, our dollars had to work harder than ever. As we examined our household spending to cut costs across the board, I noticed that grocery bills represented a big chunk of our overall budget. I figured that cutting what we spent on groceries would have a significant impact and would give us a good bit of financial wiggle room. I was right!

By cruising the grocery-store aisles with a clipboard to record prices, I learned how sales cycles work and when to buy. I diligently scanned store circulars and clipped newspaper coupons to plan meals around deals. My freezer and my pantry became two of my closest friends, since they allowed me to load up when prices dropped, keeping our food costs constant.

As we all got more Web-savvy, saving money on groceries became easier than ever. Printable coupons, electronic coupons, downloadable discounts to store loyalty cards, and deals on stores' and manufacturers' websites all presented more ways to save. My strategies allowed me to not only cut back dramatically on my own family's grocery bills, but also to give back to the less fortunate through a program I called Cut Out Hunger.

Once I mastered the ways of combining sales, coupons, promotions, and rebates, I was able to buy many items for pennies, sometimes for nothing. That translated into donations for our local food bank, and a wonderful lesson for our children.

This was all too good not to share with others, so I started spreading the word through seminars and media appearances. We launched CouponMom .com in 2001 to give shoppers one easy place on the Web to learn Strategic Shopping methods, search for deals, and share success stories and advice with others. The site has also gotten a lot of media attention, and I've appeared on both *Today* and *The Oprah Winfrey Show*, sharing what I've learned with as many people as I can. Nothing makes me more excited than showing others how to get a jar of pasta sauce for free by combining sales and coupons. Or, more important, helping families significantly slash their grocery bills over time. On the website, a community has developed, and we all have a good time helping one another reach our savings goals.

Trying economic times mean that many people who in the past never gave a thought to how much money they spent suddenly need to get serious about saving. It means many families who were living on the financial edge are struggling more than ever and need the help of those who are able to give.

This book is written for every shopper who wants to save, or give, or both. I'll show you the power of planning, and how adopting simple strategies can make the most of your time and money. I'll share budget-friendly recipes your family will love, and we'll hear some inspiring stories from CouponMom.com members who are making a difference in their families— and in their communities, by adopting the Cut Out Hunger program to fit the needs of people in their areas. I'll talk about the various types of shopping styles and how my plan can be customized for any lifestyle, so that everyone can benefit. Everyone, from the rushed single professional who has barely 5 minutes to eat, much less to plan shopping trips, to the dedicated deal seeker who treats the grocery store like a big-game hunter treats a safari, can save with the strategies this book teaches.

Our kids are now thirteen and sixteen, and we have treasured the years I have been able to spend at home with them. The Strategic Shopping methods I teach in this book helped make it possible. Our grocery spending is half of what it once was. We eat budget-friendly meals and, above all else, plan our trips to the supermarket carefully.

I hope you'll have fun reading through this book while you're learning. I hope that you'll find ways to save money starting today, and that by the end of the year you will be simply astounded at how much money you are saving. And I hope that the information we review in these pages ultimately makes your dinner table a more pleasant place where you can have a little less worry and just enjoy wonderful mealtimes together.

One

Strategic Shopping

Myth: Saving money on groceries means eating the same boring meals every day of the week.

Myth: Saving money on groceries means spending half your life shopping to find good prices.

Myth: Saving money on groceries means serving your family nothing but processed junk, since that's the cheapest way to put food on the table.

Fact: Wrong, wrong, wrong!

I've been spreading the bargain-shopping gospel for more than a decade now, and I've run into these misconceptions time and again. In this chapter we're going to discuss:

- how to turn your grocery store into a paradise of great buys with a concept I call Strategic Shopping
- the principles of Strategic Shopping and how they can help you save, no matter your "shopping personality"
- numbers that illustrate how it literally pays to apply Strategic Shopping methods at the market

What Is Strategic Shopping?

The most effective diets aren't the ones that force you to eat entirely new foods or to eat just one thing over and over. They're the ones that teach you to improve your eating habits for the long term. Let's put your grocery budget on an effective, long-term diet. Strategic Shopping is not about changing the way you eat. It is about changing the way you buy the food that you like. You can have your cake and eat it, too—as long as you use a coupon and wait for it to go on sale!

Strategic Shopping does not require you to lower your food quality standards, give up your preferences, or take hours a week to plan and shop. The goal is just the opposite. My plan helps you create customized shopping approaches that save time and allow you to serve your family tasty and healthy meals—all while cutting your grocery bill in half.

It can take time to shop strategically, but the Coupon Mom program along with the CouponMom.com website saves you time by finding the best grocery deals at both local and national stores. Our team of researchers conducts price comparisons, and that information is entered regularly into the price database, allowing you to quickly find the best deal. The coupon database alerts you to additional savings opportunities. Using the Coupon Mom No-Clip System means you simply need to save the circulars each week, then check the website to know exactly which circular to pull. Finally, the Coupon Mom Forum offers tons of great strategies from members all over the country.

Once Inspired, She Now Inspires Others

"In September 2008, I was shopping at Kroger and the lady in front of me was checking out and saved a boatload of money. I still remember her saying, 'I just love watching all the totals come down every time.' It got me thinking, if she can do it, why couldn't I? I just got fed up with spending a lot every

week and not really getting that much. It felt like I was just opening my purse and saying, 'Here, take it all!' I went home and Googled coupons and stumbled upon CouponMom.com. I am now totally addicted to the site. I think by far the most valuable asset to Coupon Mom is the Forum. The experts there answer any of your 'newbie' questions, and shoppers post the findings and deals they've gotten.

I feel like I haven't mastered the art of couponing, but I have seen a lot of good results so far. I have had people behind me in line make comments about how much I saved. I even had a lady come out in the parking lot once and say, 'I don't mean to be nosy, but I was just curious how much you saved, after seeing you hand over a pile of coupons to the clerk.' I also noticed a lot of curious glances at my binder in my shopping cart. I almost always have someone make a comment about how 'organized' I seem to be with my shopping. I have been spreading the word to those around me about tidbits of information on how to save. And yes, it is very exhilarating to see your total bills go down to a quarter—or even half—of what they were!"

—*Melissa Everidge, Dayton, Ohio*

The Principles of Strategic Shopping

Once you grasp these three basic ideas, it quickly becomes easy for you to start saving thousands of dollars a year on groceries. They are:

1. **Know your prices:** Try this little experiment. Close your eyes, reach into your pantry, and pull out the first item you touch. Now ask yourself how much that item costs. Maybe you have a general idea, within a few cents. But maybe you have no idea how much it costs—you simply toss it into your cart week after week without even giving its price tag a glance. If this is the case, you have a serious savings opportunity staring you in the face! Become familiar with the price ranges for the items you buy most regularly. This knowledge helps you recognize a deal when the item is discounted, or when you

have a coupon. This book will teach you to research prices, and will provide many price comparisons. Over time you'll learn when a deal is really a deal, and how to plan purchases for when items are on sale and you have coupons. In other words, how to think strategically!

2. **Know your store savings programs:** You might be walking past savings opportunities every time you hit the grocery store, without even knowing it. I'm here to help you fix that! Each store has its own savings programs and policies, but not all are proactive about cluing shoppers in. It's up to you to educate yourself about stores' savings programs and policies. I'll teach you the right questions to ask to learn what your stores' programs are, and how they can save you money. We'll also review the savings programs offered by a number of national and regional stores, and how you can use them to your best advantage.

3. **Know your coupons:** The grocery-store coupons in your kitchen drawer right now are either like cash or confetti. Use them wisely and they're essentially legal currency. Lose them, forget they're there until they expire, or accidentally trash them and they're just slips of paper. I'll teach you where to find the most coupons, including electronic and printable coupons that even the busiest shopper can use. I'll show you how the Coupon Mom system can save you time by pointing you directly to the coupon you need for any given shopping trip. Together, we'll have a serious impact on your grocery bill without costing you a lot of time. Even if you have just 15 minutes per week, I'll show you how to whittle down your grocery bill.

The Strategic Shopping Action Plan

You'll need to adopt some new habits in order to become a Strategic Shopper. These simple but powerful methods are easy to work into your shopping plan and will yield tremendous savings over time.

Stock up on savings: An item you buy each week goes on sale. The store adds to the discounting possibilities by running a promotion, perhaps offering greater savings if you buy three or more. And you will save even more if you have coupons for the item. To the Strategic Shopper, this is like New Year's Eve and the Fourth of July rolled into one! Don't light any firecrackers, but do celebrate by stocking up when these off-price opportunities combine for ultimate savings. If you stock up when prices are at their lowest, you keep your costs consistent. Even after prices return to normal, you'll be able to "shop your freezer" and continue to enjoy items bought at the sale price. Once this becomes a habit, you'll wince at the very notion of paying full price.

Plan to save: Success doesn't just happen in life, and savings success doesn't just happen at the grocery store. The single most crucial component to cutting your grocery spending is planning ahead. An organized shopping list, combined with careful meal planning, can take between 5 minutes and an hour to create, and your savings will reflect the effort you put into planning. Chapter 4 gives details for effective shopping planning, with tips on strategies for every lifestyle.

Any Shopping Personality Can Save

Shoppers' personalities, like personalities in general, vary dramatically, but Strategic Shopping fits anyone's lifestyle. There are three types of shoppers—Busy, Rookie, and Varsity. Busy Shoppers have very hectic lifestyles with very little time to plan or shop. Rookie Shoppers are interested in learning new ways to save but may be unfamiliar with the Strategic Shopping concept. Varsity Shoppers walk into the grocery store like a boxer entering the ring and love the thrill of the bargain hunt. This shopper doesn't mind spending the time to plan a shopping trip down to the last grain of salt, and doesn't hesitate to visit several stores to find the best deals on all needed items.

What do all three types have in common? They all stand to save money by putting Strategic Shopping to use! This book provides tips geared toward all shopping styles, to help make the most of anyone's time in the grocery store. For example:

If you are a Busy Shopper, you may not have time to plan before going to the store, so this book will teach you how to plan your shopping trip in less than 5 minutes after arriving at the store to save 20 to 25 percent off the full price of groceries. I'll also share simple strategies for getting the most value out of your food dollar when buying meat, chicken, fish, produce, dairy products, and more. For example, simply weighing a few heads of lettuce to determine the largest one results in 25 percent more lettuce, since lettuce is usually sold by the head rather than by weight. Another example: If you check the meat markdown bins for same-day meal options, you can save 50 percent or more. In-store savings strategies do not require extra planning or shopping time but can have a major impact on your overall grocery spending. And simple strategies, such as being flexible about which brands you buy, can cut your grocery spending without any planning at all.

If you are a Rookie Shopper, you are willing and able to spend a bit more time planning. I will show you how 30 minutes of planning can result in savings of 40 to 50 percent, if you plan meals around each week's store bargains. I'll teach you how to combine store savings programs with the different types of coupons to pay the lowest price for your groceries. You'll learn how to use the Coupon Mom system for your preferred store to point you quickly to the best prices, and how to spend a little time checking various stores' sales before leaving home to weigh various sources for finding the best deals.

If you are a Varsity Shopper, you are not kidding around. You're here to save, and save big. You are willing to spend an hour or more each week to map out shopping strategies, or to scour multiple stores for the best prices. In return, you can expect to pay 60 to 70 percent off full price.

Here's a look at how each of our three shoppers might fare at the grocery store by putting Strategic Shopping methods into practice. Let's say a store is offering a weekly promotion giving shoppers a free gallon of milk with the purchase of three boxes of Brand X cereal when they use their store loyalty card.

The Busy Shopper learns to check the store's ad upon arriving at the store to discover the featured sale items that would be cost-effective menu items. Naturally, the Busy Shopper notices the front page advertising the cereal promotion. This shopper might have been planning to buy milk and two boxes of a different cereal, but since he or she is flexible about brands and willing to buy more than is needed that week, buying the featured cereal turns out to be smart savings strategy. Scanning the ad translates into savings.

Our Busy Shopper has also learned to look for in-store coupons displayed in aisles, in shelf boxes, or on product packages, and grabs a $1 off coupon for Brand X cereal on a display, adding to the savings. This shopping success story took very little planning, just a careful eye and flexibility.

Full price of Brand X cereal: $4 per box
Sale price of Brand X cereal: $2 per box
Price of one gallon of milk: $3.75
Price of store loyalty card: Free

If the Busy Shopper had purchased only two boxes of sale-priced cereal and the gallon of milk, the cost would have been $7.75. By using the promotion and coupon she brings the cost down to $5 for three boxes of cereal and the gallon of milk after using the $1 coupon and her store loyalty card. A few simple strategies netted $15.75 worth of groceries for only $5 with a few simple steps, an overall savings of $10.75.

BUSY SHOPPER SAVINGS

full price of 3 boxes cereal and milk	$15.75
sale savings on cereal—3 boxes	-$6.00
free gallon milk	-$3.75
coupon savings	-$1.00
total cost	$5.00
total savings	**$10.75**

The Rookie Shopper has learned to spend 30 minutes a week creating a Strategic Shopping plan before leaving home, reviewing store ads and creating a list of meals for the week using sale items. This shopper might prefer a different store but chooses to shop at the store offering the Brand X cereal promotion. Because the Rookie Shopper has taken the time to ask about coupon policies at various stores, he or she knows that more than one box of Brand X cereal can be purchased on sale, and thus searches for multiple coupon sources. Clipping a newspaper coupon, printing another from a website, and downloading an e-coupon to that store's shopper loyalty card means the coupon savings triple when you have three coupons to buy three of the same item at a bargain price All this planning pays off, and the Rookie Shopper spends a total of $3 for the three boxes of cereal and the gallon of milk, a savings of $12.75.

ROOKIE SHOPPER SAVINGS

full price of 3 boxes cereal and milk	$15.75
sale savings on cereal–3 boxes	-$6.00
free gallon milk	-$3.75
printable coupon	-$1.00
electronic coupon	-$1.00
newspaper coupon	-$1.00
total cost	$3.00
total savings	**$12.75**

The Varsity Shopper is always planning for the next great deal. The Brand X cereal-and-milk promotion is an invitation to launch a serious savings attack. The promotion's fine print indicates that each shopper can take advantage of two deals per transaction, meaning any one shopper can buy six boxes of cereal and get two free gallons of milk. Our Varsity Shopper trades coupons with friends and has four newspaper coupons as well as the printable and electronic coupons that the Rookie Shopper used. The Varsity Shopper subscribes to the Brand X e-mail newsletter, which alerts users to an incredible deal: Buy six boxes of Brand X and fill out a printable form on the Brand X website for a $5 mail-in rebate. By combining sale prices, store promotions, multiple coupons, and the printable mail-in rebate, the Varsity Shopper purchases six boxes of cereal and two gallons of milk for only $1—plus the cost of a stamp to mail in the rebate!

VARSITY SHOPPER SAVINGS

full price of 6 boxes cereal and 2 gallons milk	$31.50
free milk—2 gallons	-$7.50
sale savings on cereal—6 boxes	-$12.00
printable coupon	-$1.00
electronic coupon	-$1.00
newspaper coupons (4)	-$4.00
total cost at register	$6.00
mail-in rebate refund	-$5.00
net cost after sale, coupons, and rebate	$1.00
total savings	**$30.50**

A Final Word

The quiz in the next chapter will help determine your shopping personality, and throughout the book I'll make recommendations that will fit the various shopping styles. As you put your own plan into practice, you may find that you are willing and able to progress to the next level of shopping strategy to save even more. When you approach Strategic Shopping based on your preferences, time constraints, and shopping personality, you are much more likely to be successful in the long term and to save money consistently as you develop new savings habits. All types of shoppers can save, and I'm here to help everyone do it!

Two

What Kind of Shopper Are You?

We're all different, and our shopping styles are all different. Who you are as a shopper can have a big impact on how much you spend. But don't get discouraged if you don't seem to have bargain-hunting DNA. No matter which shopping personality type best describes you, everyone can save money at the grocery store by putting Strategic Shopping to work. In this chapter we're going to discuss:

- the different types of shopper personalities
- a fun quiz to help you figure out your shopping style
- strategies for saving, no matter what your supermarket personality is!

The Science of Savings

When we hear the phrase "Nielsen ratings," we often think of television shows, since research conducted by this global firm often dictates which shows will make it. But the company, founded in the 1920s, performs a vast array of market research, including what makes shoppers tick. A Nielsen study of shopper behavior, which reviewed consumers' shopping behavior across thirty different food categories, defined four specific distinct shopping "identities." Many of us likely have multiple supermarket personalities, adopting several different modes of shopping during a single trip to the supermarket, depending on the items we're purchasing.

Here are the four shopping personality categories. I bet you'll start to recognize yourself as you read through them!

Auto-pilot: You can set your clock by this shopper's weekly trip to the grocery store. He or she makes purchase decisions largely based on habit and is not interested in trying new products. This shopper's style is "grab and go." Typical products purchased in auto-pilot mode include mayonnaise, margarine, nuts, coffee, hot cereal, bottled water, carbonated soft drinks, coffee, popcorn, and cold cuts.

Variety-seeking: This shopper likes to browse in search of new products, often tossing things like chewing gum, breakfast bars, frozen snacks, cold cereal, frozen entrées, cookies, and salad dressing into the cart. He or she tends to get bored by buying the same things each week, so is always on the lookout for new options and surprises in these product lines.

Buzz: This guy or gal is the advertiser's dream shopper, since he or she is heavily influenced by marketing and new product introductions. True to their nickname, they are open to "buzz" and respond to engaging advertising. Typical products for buzz shoppers include ready-to-drink tea, smoothies, yogurt drinks, sports drinks, energy drinks, and chocolate. Marketers know they can reel in buzz shoppers by introducing "new and improved" varieties, new packaging, or catchy ads.

Bargain-hunting: This shopper is going to stretch a dollar until George Washington cries out in pain. He or she plans a trip to the market like NASA plans a trip to the moon: with careful analysis and precision. This shopper is on a mission to save and is driven by deals, promotions, and comparing prices. Bargain-hunting products include canned tuna, canned tomatoes, canned fruit, and pasta sauce.

The study did not include the average weekly grocery bill or the general health and nutrition of each kind of shopper, but it's not hard to guess. I'd be willing to bet that the auto-pilot, variety-seeking, and buzz shoppers have higher bills than the bargain-hunting shopper. Because you are reading this book, I will assume that no matter who you are when it comes to shopper identity, you're interested in becoming more of a bargain hunter.

If the first three categories describe you more accurately, don't worry! We're going to talk about how to wake up your inner auto-pilot so you don't roll past bargains, train your inner variety seeker to move quickly in search of savings, and tame your inner buzz gene so that you're guided by savings and nutrition rather than catchy advertising. But it's going to take some effort on your part. I once worked with a woman who asked for my help in trimming her grocery store bill. As a proud bargain hunter, I was happy to share strategies, such as making a detailed shopping plan and shopping as quickly as possible. But although I spent a few hours reviewing Strategic Shopping with my new friend, it was clear that her buzz and variety-seeking traits were going to make my job difficult.

Jennifer went through the aisles very slowly, looking up and down for products that caught her eye, even when they weren't on her carefully planned list. She liked trying new things, so she chose many new items each time she went to the store. Most of these were junk food and snacks, and in fact these unplanned extras ended up comprising more than 25 percent of her bill. Buying these products was fun for her, but she was wasting loads of money and her shopping trip took twice as long as mine did. Though she had a grocery list, snacks and new treats seemed to jump into her cart!

Shopping with my Strategic Shopping methods can be still be fun, because as I think most of us would agree, it's a lot of fun to save money. But they make trips to the store a more targeted mission. By applying smarter strategies, Jennifer could easily pare down her grocery spending, pocket the extra cash, and save it for an activity the whole family could enjoy. That's *my* idea of fun!

Turning Strategic Shopping into a Family Affair

"I have been using coupons since I became a stay-at-home mom eight years ago. My girls are eight, six, four, and two. It started out with simply asking the companies for any extras and signing up for their e-mails and newsletters. Then I found CouponMom.com several years ago. I treat this as my job to see how much I can save my family.

My sister and I use a buddy system even though she is 60 miles away. We call each other and go over our lists for the week to make sure we haven't missed anything. We also buy each other items if our stores are out of them or if we find something on clearance. Plus, we get to brag to each other about our finds. It is so great to have a buddy!

My kids donate extra birthday and Christmas presents to Toys for Tots each year. I contribute to food drives in my community, and I have donated to individual families in need. I have been known to print out lists of coupon websites I use for friends and family, especially those with new babies. I have been to a few coupon parties that my sister has given in her own home. My friends and my children call me the Coupon Queen!"

—Amy Moon, Conyers, Georgia

Saving Can Still Be Fun

Even die-hard variety-seeking or buzz shoppers can save money, if they apply some deliberate measures to their trips to the store. Try letting corporate marketing campaigns work for you, rather than the other way around. When companies trot out new products, they often flood consumers with coupons, promotions, and special prices in order to start building an audience for those products. Make these great introductory deals a part of your shopping plan—but have the discipline to remove items from your list once the bargain rates come to an end.

Turn Off the "Auto-Pilot" to Save

I once went shopping with a typical auto-pilot shopper, a busy single professional who needed to shop as quickly as possible and not spend a lot of time shopping. We met at the grocery store with identical lists and set off to compare results. At the end of our trip, having bought the same items, she had spent $250 and I had spent just $75! The difference was our shopping strategies. I had done my homework and had reviewed the store's sales circular ahead of time to learn which items were on sale. Additionally, my well-organized coupons allowed me to match sale items with coupons, to lower my bill even more. My auto-pilot friend opted mostly for her favorite name brands and grabbed whatever items usually stocked her pantry. She hadn't taken the time to scan the sales flier or clip coupons, and she bought only items she was familiar with, since she generally bought the same list week after week. All those decisions ended up costing her money. Planning ahead may seem time-consuming, but you get real savings as your reward.

What's Your Shopper IQ?

In addition to the Nielsen study's shopping categories, I find that many people are Busy, Rookie, or Varsity Shoppers. Before we begin cutting your grocery bill, let's figure out your shopping style so that I can help you create the savings shopping plan that will work for you and your family. Choose the answer that best fits you, and tally the points at the end.

1. Do you enjoy grocery shopping?
   A. I'd almost rather starve.
   B. It's not my favorite thing, but it's not the worst chore in the world.
   C. I look forward to it!

2. Do you make a list before you shop?
   A. Never. I just grab whatever seems appealing and not too expensive, and hope for the best.
   B. When I have time.
   C. Of course! Shopping without a list is like taking a trip with no map!

3. Do you stick to your list when you shop?
   A. I've usually lost it before I get into the store.
   B. I use it as a guide but feel free to grab a few other things as well.
   C. The list must be obeyed.

4. Do you always buy the same brands?

   A. Always.

   B. Mostly, but I've been known to choose private labels on occasion.

   C. Brands mean nothing to me. If it's cheap, on sale, or I have a coupon, it's in my cart.

5. Where do you shop the most often?

   A. At the store closest to my house.

   B. At the cheapest place I know of.

   C. I'll hit three, four, even five places if I have to, to score the best bargains.

6. How often do you grocery shop?

   A. When it's either that or feed the kids frosting for dinner.

   B. Once or twice a week.

   C. So often that other shoppers ask me where stuff is.

7. Do you use your store's discount card?

   A. I used it to scrape ice off my windshield last winter. Haven't seen it since.

   B. If I have it with me. But if I've changed purses recently, all bets are off.

   C. Are you kidding? I'd have the card's bar code tattooed onto my forearm if I could.

8. Do you use grocery coupons?

   A. That's way too much trouble for someone as busy as me.

   B. If I remember them, which is maybe half the time.

   C. No coupons, no groceries.

9. Do you print grocery coupons?

   A. How do you do that?

   B. I tried it once, but it seemed like a lot of trouble.

   C. Always.

10. Do you use electronic coupons?

    A. What are they for, buying robots at a discount?

    B. Once or twice, but it took too much time.

    C. Always—click or snip, it's all good!

11. Do you belong to Upromise?

    A. Upromise to tell me what that is sometime?

    B. I think I joined once and then forgot to ever log on again.

    C. I check Upromise like my kids check their Facebook accounts.

12. Have you ever purchased grocery items free with coupons?

    A. Is that like a "five-finger discount"? Of course not!

    B. Once in a while.

    C. Why do you think I was high-fiving every other shopper in line the other day?

13. Do you ever shop at the drugstore?

    A. Never. Way too expensive.

    B. When I'm getting prescriptions filled, I'll grab a few necessities even though the prices do seem higher.

    C. Yes! I get drugstore bargains at least once a month.

14. Do you take your grocery coupons with you on vacation?

    A. Please. I'm lucky if I remember my sunscreen.

    B. No, but I shop the sales at the grocery store.

    C. For me using coupons *is* a vacation! So I wouldn't dream of leaving them at home!

To calculate your score, give yourself one point for every A answer, two points for B answers, and three points for C answers.

If you scored between 14 and 21, you are a Busy Shopper. You are juggling a lot and have barely enough time to get to the store, much less chart a course for everything you'll do once you get there. This book will teach you how to plan your shopping trip in less than 5 minutes, helping you save 20 to 25 percent off full-price groceries as a result. We'll also teach simple strategies for getting the most value out of your food dollar when buying meat, chicken, fish, produce, dairy products, and more. Simple in-store savings strategies do not require extra planning or shopping time but can have a major impact on overall grocery spending.

If you scored between 22 and 36, you are a Rookie Shopper. You're interested in savings strategies but want to get better. Rookie Shoppers who will spend 30 minutes planning a trip to the grocery store can wind up saving 40 to 50 percent. We'll also teach you how to plan your meals around each week's bargains, and how to combine store savings programs with all types of coupons to pay the lowest price for your groceries. You can use the Coupon Mom system for your preferred store to save time in finding the best deals each week.

If you scored 37 or higher, you are a Varsity Shopper. You're already familiar with store sales and coupons, and you don't mind spending an hour to plan your shopping for the week. This longer prep time can result in your grocery bill being chopped by 60 to 70 percent. Since you're pretty good at getting good deals at your supermarket, we'll teach you to consider shopping in drugstores, discount stores, and alternative grocery stores, where you will cherry-pick the best bargains. The Coupon Mom system makes it easy to search the store deals without leaving your home, and with a master plan at the beginning of the week, you'll learn to add stops to several stores so you're able to take advantage of bargains without making extra trips.

A Final Word

There's one thing that Busy, Rookie, and Varsity Shoppers all have in common. They all have the potential to get more out of their grocery dollars. Strategic Shopping methods can be applied to anyone's lifestyle, whether you're a dedicated coupon clipper feeding a large family or an on-the-go professional cooking for one or two most nights, with little time to shop. The longer you put Strategic Shopping to use, the better you'll get at it, and the more you'll save!

Three

Think Like a Saver:
The Strategic Shopping Mentality

Some people hate grocery shopping and treat it like a chore they must endure. Others love going to the supermarket and enjoy running into friends and discovering great new products. I view grocery shopping as a mission. My goal is to feed my family the healthiest, tastiest meals possible while spending the least amount of money. What's most important to understand about Strategic Shopping is that the system isn't just about the amount you spend—it also teaches you how to use the items you buy to get the most value for your grocery dollar.

In this chapter we're going to discuss:

- creating a budget and clear goals and then tracking your spending
- tips to avoid spending more than you intend to at the grocery store
- ways to maximize your food dollar at home and on the road, so you don't unwittingly sabotage your own Strategic Shopping!

The mantra of Strategic Shopping is simple: "Saving money on groceries isn't about changing the way you eat; it is about changing the way you buy the food that you like." To live by these words, you need to combine smart shopping and smart food management. Low prices are only half the secret to cutting your grocery bill in half. The other half is preparing, storing, and cooking foods in ways that wring the most savings out of items you place in the cart each week.

These eight steps will get you started:

1. **Plan a grocery budget:** If there were ever a more detested word in the English language than "diet," it would have to be "budget." I don't like the B-word any more than you do, but this is a vital first step. Knowing exactly how much you can afford to spend keeps you on track from the beginning and forces you to think strategically. Shoppers without a budget can fall into the "savings game" trap and undermine their own efforts. For example, if your goal is to achieve the highest percentage savings on your groceries, paying $1 for a sale-priced rice mix to save 50 percent makes sense. But if you are thinking strategically, with a budget in mind, your goal is to get the most food for your dollar. In that case, spending the same $1 on a full-priced bag of plain rice that has twice as many servings makes more sense. Setting a dollar amount rather than a savings percentage as your goal helps you to "buy smart."

2. **Set measurable goals:** How many New Year's dieters give up by Valentine's Day? The reason so many people bag their resolutions is that they fail to set measurable goals. Resolving to lose half a pound a week with sensible food choices and exercise is a lot less exciting than declaring a goal of losing 100 pounds, "even if I have to starve myself." Putting your grocery budget on a diet works much the same way. If your goal is to cut your $700-a-month grocery bill down to $500 a month, break it down and set a limit of $115 each week. Even small steps can start showing a difference immediately, keeping you motivated. Keep track of what you spend by saving your receipts so you can chart your progress. I save grocery receipts in an envelope that's posted on the

refrigerator. (If other family members go to the grocery store, they know where to put the receipt!) I keep a running total of the amount spent on the outside of the envelope, making it easy to track our spending throughout the month. At the end of the month I total the receipts and feel a sense of accomplishment when I've met my goal.

3. **Spend cash to stay on budget:** Nothing will enforce a strict budget like paying only with cash. When the dollars are gone, you're done! For a television feature last year, I went on a shopping trip to prove that you can feed a family of five a healthy diet, including three meals a day and snacks, on $100 per week. I was given $100 cash in an envelope. I stretched that $100 with sales and coupons, and kept a running total of my purchases with a calculator as I shopped to make sure I stayed within my budget. When I got to the register the total rang up to $103. A challenge is a challenge, so I removed the least essential item to stay in budget. As it turns out, I *had* stayed within my budget, but a computer error caused an accidental overcharge. Because I always review my receipts, the mistake jumped out at me and I promptly requested a refund. Although the point of the television feature was to teach viewers how to save, I learned an important lesson myself that day. Keeping a firm budget and using an all-cash approach allows no wiggle room, and carefully going over receipts sometimes turns up costly errors. Applying that level of diligence along with Strategic Shopping skills will allow you to bring home the healthiest, most practical food items for your family while spending less money to do so. Does this take longer than simply popping into the store and grabbing whatever seems appealing? Of course it does. But if the result is saving hundreds, even thousands, of dollars a year, isn't it worth your time?

4. Don't let your food dollars go to waste: According to USDA studies, 10 to 40 percent of a family's grocery spending is

Patience Is a Strategic Shopping Virtue

"I've been saving since I had a regular job at fifteen. My parents always taught me to put some of my weekly pay away into a savings account, never have any credit-card debt, either save for items or pay for them with cash, and to go to the sale rack first. But I thought coupons were a waste of time and energy.

I will admit to being frustrated during months one and two of my strategic shopping plan. I could see my stockpile growing, but I was spending the same amount of money as I was before CouponMom.com. It was during month five that I really started seeing the fruits of my labor—of being able to start cherry-picking deals and knowing the difference between an okay deal and a great one. Have patience: patience to wait to use a coupon, patience to grow your stockpile, and patience to whittle down your grocery spending.

Before CouponMom.com I was spending between $650 and $700 a month for grocery, health, and beauty items. At the end of month five, I'm down to $475 per month, and I'm hoping to get it down to $400 after nine months. I use Aveda shampoo and conditioner and MAC makeup, so there are some splurges in the $475. I know on coupons alone I save between 40 and 45 percent every month. Shaving money off our grocery bill has allowed us 'margin' in our financial, personal, and spiritual lives. I'm glad I stuck it out!"

—Kelly Snyder, Lenexa, Kansas

wasted. Avoid throwing your money down the drain by working to reduce your waste to zero. Here are some tips to keep you from throwing your food dollars away:

- Plan your shopping lists carefully, and stick to your lists.
- Serve reasonably sized portions to children.
- Serve leftovers one night a week.
- Designate one refrigerator shelf for clear containers of leftovers.

- If you can't use leftovers within two days, freeze them immediately for future use.
- Eat leftovers of the previous night's dinner for lunch the next day.
- Think creatively when reusing leftovers, and create menu plans with leftovers in mind. Leftover veggies can become a healthy salad. Leftover chicken or beef can have a second life in soup.

5. **Live by the 5-minute rule:** If it takes you 5 minutes or less to prepare an item instead of buying it pre-cooked, pre-washed, or pre-cut, then it is well worth your time to save the money by doing it yourself. You'll end up earning an hourly "wage" of $50 or more when you wash your own lettuce or make your own tuna salad.

6. **Cook meals at home:** Cooking shows starring celebrity chefs are fun to watch, but you don't have to be one of them to feed your family tasty and nutritious meals. Learn to master a few favorite dishes that do not require many ingredients or take much time to prepare, and you'll be able to feed your family a healthy diet at a low cost without a lot of effort. Recipe websites, cooking magazines, and cookbooks you can borrow from the library are great sources of inspiration.

7. **Steer clear of fast food:** Think about what people in a drive-through line are doing: throwing money out the window. Don't pay the high cost of convenience dining when you're struggling to get your overall food budget under control. It's possible to save hundreds, or thousands, of dollars a year from your household budget by eating breakfast at home and packing your lunch. Bring coffee or soft drinks and snacks from home to save on the high cost of vending machines or coffee shops. These habits are good for your health as well as your budget. When you're not frittering your food budget away one latte at a time, you can afford the occasional treat of a fine, high-quality meal out with your family.

8. **Consider other options:** When I first began to tackle our family's grocery budget, I read several books on frugal grocery shopping, frugal cooking, and strategic meal planning. They taught me that saving money on groceries could be a fun game of finding clever ways to stretch my grocery dollars in every food category. But Strategic Shopping doesn't mean just using coupons and buying things on sale. In order to get the most value out of my food dollar, I learned to find less-expensive, comparable substitutes for common foods, and sources other than the grocery store for finding bargains on what we eat. Even if you aren't a coupon user, you can save plenty of money by knowing how to make smart choices in each department of the grocery store. This book will teach frugal strategies by department, suggest simple substitutions to save, and also suggest alternative shopping options to save money on non-food items.

She's Won Him Over!

"I have found that I really enjoy couponing. It always seems like I'm having a contest with myself each week to get the best deal for my family. My husband just shakes his head. He used to complain about all of my stockpiling but changed his mind when he was laid off in December. Thanks to all the deals I was able to get before then, I have had so much stocked up for us that it has really helped us with the loss in pay. I haven't paid full price for any toiletries in over a year. There are certain items that I won't pay more than 50 cents for. At one point I would have thought that seemed crazy, but now it seems crazy to pay more than that."

—Amy Warren, Roanoke, Texas

Read This Before You Set Foot in the Grocery Store!

Grocery retailers want shoppers to spend as much as possible, and they use clever merchandising strategies to entice consumers to part with more money than they might have intended. Review these ten tips before you go shopping to avoid falling into spending traps!

Never shop when you are hungry: Eat, then shop. It's very difficult to be a disciplined shopper when you are hungry.

Shop alone if you can: Shopping with a friend or family member can get you off track.

Use the store ad to plan your trip, but do not assume that every item in the store ad is a deal: According to *Consumer Reports* magazine, 75 percent of shoppers rely on store ads to plan their trips. Most shoppers do not realize that product manufacturers pay for most of the advertising space in a store's weekly ad. As a result, a product's sales can increase by 500 percent when its manufacturer buys space in the store ad. Be aware—products may be featured regardless of their prices. However, you can be reasonably sure that the front-page items are deeply discounted.

Compare unit prices: The size of a package can be deceptive, and the largest size isn't always the least expensive on a unit-cost basis. Pay attention to the sizes of different flavors or varieties of the same product, since specialty varieties may have fewer ounces in the package than the basic version.

Skip the high price of convenience: Buy food in its most basic form to get the most food for your dollar.

Beware of special displays: Don't assume that special displays or displays at the end of an aisle are the best price. They may actually be selling at full price.

Don't fall for multiple pricing gimmicks: Stores frequently post prices such as "10 for $10" when the items actually sell for $1 each, regardless of the quantity purchased. Unless the sign says you must buy ten, you can assume there is no minimum purchase requirement.

Check different departments: As strange as it sounds, a store may beat its own price sometimes. A type of cheese sold in the deli department might cost more than a different brand of the same type of cheese sold in the dairy department. One brand of a type of nuts in the produce department might cost less than a different brand of the same type of nuts in the baking aisle. Often, the quality is the same.

Watch prices at the register and check your receipt: Grocery stores change thousands of prices on items each week. That means there are thousands of opportunities for pricing errors. Some stores will give you an item free if you are overcharged, but it's up to you to point it out. At the very least, pay the correct amount.

Stick to your list and shop as quickly as possible: The longer you hang around, the more likely you are to veer from your list and spend more than you'd planned to. Get in and get out!

A Final Word

The great thing about Strategic Shopping is that it will work for anyone. Start putting these methods to work for you now, and by the end of the year you'll be amazed at how much you have saved over time. Your Strategic Shopping plan—and success—is up to you. If you're willing to put in the time, the methods I teach can dramatically reduce how much you spend week after week. But even if you have next to no time to plan your grocery shopping excursions, adopting a Strategic Shopping mentality will save you money.

Four

— — —

What's the Plan? Save with Grocery Lists and Meal Planning

Some of the most powerful weapons you have in the battle against high grocery prices are a pen and a piece of paper. Simply writing down what you plan to buy—and sticking faithfully to that list—can help keep your grocery bill under control. Similarly, charting out menu plans for the week keeps each meal affordable. In this chapter we're going to discuss:

- the most successful ways to plan a budget-minded shopping trip, and how each shopping "personality" can benefit from planning
- statistics that show the significant impact that planning ahead has on your overall grocery spending
- how to combine meal planning and sale items to feed your family for the least amount of money

Plan, Then Shop

Even if you shop without coupons, a well-planned grocery list, created by scanning the store's sales circular for deals, serves as a discount "coupon" of sorts. Sticking to your list easily shaves 25 percent or more off your total bill. You can expect to chop your bill in half if you'll go the extra step and list every item you need for at least a week's worth of meals and snacks, as well as paper and cleaning products and toiletries. Planning ahead makes the best use of your grocery shopping time and eliminates those in-between trips for the one or two items you forgot the first time. How many times have you dashed to the store intending to grab just that gallon of milk or loaf of bread you missed the first time, only to return home with a trunk full of items that somehow jumped into your cart?

By the Numbers: Stats Prove Planning Works

Don't just take my word for it. I've got Ivy League research backing me up! Research from a 2009 study published by the University of Pennsylvania's Wharton School of Business found that efficient shoppers with detailed shopping plans do a better job of sticking to their shopping lists and budgets. In the study, shoppers who described themselves as "fast and efficient" made 82 percent fewer impulse purchases than other shoppers. The study also found that unplanned purchasing goes up by 23 percent if the shopping trip itself is unplanned, but it goes down by 13 percent if it's a major or weekly trip. In other words, making one well-planned shopping trip per week is the key ingredient to slimmer grocery bills.

Spend Time to Save Time—and Money

Has this ever happened to you? It's close to dinnertime, and you realize there's nothing in the fridge. You dash over to the market to grab a few things. You haven't had time to make a list, much less clip coupons, so you keep an eye out for sale prices and hope for the best. Once you're home, though, you realize some key ingredients are missing. With the clock running out and no time to run back to the store, you simply order pizza. Not only have you wasted a trip to the store and shelled out cash unnecessarily for the pizza, you're going to have to return to the supermarket at some point so you can feed your family the next day.

A few minutes of planning would have made better use of your trip to the grocery store, and there would have been no reason to order out. Yes, it takes a little time to get your grocery-store strategy in order, but the results are saved time and money and healthier meals.

Have I convinced you that planning is essential to saving money at the grocery store? Let's turn you into a planning pro!

Four Steps to Creating Your Shopping List

1. Check to see what you already have on hand to turn ingredients in your kitchen into meals. (If you already have eggs, milk, and syrup, you just need some bread to make French toast, for example.) Plus, this keeps you from accidentally duplicating items you've already purchased, which can be important if you have limited storage space.
2. Check your stores' featured sale items and coupon bargains before leaving home, so you'll know exactly where to find the best deals.
3. Plan specific daily menus around your on-hand ingredients and store bargains.
4. Your current food inventory + needed items bought on sale and with coupons = your shopping list!

What's for Dinner? Bargain-Based Menu Planning

Just as planning your shopping trip saves time and money, so does planning your weekly menus. This should take just 10 or 15 minutes each week. Ideally, you will want to set aside one hour each week to plan meals, make your shopping list, and cut out any coupons you need. But even if you're having a particularly time-crunched week, don't give up—even the Busy Shopper can save money with some crash-course planning at the last minute. Keep a pen and small spiral notebook in your car or purse and take them into the store with you. Pick up the store's weekly sales circular as you enter the store, and quickly jot down the best bargains you spot. Even this little bit of effort will help you stay focused while you shop, reducing impulse spending.

Which Comes First, the Menu or the List?

Even shoppers who do religiously make lists sometimes prefer to sketch out meal plans first, before creating their shopping lists. They generally do not take the store sale items into consideration before planning their meals. If the items they need for the meals they want to cook just happen to be on sale, they simply luck into bargains. But the dedicated Strategic Shopper isn't going to rely on a chance encounter with a rock-bottom sale price! Follow these steps to go after bargains rather than waiting to stumble across them—and get ready to save 50 percent or more on your groceries.

Scan the week's calendar to figure out what everyone's going to be eating and when: Meals at the dining-room table aren't the only time your family eats! Remember packed lunches, school or sporting events, and social outings, so that this extracurricular eating doesn't translate into extra trips to the store. There's no quicker way to toss cash out the window than waiting until the last minute to pick up refreshments for your child's homeroom party or a business associate's cocktail hour. Thinking through your family's culinary calendar helps you prepare to make every bite a bargain.

Keep an eye on your refrigerator's perishable items: According to research from the University of Arizona's Bureau of Applied Research in Anthropology, the average household ends up wasting an average of 14 percent of its grocery spending by throwing away unused or spoiled food. Even worse, 15 percent of that waste includes products that were never opened and were still within their expiration date! (This statistic really makes me cringe—why not just set dollar bills on fire while we're at it?) The study also found that a family of four ends up throwing away an average of $590 of perishable groceries per year, such as meat, produce, dairy, and grain products. You can save an average of $50 per month by avoiding overbuying perishable foods. Check your supplies before shopping and estimate the exact amount you'll need to buy for the next week. This is also a good time to throw away outdated leftovers, make sure perishable items are in view, and use up good leftovers for that day's meals.

Check the pantry and freezer to make sure you have adequate staples on hand for easy "convenience" meals: Have a few easy meals in mind, such as pasta, soups, chili, soft tacos, homemade pizza, or chicken pot pie. Simple dishes that can be made with items you already have on hand can save you the expense of that last-minute call for pizza delivery because "There isn't anything to eat." Learn to create meals with easy-to-store items, such as canned beans, tomatoes, cream soup, dry pasta, jarred pasta sauce, pizza-crust mix, corn-muffin mix, bouillon cubes, and canned chicken or tuna. My freezer is typically stocked with staples, such as shredded cheese, low-fat smoked sausage, tortillas, frozen vegetables, and frozen containers of browned ground beef or diced cooked chicken that I've prepared earlier in large batches to have on hand for quick meals. The recipe chapter will give you more ideas for using common staples to make quick and tasty meals.

Don't snack on dinner! Keep munchies around so your family doesn't graze on the ingredients you were planning to use as the night's main course. I keep inexpensive items, such as popcorn, pretzels, Popsicles, crackers, peanut butter, and brownie mixes (purchased for pennies with coupons) on hand for quick treats. I also keep a container of frozen banana slices in the freezer to make inexpensive, healthy fruit smoothies in the blender by adding just milk. I buy yogurt, crackers, fruit, carrots, and celery in quantity and let my family know that these healthy treats are always available.

Celebrate Leftover Night once a week: Keep any leftovers on one shelf of the refrigerator in clear containers, so you can see what you have to use up. This ensures that leftovers become tasty soups or casseroles instead of scary science projects. Let this become a fun family project, too. On our Leftover Nights, each family member may have a different entrée and vegetable from meals we've had that week. A green salad for everyone completes the meal.

Repurpose ingredients: Easy recipe ideas give new life to leftover items that might otherwise get thrown away. Let's say you have a bit of leftover cooked rice and some cooked broccoli. It's not enough for another four servings of rice and broccoli, but that doesn't mean it's time to toss it! Add $1.50 worth of eggs and cheese and you have a lovely dinner frittata. Similarly, a couple of pieces of leftover chicken from last night's meal become the building blocks of easy homemade soup served over rice when combined with fresh or frozen vegetables and chicken broth or bouillon. The next time you're tempted to trash leftovers simply because it seems like "not enough to save," imagine me and the two million members of the CouponMom.com community shouting, "Stop!" Then flip to the recipe chapter of this book for great ideas on turning leftovers into great meals and working "planned leftover" strategies into your weekly menu creation to simplify meals and save money.

Once you know what you have on hand, review your grocery store's weekly circulars for sales on entrée items like beef, chicken, or pork: Then plan the week's meals around the best deals. Because featured main-dish items are generally 50 percent off or more, it makes sense to stock up and freeze. That way, this week's bargains become next week's meals. If the featured sale item on any given week doesn't appeal to your family, you can still keep menu prices under control by "shopping your freezer" and dining on last week's sales items. Scan several stores' weekly sales circulars and plan more than one trip if you determine it's worth your time.

Review your store's ad for bargains on side items you need to round out your meals, and stock up when prices plummet: If prices for sides are marked down 50 percent off or more, it's a good idea to buy enough for two weeks if you can afford it. Spending the extra amount to buy more when the item is on sale keeps you from paying full price when the sale period ends. When you need items that aren't featured in your store's weekly sales flier, compare various brands to ensure that you always pay the lowest price.

Put other shoppers to work for you! Grocery deals websites and blogs have valuable information that other people have discovered. A store ad may show that Brand X pasta sauce is on sale for $1.50, but this may be just the beginning. Information on a grocery deals website may alert you to a newspaper coupon good for $1 off two jars of Brand X pasta sauce, and note that an in-store promotion features a $2 box of pasta free when you buy two jars of the sauce. Buying one jar of pasta sauce at the sale price is fine. But by taking advantage of research other shoppers have compiled, you'll actually get more than twice as much food: two jars of pasta sauce and a box of pasta. You can unearth these enticing finds by running an Internet search for the name of your grocery store and the word "deals" to turn up helpful sites and blogs. My website, CouponMom.com, lists grocery deals every week for thousands of stores across the country.

Tell the Web what you have on hand and let it tell you what to cook:

Many recipe sites feature a nifty recipe-search tool. Enter the ingredients you have, and a list of recipes pops up featuring those ingredients. The sites I like include Allrecipes.com and the food manufacturers' sites for the products I have on hand.

Create menu cards: Write down what you plan to feed everyone that week on an index card or piece of paper and post it on the refrigerator. Make reminder notes to yourself to take ingredients out of the freezer ahead of time. And include a list of snacks so your family members can assess their nibbling options at a glance.

Scan coupon websites and review the clipped coupons you have on hand: Keep them neatly organized or attach them to your shopping list so you're ready to whip them out at the register.

Train yourself to resist temptation: The aisles of a grocery store can be like a highway lined with billboards, each trying to lure you into spending money. By planning ahead, you can keep clever merchandising displays from derailing your thrifty shopping intentions. A 2005 Arbitron study found that 40 percent of "smart shoppers" who consulted sales circulars and collected coupons still made unplanned purchases after hearing an audio advertisement for a product over the store's loudspeakers. The study also found that 35 percent of "smart shoppers" purchased a different brand than the one on their list after hearing an audio advertisement in the store. I'm not suggesting you wear earmuffs, although I suppose that might work. But do know that the longer you stay in the store, the more likely you are to succumb to store merchandising. A carefully planned list and strategy helps you get in and get out quickly, before marketing ploys snare you in their catchy clutches.

Shopping Strategies for Every Shopping Personality

If you are a Busy Shopper without a lot of time for coupon clipping and organizing, you can start making a dent in your grocery bill by spending 5 minutes to work these simple steps to your routine.

Stock up on staples: A full pantry and freezer are the Busy Shopper's best friends. Keeping a good supply of staples on hand cuts down on those unplanned—and costly—trips to the store. Create your own list of pantry and freezer staples for your favorite easy meals that can be prepared with simple staples, and then load up when you find good deals.

Manage leftovers: One shelf of your refrigerator needs to become the Leftover Holding Area, where surplus ingredients await their next chance to grace your table. For the average family of four, eliminating food waste translates to at least $50 per month in grocery savings.

Don't shop empty-handed: Check your current grocery supplies and plan meals with what you have on hand as well as any leftovers. Then list the basic items you need (in a general sense, such as "green vegetables" or "cereal"). Watch for sale prices in the store for those items when you shop, and let the list be your guide.

Grab the loss leaders: Loss leaders are just that: items the store knows it will take a loss on but will lead shoppers to its doors. Scan the store's weekly advertising circular for featured sale items. (If you don't have time to read it at home, pick one up as you enter the store.) Glancing at the circular's front page for 15 seconds will alert you to deals such as chicken or beef for 50 percent off or "buy one, get one free" promotions. Stock up when prices drop to keep your costs consistently low.

If you are a Rookie Shopper with a little more time to spend, you can save by putting the Busy Shopper strategies to use and then doing a little extra planning.

Find all the best grocery and coupon deals before you shop: Your store's weekly ad or the CouponMom.com's Grocery Deals list points you to the best sale prices and promotions for the items you need. You don't necessarily have to go to more than one store to save, but if you have more than one grocery store nearby, it makes sense to review all of the stores' circulars or deals lists to see who has the best bargains. Write down specific sale items that fit your general list (such as "fresh broccoli"), cut out or print the coupons you need, and take advantage of any special store promotions that require purchasing a specific combination of items. For example, a promotion might offer a free gallon of milk with the purchase of three boxes of cereal.

Create bargain-minded menu plans: Online recipe sites can help you tailor meals around deals. Find recipes that suit your tastes and time constraints, and consider doubling the recipes to save time as well as money.

The Varsity Shopper, who prepares for a trip to the grocery store like a soldier preparing for battle, can combine the strategies of the other two types and then accelerate the savings even further.

Study all the store sales: Rather than reviewing and selecting only one store's sales, peruse multiple store circulars and Grocery Deals lists on CouponMom.com and grocery deals blogs.

Create a shopping master plan for the week: Cherry-pick the best bargains from each store and create short lists per store at the beginning of the week. Attach the necessary coupons to each list.

Manage your master plan easily: As a Varsity Shopper, you travel with your coupon organizer like the president travels with the nuclear codes. Its valuable contents are never far from your reach. Set up the organizer with one section designated for each store list, or put all the lists with attached coupons in a special file. Because it's always with you, it's easy to make quick stops at each store as you're running errands or while commuting, to make each trip an efficient use of your time.

Shop with food safety in mind: If you're going to be hitting numerous stores, it's a good idea to keep a cooler in your car. That way, perishables you pick up during your first trip remain properly refrigerated throughout the duration of your bargain-hunting odyssey.

A Final Word

Regardless of your shopping personality, you can save money and time by planning. It takes time for a new habit to become routine. If working up a comprehensive shopping list for an entire week seems overwhelming, start small with a few planning strategies. Runners don't get ready for marathons by running the entire 26 miles on the first day of training!

Five

— — —

By the Numbers: Learning Prices to Detect the Best Bargains

Prices at the grocery store change like the tide. First they're high, then they're low. If you're not paying attention, it's easy to get swept away by all the fluctuations. But Strategic Shopping can ensure smooth sailing—and consistently low prices.

In this chapter we're going to discuss:

- using a price book to get your costs down and keep them there
- tracking unit cost and comparing various items to determine which sizes and brands are the best deals
- empowering yourself by ensuring that prices are correct, asking for rain checks or store guarantees, and returning items that don't meet your standards

Your Price Book: The Ultimate Tracking Device

If knowledge is power, then tracking prices for a few weeks in your grocery store is going to make you an invincible shopper. By arming yourself with data built up over a period of time, you'll be able to apply a critical eye when cruising the aisles and know when a sale is really a sale. Then when you stock up when prices hit their lowest, you'll be able to avoid purchasing at peak cost, allowing your family to eat for the same amount week after week.

It's up to you to decide how much effort to put into your price book. You can track numbers at various stores around town or stick to your regular market to establish concrete trends there. Your price book is going to require an investment of time, but once you've established a pattern, it'll easily pay for itself.

Clipboard Chic

For me price-booking used to be sort of a solitary pursuit. In my first eight years of scanning price tags at numerous grocery stores for the CouponMom .com website, I was often the only shopper with a clipboard in hand. But I've noticed that's changed this year. Suddenly a clipboard seems to be the must-have accessory at the grocery stores in my area, as my fellow shoppers have become keenly interested in saving.

Cheap may be the new black, but I don't think that keeping a price book is a passing fad. Once you start spending dramatically less to feed your family, it's hard to go back to full price! Other shoppers have told me varying stories of how much they save by using a price book, and everyone's preferences vary by household. So it's really up to each one of us to make a price book work for our families. Doing your own price comparison is a critical first step to reducing your grocery spending on items you prefer.

The easiest way to get started is to check advertised sale prices once a week and begin logging in the numbers. Use a small, inexpensive spiral notebook that will fit into your purse or glove compartment, so it's easy to take shopping with you. Use one page per item to track numbers each week. This system would work fine for tracking twenty items or fewer each week.

Sample Page in a Small Price Book
Flour, 5 lb., all-purpose store brand
Fred's Market, May 1, $2.19
Wal-Mart, May 10, $1.79
Aldi, May 13, $1.69
Kroger, May 14, $1.99 (name brand on sale with coupon, $1.49)

Once you get the hang of it, you might want to step up to a full-size spiral notebook and list several items per page. It's helpful to stay organized by designating one page for each department, such as dairy, produce, meat, or cereal. List items on the left side of the page, with columns for each week that you track prices. Use a separate column for each store that you decide to track under each week.

I probably don't need to say this, but keep it simple. Whether you decide to stick with the small purse-size notebook or graduate to the full-size notebook, don't spend a lot. That would defeat the purpose!

An alternative to using notebooks is to enter your price information into computer spreadsheet software. Entering the data into a spreadsheet makes it easy to compare total and average prices.

SAMPLE SPREADSHEET OR PAGE IN SPIRAL NOTEBOOK

Dairy Dept.	Week of 4/20		Week of 4/27		Week of 5/4	
Item	Store A	Store B	Store A	Store B	Store A	Store B
milk, low-fat, 1 gallon						
eggs, 1 dozen large						
cheddar cheese, 8 oz.						
orange juice, 64 oz.						
flour tortillas, 10 ct.						
butter, 1 lb.						

Index cards can also be handy for tracking prices. Using one card per item, it's easy to note prices, store name, and date on the item's card. As you are making your shopping list or checking to see if a store's so-called sale price is a good deal or just a snappy come-on, you can flip to the corresponding card to easily discover whether you have a bargain or a gimmick on your hands.

SAMPLE INDEX CARD

Flour, 5 lb., all-purpose, store brand (baking section of file)	
Fred's Market	May 1, $2.19
Wal-Mart	May 10, $1.79
Aldi	May 13, $1.69
Kroger	May 14, $1.99 (name brand on sale with coupon, $1.49)

Are We There Yet? Tracking Takes Time

To really know whether a deal is a deal, you need to be familiar with how the numbers increase or decrease over time. It's a good idea to track prices for at least six weeks, ideally up to twelve weeks, to have a true sense of what the best prices are for the items on your list. During this period you'll learn how often items are sold at a discount. Some price cycles are short, with items going on sale every other week. For others, it may take you that initial twelve-week time frame to discover when prices truly hit their bottom.

I get that we're all busy, and your family needs to eat today, not three months from now. So start with a small yet powerful list. Pick ten or twenty of the highest-cost items you purchase each week and start tracking those for the quickest, most significant impact. As you expand to include more items, continue to identify what your household's high-impact items are, and start tracking those first.

Here's an example. You may use 6 pounds of boneless chicken breast per week for your household, and only one can of cooking spray per month. The chicken ranges in price from $2 to $5 per pound, while the cooking spray ranges from $1 to $1.69. It's not hard to figure out where you have the greater opportunity for savings. By timing things right, you can potentially save $18 per week on chicken, or 17 cents per week on cooking spray. A quick look at the numbers and it's easy to see where your price-tracking time is best spent.

Furthermore, if you find that chicken goes on sale every other week and begin buying a two-week supply, you will flatten your cost over time. By freezing what you can't use right away and thawing it as you need it, you keep the cost consistent week to week. If that means paying $2 per pound every other week instead of $5 per pound every week, you're racking up $468 in savings per year on chicken breasts alone. If I handed you a spiral notebook and offered to pay you $468 a year to start checking prices each week, would that be worth your time? It's worth mine!

Crunch Those Numbers

Simply looking at price tags doesn't tell you the whole story. It's important to track prices per ounce, not just prices per container. One store's private-label ice cream may come in a 48-ounce carton, while another's may come in a 64-ounce carton. You need to calculate the cost per ounce, not the cost per carton, to determine the best price on ice cream. This approach is particularly important if you are comparing supermarket items to the same brands available at a wholesale club, since the wholesale clubs typically have much larger packages than supermarket items.

You also need to evaluate the difference in cost between different-size containers for the same item. It's not unheard of for an item to beat its very own price depending on how it's packaged. Don't go on appearance alone. Whip out your calculator and start figuring. In my pricing research, I was amazed at how deceiving packages could be.

It's natural to assume that the larger-size container, offering the greatest number of servings, results in the lowest per-unit price. Not so fast. If I have a coupon, especially one that can be doubled, the savings might whittle the cost of the smaller-size item down to nearly nothing. It might even be free. That theory doesn't always apply, though, so it's important to calculate before you buy.

And appearances can be misleading. Don't make assumptions on the best price solely on what an item looks like. Two containers of yogurt may look identical, but a closer inspection might reveal that one is a 6-ounce container while the other is a whipped variety, offering 4 ounces at the same price. By tossing what looks like the same thing into your cart, you could pay 50 percent more without realizing it.

Cereal Numbers

I have found the cereal aisle to be one of the most confusing departments for comparison pricing. Not only are there multiple brands for similar varieties of cereals, but each brand also comes in multiple sizes. Again, your calculator is your friend here. Look at the number of servings on the box and evaluate your cost per serving, since it is nearly impossible to know which size offers the best value simply by looking at the boxes.

Here's an example. I wanted to know which brand of frosted cornflakes cereal cost the least. I compared name-brand Frosted Flakes with the store variety but still had five options to muddle through. The name-brand cereal came in small, medium, and large family-size boxes. The regular store brand came in just one size but also sold the cereal under its "value" store label in the generic white box.

With no analysis available to me, I might assume that the "value" brand was the best bargain, with the name-brand options costing far more. Wrong! By running the numbers I quickly determined that the family-size box was actually the most expensive size. The "value" brand was more expensive than the higher-quality-tier store-brand option.

Cereal Variety and Size	Price	Cost per Ounce	Cost per Serving
Kellogg's Frosted Flakes, 17 oz.	$2.94	17 cents	18 cents
Kellogg's Frosted Flakes, 23 oz.	$3.21	14 cents	15 cents
Kellogg's Frosted Flakes, 27.5 oz. family-size	$4.99	18 cents	20 cents
store brand, 17 oz.	$1.89	11 cents	12 cents
store "value" brand, 8 oz.	$0.99	12 cents	14 cents

As it turns out, the medium-size box of Kellogg's Frosted Flakes was the best value out of the name-brand options. By using a $1 coupon, the medium-size box would still have had a lower per-serving cost than the smallest box. And the "value" brand wasn't the best value, either.

The larger box of the store brand's frosted cornflakes cereal had the lowest unit cost.

It may seem like a lot of trouble to save a few pennies, but keep that calculator handy.

Even though the price difference is only a few cents per serving, it can add up over time. If four family members each had one small bowl of cereal per day over the course of a year, the total savings of buying the medium-size box of Kellogg's versus the family-size box of Kellogg's would be $73 per year. That's a significant savings realized without even changing your preferred brand of cereal.

Fact or Fiction? The Real Story on the Best Prices

Making orange juice from frozen concentrate is always cheaper than buying it from the carton. Purchasing a 32-ounce tub of yogurt is always cheaper than buying it in individual containers.

Right?

Not always. Comparing prices tells the true story. When I compared my store-brand varieties' sizes, the least expensive options were the 64-ounce jug of orange juice and the individual 6-ounce containers of yogurt. How many shoppers automatically grab what they think are probably the least expensive containers and needlessly bulk up their overall bills?

Of course, prices change, and it's certainly possible that the biggest container of yogurt is sometimes also the cheapest. But don't assume. Do the simple calculations to determine the best price each week on the items you buy.

Easy Ways to Save

As we learned with our example of paying $2 per pound versus $5 per pound for chicken breasts, attacking the highest-impact items on your grocery list is the best way to quickly wring savings out of your shopping trip. Here are some simple concepts for getting the most out of your grocery dollar.

Stock up during sales: Using your price book as a guide, pounce when items go on sale at their lowest cost. Because you've tracked prices over time, you'll also know how often things go on sale. My favorite brand of chicken goes on sale at my store once every four weeks. If I shopped at only one store and bought only that brand, I would buy four weeks' worth of it for the freezer, or about twelve packages of chicken for my family.

Remain flexible to other brands: Somebody's going to put chicken on sale every other week. It might not be my preferred brand, but by remaining open to other labels, I increase my opportunities to save. If I am willing to buy whichever brand of boneless chicken breasts is on sale, I have an opportunity to buy it at the best price every two weeks. That way, I don't need to buy as much at any one time.

Remain flexible to other stores: Supermarkets love loyal customers. The less willing you are to hit the road, the less likely you are to discover better deals elsewhere. It's worth your time to shop around. If an item on your list isn't on sale at one supermarket, chances are another has it on special. Once you learn where the deals are, you'll know which store to hit for certain items, lessening your need to buy huge quantities when you do find a deal.

Make simple substitutions: If boneless chicken breast was selling for $5 per pound at my store and I was out of chicken, I would be willing to buy whatever the sale-priced chicken variety was and alter my menu plan. Whole chickens at 69 cents per pound would start looking pretty good.

When in doubt, do without: If no variety of chicken was on sale that week, guess what: We would not eat chicken that week. I've come up with all sorts of clever and frugal menu items over the years, but I have never paid $5 per pound for chicken breasts!

Make sure the price is right: The typical supermarket may have as many as five thousand price changes per week. That's five thousand chances that something might go wrong, whether it's an outdated tag or a price that rings up incorrectly for some reason. Pay attention as the cashier checks you out, and study your receipt to make sure you're paying the correct price.

Take advantage of price guarantees: Some stores will give you the item free if you point out a price discrepancy. At the very least, the store will make an adjustment and charge you the correct price. I've caught pricing discrepancies dozens of times over the years that have added up to real money. It pays to pay attention!

Get rain checks: Stores often run out of their featured sale item, which is annoying but does not necessarily mean you've missed the sale. Take a few minutes to request a "rain check" for the item at the customer service department. This allows you to purchase the item at the advertised sale price when it's available again. While you're waiting for the store to restock, keep an eye out for coupons. You could get it for even less.

Don't be afraid to return defective products: There have been times when I've purchased meat, chicken, pork, or fish that hasn't smelled quite right when I opened it. No bargain is worth risking your health, so toss anything that seems unfit to eat. When this has happened, I cut off the price label of the product, wash it, and stop at the store's customer service counter on my next shopping trip to get a refund. One time I purchased eight pork tenderloins when they were selling for 50 percent off and put them in the freezer. When I thawed one that wasn't up to par, I took all of them back to the store and got a $42 refund. That was definitely worth taking the extra 10 minutes rather than throwing them all away. Refunds are much easier with a receipt, so get in the habit of saving your receipts for at least a couple of weeks after you shop.

Take advantage of store-brand guarantees: Some stores will guarantee the satisfaction of their products with a money-back guarantee. Even if the product meets the food safety test, if you don't like the product as much as the national brand, the guarantee entitles you to return the product to the store for compensation. For example, my local Kroger store has a Try it, Like it, or Get the National Brand Free policy. If I really didn't like their private-label graham crackers, I could return them and get a free box of the Nabisco or Keebler variety at no extra cost. My store's policy limits the guarantee to items priced at $5 or less. It's possible that your store has a similar policy but doesn't advertise it, so be sure to ask the customer service desk whether or not they have a store-brand guarantee.

A Final Word

Getting the most use out of Strategic Shopping methods like a price book or saving with store guarantees or rain checks takes some confidence. You have to not mind being the shopper carefully trolling the aisles with clipboard in hand. You have to check any trepidation you might feel about asking for refunds or guarantees. Here's an easy way to feel more at ease: Tell people what you're doing! I haven't found a store employee or fellow shopper yet who did not respond positively when he or she learned that my grocery-store routines were all about saving money to feed my family.

Six

– –

Super Savings at Supermarkets

People ask me all the time which supermarkets have the best prices. My answer? All of them! Part of Strategic Shopping is learning your store's savings programs. Once you've mastered them, you can combine coupons and time purchases to coincide with sales. As a result, you can find great deals at any store. It just takes a little detective work on your part.

In this chapter we're going to discuss:

- the questions to ask at your store to make the most powerful use of your coupons
- various savings programs at some major grocery-store chains, and strategies for ferreting out savings opportunities that might not be immediately apparent
- the hidden bargains on non-food items that can be available at the supermarket

Here's Some Good News: Hidden Deals at Your Store

Pull your trench coat out of the closet—it's time you became an investigative reporter. The topic of your sensational scoop: the best bargains at your grocery store. Each store's policies vary, so I'll tell you the right questions to ask store employees. But the most important thing to remember is to be *sure* to ask. Every supermarket, drugstore, discount store, wholesale club, and even discount food outlet has unique pricing, promotion, and/or coupon policies. While stores advertise some of their policies, many more are available on an "on request" basis. It's up to you to sniff out those hidden deals.

Here's an example. One of the markets in my area is glad to accept its competitors' coupons. But this is something of an open secret. You won't find this generous policy printed in any store ads, on store signs, or even on its website. I learned of this great savings opportunity only when a store manager told me about it. I later verified with managers of other stores in the chain that it is indeed company policy. I even noticed that the cash registers have special keys for ringing up competitors' coupons. Talk about valuable insider intelligence!

If you're on the shy side, you might be hesitant to ask about unadvertised savings programs. But putting the little-known policy about competitor coupons to work has saved me hundreds of dollars over the years. Let visions of dollar signs dancing in your head banish your bashfulness. Let's take a look at some of the most common savings programs, and the questions you need to ask to make your grocery dollar go the furthest.

Savings Programs Available at Supermarkets

Stores use dozens of marketing approaches to lure shoppers, but while these promotions are meant to drum up business for the supermarkets, Strategic Shoppers find ways to turn them into great savings opportunities.

I rarely meet shoppers who are aware of all of their stores' savings programs, so this chapter should be a real eye-opener. You'll want to confirm specifics with your store's employees, but here's an overview of the deals that may translate into bargains hiding in plain sight at a store near you.

Store Loyalty Cards

Most large supermarket chains have a store loyalty card that allows you to save while allowing the store to gather data about you. For example, you can sign up for the Kroger Plus Card at Kroger, the Club Card at Safeway, the Preferred Savings Card at Albertsons, and the Price Plus Club Card at ShopRite, either in-store or on the stores' websites. Using them allows you

to benefit from sale discounts, bonus coupon values, and promotional bo-
nuses, such as fuel-center discounts or a free turkey during the holidays.

Some stores even offer rebates on your total spending in the form of
store credit. For example, Ralphs, a chain in Southern California, offers a
Ralphs Rewards loyalty card that gives shoppers points at a rate of 1 percent
of their total spending. Shoppers then receive rewards certificates each
quarter that can be used on future purchases. Similarly, CVS/Pharmacy
drugstores' ExtraCare loyalty card program offers Extra Bucks rebates at a
rate of 2 percent of total spending. Both stores offer bonus rebates during
special promotional periods.

Some people don't like stores that require shoppers to use loyalty cards
to receive benefits because they consider it an invasion of privacy. I understand this legitimate concern. To allay any fears about privacy, check your
store's website and click on the "privacy policy" link. This should take you
to information explaining exactly how the store uses personal information
it gathers from loyalty cards. I've checked a number of store sites for privacy
policy information. Each policy I reviewed clearly states that the store does
not sell customer e-mail or mailing-address information to other parties.
Stores that do sell this type of information are legally required to say so in
their privacy policies.

I think the benefits of using a loyalty card far outweigh any privacy
concerns. After all, I shop in plain view of other shoppers, so I don't consider my trips to grocery stores to be covert operations. The way I see it,
allowing supermarkets to track my purchases actually puts them to work for
me. Information gathered from my shopping trips over time helps the store
tailor coupon offers specifically for my family. As a result of my regular
loyalty card use, I frequently receive coupons mailed to my home or generated at the cash register for the items I regularly use.

Not only are these coupons generated with my purchasing patterns in
mind, they often exceed the deals available from newspaper coupons or
store circulars. I decided to track the savings available by using loyalty card–
generated coupons. In three months I received $136 worth of coupons and
used $85 worth of them immediately. When you add those coupons on top
of other types of coupons, as well as store promotions and other deals, it's
easy to see how the savings start piling up!

Be sure to completely fill out the loyalty card form when you sign up. Providing your correct address brings bargains right to your door. If you have a loyalty card but aren't receiving coupons in the mail, it might be that you didn't fill out the form completely when you signed up. If this is the case, you're getting only half of the benefit of loyalty card membership, and I recommend that you sign up again for a new card. Be sure to fill out the form completely this time!

Coupon Policies

Think of coupons as cash that you can either put into interest-bearing savings accounts or bury in the backyard. They're going to save you money, but it's up to you to learn how powerful they can be. I'd challenge you to consider the face value on a coupon as merely the starting point.

Coupon policies are frequently driven by local competitive pressures, which can vary by state, city, and even neighborhood. Most supermarket chains have official corporate policies, but individual stores may have the flexibility to tweak those policies. Coupon policies may vary, then, not only from chain to chain but also from store to store within a chain. You need to be sure to ask so that you know exactly how coupons work at your store.

Here are the questions to ask at your store to get the most value from your coupons:

- **Do you accept manufacturers' coupons?** Almost all supermarkets do, although some discount stores and food outlets do not.
- **Do you double or triple coupon values? If so, to what limit?** If your store doubles or triples coupons, they most likely do that every day of the week, up to a certain value. Some stores double coupons up to 50 cents, meaning your 50-cent coupon would be worth $1, but a 75-cent coupon is just 75 cents off. (It's curious to note how many store or manufacturer coupons offer 55-cent discounts, just over the amount that can usually be doubled.) Some stores double coupons up to 99 cents, and on rare occasions some will double or triple the value of higher-value cou-

pons for a limited time, so make sure you keep an eye out for these tremendous opportunities. Triple High-Value Coupon Day is like Super Bowl Sunday to the Strategic Shopper!

- **Do you accept expired coupons?** Some stores do not double coupons but will accept expired manufacturers coupons as an alternative. If your store does not accept expired coupons, be sure not to accidentally use them. The store won't be reimbursed for their value in those cases. The CouponMom.com community always plays fair!

- **Do you offer store coupons? Where can I find them?** Some stores have coupons in their weekly flier, on their websites, in special sections of the Sunday newspaper, in brochure racks in the store, or even in store magazines. For example, you can print store coupons from Target.com; clip weekly coupons that let you buy a pre-selected grocery item for a penny, called the 1-Cent Mystery Item Coupon, from the Sunday Publix circular; or clip coupons from the ShopRite or Safeway sales circulars.

- **Do you accept competitors' coupons?** If your store does accept competitors' coupons, get ready for serious savings. Sign up for the e-mail newsletters and loyalty cards for the various supermarkets and drugstores in your area; look in other stores' weekly sales fliers for store coupons; print store coupons from the SuperTarget, Walgreens, or Rite Aid website; and collect in-store coupon booklets at grocery and drugstores. This gives you a massive coupon collection. If your store accepts coupons from multiple sources, your savings opportunities expand tremendously.

- **Do you accept Internet coupons?** Hundreds of dollars of savings are available absolutely free (other than the cost of printer paper and ink) from websites. Most stores accept Internet coupons, but some won't, due to concern over counterfeit coupons. If your store accepts printable coupons on a case-by-case basis, follow these guidelines to increase the likelihood that you'll be able to use them. Naturally, you want to use only coupons that you've printed from legitimate sites, including CouponMom.com, Coupons.com, SmartSource.com, and RedPlum.com.

° Do not cut the coupon out after you print it, so that you can show that the coupon was printed from a legitimate site.

° Legitimate Internet coupons should say "manufacturer coupon" and include valid remit addresses for the manufacturer and bar codes that can be scanned.

° Ask to speak to the manager if the cashier does not know whether or not to accept the coupon.

° Visit the store's corporate website and look for the coupon policy. For example, to find the Wal-Mart policy on Internet coupons, log on to www.walmartfacts.com and search for "coupon policy," or find the policy directly at http://walmartstores.com/7655.aspx. If you're not able to find the Internet policy on a store's website, send an e-mail requesting policy details to the customer service contact. Print the e-mail you receive in response and keep it with your coupons. If a store clerk is unsure of his or her own corporate policy, you'll be able to offer your written proof as guidance.

° Many stores now allow shoppers to print coupons from their own websites. Take the entire printed page with you to the store. If a cashier questions the coupons, you can show that you printed them directly from the store's website.

"Buy One, Get One Free" Deals

These promotions offer 50 percent savings, but Strategic Shoppers know how to get an even better deal using coupons. If you're careful, you might turn this promotion into a "get two free" deal. Here are two savings scenarios:

1. **The first item rings up at full price, and the second item is zero.** In this case, you would need to buy two items in order to realize the BOGO savings. If you have more than one

coupon for the BOGO item, you may be able to use two coupons, one for each item, to save the most. Using two coupons on a BOGO deal may make the entire purchase free. Example:

Brand X crackers are usually $2 per box.

This week, Brand X crackers are buy one, get one free, meaning your average cost for each box is $1 ($2 divided by two boxes = $1 per box).

If you have one coupon for $1 off Brand X crackers, your average cost is now 50 cents per box ($2 minus $1 coupon = $1 divided by two boxes = 50 cents per box).

If you have two coupons for $1 off Brand X crackers, you would save the most, and you would get two boxes of crackers free ($2 minus two $1 coupons = free!).

2. **Each item rings up at half-price.** If the store charges half-price for each BOGO item, then you do not need to buy two items. If you had only one $1 coupon for Brand X crackers, you would still get the item free, since the BOGO crackers would actually ring up at $1 per box. If you had an odd number of coupons, such as three, you would get three boxes free. This is the most desirable BOGO policy for Strategic Shoppers, since you can maximize your savings easily.

To make the most out of BOGO deals, you need to know exactly how they work. Otherwise, it's easy to spend more per item than necessary. In the second example, where each item rings up at half-price, a shopper who buys only as many items as he or she has coupons for will get each item for free. Buy two items with one coupon and your savings decrease.

To learn how BOGO deals work at your store, ask! Or review your receipt the next time you buy items offered with BOGO deals to determine how they ring up. Keep in mind that each store may handle this differently. While BOGO items often ring up for half-price at grocery stores, drugstores typically charge full price for the first item and nothing for the second. In other words, you must purchase two items at drugstores in order to benefit from the BOGO deal, but it might not be necessary at grocery stores.

Multiple Item Pricing

Here's a secret for you. That "10 for $10" promotion at your grocery store could just as easily read "1 for $1." The "3 for $5" promotion could also read "$1.67 each." The multiple-pricing pitch is a common way supermarkets try to get shoppers to fill up their carts. If you are feeding an army, you might need all ten items. But if you aren't, you can bring the promotion more in line with your family's needs. In most cases, shoppers do not need to buy multiple items in order to pay the discounted price. Read the tag carefully to be sure. If it does not say "minimum purchase 10" or "pay $1.50 each if less than 10 purchased," you can assume that a smaller quantity will still be sold at the multiple-item price.

Even more confusing than the "10 for $10" pitch is the "10 for $10" mix-and-match sale. Ads promoting such deals often feature pictures of qualifying items, leading you to believe you need to gather ten of the assorted items in order to get them for $1 each. Again, read the wording carefully, but in many cases you're able to buy just what you need for $1 each.

Ideally, you want to buy only as many items offered at the multiple-item price as you have coupons for. Combining store and manufacturer coupons with BOGO offers often results in completely free items. The only thing better than BOGO is getting all of the items for free!

Special Discounts or Rewards Programs

Some stores honor senior citizens by offering discounts, such as 5 percent off on Wednesdays. Your store may also have rewards programs that offer additional savings, such as a Baby Club or a Pet Club to entice shoppers to buy their diapers or pet food there. When you sign up for these special shopping clubs, you may receive special coupons in the mail for items the store figures members will use. For example, members of my supermarket's Baby Club get coupons for baby products as well as convenience dinners, such as rotisserie chickens in the deli, and inexpensive photo development. Even if you do not spend enough to earn large rewards, the coupon savings definitely justify the time you take to fill out the enrollment form. Check at the customer service counter to see which programs your store offers.

Rain-Check Policy

One of the best tools in the Strategic Shopper's savings arsenal is the rain check. This allows you to buy at the sale price when the item on sale is out of stock. You might find a coupon for the rain-checked item by the time it's in stock again, resulting in an even deeper discount.

Price-Matching Policy

Some stores will match competitors' advertised sale prices, but it's up to you to ask. If several stores have items you need at low sale prices and one of your stores matches prices, you can save time and money by taking all of the stores' circulars to the price-matching store to get the lowest sale price for the items all in one place. Wal-Mart will match other stores' prices, but you must bring in the printed ad showing the lower prices. Ask employees at your supermarket what that store's price-matching policy is.

Upromise Program Participation

Upromise is a free service that rewards members with cash rebates on all kinds of everyday purchases at many online and traditional stores, including supermarkets and some drugstores. Your rebates can be directed toward a college savings plan or redeemed for cash. Launched in April 2001, Upromise has more than ten million members today. Its program works at more than 21,000 grocery and drug stores, 10,000 gas stations, and 8,500 restaurants, as well as hundreds of retail store locations and online shopping sites. Most major supermarkets participate in the Upromise program. Once you sign up at Upromise.com, register your store's loyalty card in your Upromise account. When you buy qualifying items, the rebate amount is automatically added to your Upromise account. The site also offers eCoupons. You can download the coupon value for specific items to your account. The Upromise eCoupon amount does not come off at the register but is automatically deposited to your Upromise account when you purchase those items.

Price Accuracy Guarantee

Supermarkets generally offer some kind of price-accuracy guarantee. This means that if the register incorrectly rings up an item, the price will be corrected—and you might even get the item for free. But again, it's up to you to point out any discrepancies. Grocery stores change thousands of prices each week. It's understandable that a mistake might occur once in a while. So get into the habit of watching prices ring up at the checkout, and hang on to your receipts. If you spot an overcharge after you've left the store, take your receipt to the customer service department on your next visit. You should be able to get a refund for the price difference or for the full amount, depending on the store's policy.

If you accidentally picked up the wrong size or variety off the shelf and bought a more expensive item than the sale-priced item you intended to buy, you can return the item for a refund on your next visit.

To avoid overpaying for groceries and to keep from having to return for refunds, I always ask the cashier to wait until I've unloaded all of my groceries before he or she starts ringing up my order. That way, I am able to watch the register ring up prices as they are scanned so that I can catch any errors on my part or the register's part and correct them immediately.

Store-Brand or Private-Label Guarantee

Many supermarkets stock a wide variety of private-label items. These are often much less expensive than their name-brand counterparts and are often just as good. (Some private-label items are actually made by the same manufacturers as name-brand items.) But it's possible that you might not like the store brands as well as name brands. To encourage shoppers to try their own labels, many stores offer money-back guarantees. If you decide the private-label items don't meet your standards, you can bring them back for refunds. Such guarantees are often printed on the packages of stores' own brands. Or ask at the customer service department.

Pharmacy Discounts and Coupons

Drugstores have gotten very shrewd at luring customers by offering gift cards or other incentives for shoppers who transfer prescriptions. Not surprisingly, supermarket pharmacies are fighting back, offering their own pharmacy-transfer coupons and discounted or free generic drugs. Your supermarket pharmacy might offer a specific list of drugs that cost as little as $10 for a three-month prescription, or $4 for a thirty-day prescription.

Some stores have even offered a selected list of antibiotics at no charge either permanently or during short-term promotions. Many supermarkets offer gift cards of varying value for transferring prescriptions. You can find these offers by reading the store's weekly ad circulars, the store's e-mail newsletter, home mailers, or the Sunday grocery coupon circular. Your store also may match other pharmacies' prices or accept prescription-transfer coupons from other pharmacies. If you're unsure about the savings available at your store's pharmacy, ask for details.

Grocery Store Websites

Your supermarket's website is a great resource for deals on lots of items, not just groceries. Store loyalty cardholders might qualify for reduced admission to local attractions, for example. You can also view the store's weekly ad, learn about special promotions, and find printable or electronic grocery coupons by visiting the store's website. If the store offers an e-mail newsletter, sign up to receive advanced information about sales and coupons. And the website is a great place to ask questions by e-mailing customer service. It's a good idea to print responses for future reference.

Custom-Made Savings Opportunities

Sometimes Strategic Shoppers have to find their own deals. Ask meat, dairy, or produce managers about special sales or markdowns. For example, your produce manager might mark down yesterday's produce at 5:30 a.m., so shopping early pays off. Your meat manager may mark down meat with upcoming expiration dates at 4 p.m., so shoppers who stop by on their way home from work can pick up bargains for that night's dinner. And your store may feature weekly Manager Markdowns that offer various items at a 50 percent savings. Mastering your store's savings opportunities ensures that you will make the most out of every shopping trip.

Unexpected Bargains: Grocery-Store Deals on Photo Development, Air Miles, Gas, and More

Big-box retailers, such as Wal-Mart or SuperTarget, offer larger grocery sections to encourage shoppers to view them as one-stop destinations for a variety of items. In response, many supermarkets have begun offering shoppers a number of non-grocery items and services. Pharmacies have long been featured inside grocery stores. Many stores also offer DVD rentals, photo centers, full-service delis, in-store gourmet coffee shops, floral departments, and fuel centers. Strategic Shoppers love it when supercenters and supermarkets fight over them. With some careful planning, we are the ones who win.

Here's an overview of some of the non-grocery deals your grocery store might offer.

Online Photo Development

Check your supermarket's website for online photo development service. If so, you're able to upload your photos online and pick up the prints at your store when you shop. This is a quick way to get prints from your digital cameras with no shipping charge and no extra trip to the photo store. Your supermarket's e-mail newsletter may feature special offers, such as free prints for new customers or coupons for free enlargements. National drugstore chains offer similar services.

Gas Stations

Supermarket fuel center prices are competitive, and some stores give additional fuel discounts based on grocery purchases. If your store sells retailers' and restaurant gift cards, you can buy them for your own use and increase your fuel savings by consolidating your spending at your grocery store.

Restaurant Meal Deals and Airline Miles

Safeway and Safeway-owned stores, such as Vons, Genuardi's, and Dominick's, reward shoppers with free United airline miles when they register their grocery card at www.grocerymiles.com. Even if you don't accumulate enough miles to get a free airline ticket, you can get free restaurant gift certificates with United Miles from Restaurant.com. Redeem airline miles for restaurant certificates online at this link: http://www.united.com/page/article/0,6722,52131,00.html.

Cheap DVD Rentals

Many supermarkets and discount stores have DVD-rental kiosks that are much less expensive than video-store rentals and quicker than rent-by-mail services. We can rent movies from our store's Redbox DVD kiosk for only $1 per night. As long as I remember to return the DVD the next day, we can rent one movie each week and pay less in a month than the cost of renting one DVD at a freestanding video store. (And it's significantly cheaper than taking everyone to the cinema, where $9 movie tickets are the norm.) Visit www.Redbox.com to find locations in your area. Sign up for the Redbox e-mail newsletter to receive one free rental immediately. You'll also receive codes for free rentals periodically.

Change Counting

You can find Coinstar change-counting machines in many stores. They can turn your coins into cash, but at an 8.9 percent fee. But if you choose to receive a gift certificate instead of a cash voucher, you can often avoid such a fee. Participating retailers vary but may include Amazon, Borders, CVS/Pharmacy, and Starbucks. Check www.Coinstar.com for details and to find a machine in a store near you.

A Final Word

Each supermarket in your area likely bills itself as the low-price leader in its market. I agree with all of them but not necessarily all the time. It's up to you to educate yourself about the savings opportunities available at various retailers. If you find yourself shopping at just one store in your area out of convenience, challenge yourself to explore possibilities at just one additional store, then another, as time allows. I'm guessing you'll decide that scoring the best possible prices will make shopping around worth your time.

Seven

— — —

Clip, Print, or Swipe to Save: Using Coupons

I f you found a $20 bill on the ground on your way into the grocery store, would you pick it up? Of course you would! But many of us are giving up the equivalent of free money by failing to work coupon use into our shopping habits. It's not quite as easy as scooping cash off the ground, but using coupons is still a relatively simple way to stretch your grocery budget.

In this chapter we're going to discuss:

- where to look for coupons, beyond your Sunday newspaper
- how to make your coupons work their hardest for you and translate into the most significant savings
- handy ways to organize your coupons to make sure you don't accidentally throw away "free money"

Don't Give Up!

"I was busy with my kids' schedule and school, the house, and my part-time job. I slacked off a little. I fell off the coupon wagon and just kept stuffing the weekly coupons in my tote bag. I also let them accumulate on my kitchen

table. I think I had four or five months' worth of coupon circulars saved at that point. I also had a ton of loose coupons that I received in the mail or from items that I had purchased and just dumped into the tote.

One Friday night after the kids and hubby were in bed, I emptied my tote bag, collated them, and start paging through each one. There were a lot of expired coupons and things that I knew I wouldn't or don't use. I cut out all the ones I wanted and tossed the expired ones. It took me about three hours to get through my collection, but it was worth it.

All the coupons I clipped that I wasn't using the following day were sorted and placed in the organizer. I did save over $100 on food shopping that day, on meats, cleaning products, paper goods, etc. So it was definitely worth the effort from the night before."

—Dawn Snyder, Philadelphia, Pennsylvania

Downturn in the Economy = Uptick in Coupon Use

The fourth quarter of 2008—with the jobs and real-estate market sluggish, the auto industry in trouble, upheaval in the banking industry creating global financial shockwaves, and the stock market taking a swan dive— wasn't exactly a time of economic jubilation in our county. But I did find at least one statistic to smile about. Coupon use soared by a double-digit percentage. Throughout 2008, the face value of coupons and the number of coupons issued increased as well. Even as things turn around, I hope new coupon users who turned their scissors into instruments of economic recovery will keep on clipping.

Overall in 2008, the average face value of coupons increased 9 percent, and the number of coupons issued increased 5 percent. And for the first time in nearly two decades, coupon redemption increased in the fourth quarter of 2008 by 17 percent, compared to the fourth quarter of 2007.[1]

A December 2008 survey suggests that as times got tough, consumers

---

1. NCH Marketing Services, March 2009.

who might have felt embarrassed about coupon use in the past quickly got over their qualms. Nearly 57 percent of consumers who responded to the survey said they were once self-conscious about using grocery coupons but were no longer squeamish about it. Some 43 percent of consumers said they had used coupons more often in the second half of 2008, and only 22 percent said they still found coupon use embarrassing.[2]

My message to that 22 percent of shoppers: There's nothing wrong with taking free money to help feed your family! Last year, 315 billion grocery coupons worth more than $400 billion were distributed, but less than 1 percent of them were redeemed. About 2.6 billion coupons were redeemed at a dollar value of $3.3 billion.[3] Increasing coupon use just 1 percent would translate into $3 billion saved. If you're still bashful, keep in mind that manufacturers don't print coupons exclusively as a charitable program (although many civic-minded companies have amended their prices, mindful of struggling families). Coupons help businesses build market share by enticing customers to try new products or choose the products the coupons are promoting.

Think of coupon use as part-time employment. If you can save $50 a week with one or two hours of planning, that's not a bad hourly wage for a "job" that requires no performance review and is entirely recession-proof!

As Seen on TV! How to Pay $17 for $96 Worth of Groceries

A television reporter working on a story went grocery shopping with me recently. She was not a regular coupon user, and throughout the trip she seemed genuinely amazed when I explained how the coupon deals worked. The real stunner for her was my final bill. The items I'd purchased rang up to $96, but with all the coupons I used, I walked out with my wallet just $17 lighter.

"When I was assigned this story I didn't understand why I would need someone to teach me how to use a coupon, " the reporter told me. "I

---

2. Study findings by ICOM Information and Communications, a provider of marketing data (Dec. 2008).
3. Carolina Marketing Services (March 2009).

thought, *Don't you just cut it out and hand it over?* I had no idea you could save this much money with coupons."

Yes, it makes for great TV when you can demonstrate such a grocery-store triumph, but this was no ratings gimmick. It's representative of the savings that any family can realize with a little effort.

Reuniting with Old Friends . . . Coupons!

"The first time I used coupons was at age 18. I went to a drugstore that was having a double-coupons promotion—unheard of at that time—and bought a bunch of stuff for my new household. After that I pretty much forgot about coupons for quite a while. I had no clue about how to 'strategically shop.' I would go through circulars and clip what I thought I might use and throw away the rest. I didn't know about Extra Bucks or Register Rewards or Single Check Rebates. I started using CouponMom.com in August 2008 and really got the system going in October when I bought over $45 of items for only $3.11. Of course this is run-of-the-mill for most savvy couponers. I was amazed that I had never caught on to this before. I also used the Strategic Shopping method at my local grocery store, which I'd never done before. It was amazing. I save probably around $500 per month, and I donate toiletries to a local charity and help out family members with miscellaneous items. I used to just save a few coupons here and there for things that I knew I'd get soon, then throw the rest away. Not now!"

—Beth Mersino, Oxford, Michigan

Finding Them Is One Thing, Knowing When to Use Them Is Another

You almost can't avoid getting your hands on a stack of coupons each week. They come in the mail. They're inserted into your Sunday newspaper. They might even be affixed to products you're planning to buy anyway. Remember, 315 billion of these things are distributed each year. They're practically raining from the sky!

But simply collecting and redeeming coupons isn't enough. Strategic

Shoppers know that the science of using coupons has more to do with knowing where to find the right coupons, how to combine coupons when possible, and when to use them.

Maybe you think coupons don't apply to the items your family uses. Or maybe you find them too time-consuming to gather and too difficult to organize. Not so! I can teach you how to spend very little time accessing the coupons that are best suited for your family to help you save on the things you buy each week. New methods of coupon distribution and free Internet resources mean that even the Rookie Shopper can put coupons to very profitable use without a lot of effort.

Of course, just as with any endeavor in life, your success at using coupons will depend on how much you put into it. If you want television reporters following you through the grocery store to document your incredible savings (or even if you just want the incredible savings, without the cameras) you'll need to scour a number of sources to come up with numerous coupons. And you'll need to pay attention to timing. Just because you clip a coupon today doesn't mean you need to rush out to redeem it tomorrow. Learn to wait until items for which you have coupons go on sale, then spring into action. Because manufacturers often use various means to distribute coupons, it's likely you'll have several when the item they're promoting goes on sale. When that happens, you can stock up for next to nothing.

Think of coupons as your family's financial rocket boosters. Once you've launched Strategic Shopping, fire up the coupons to really give your savings a jolt. Once you've clipped or printed a coupon, the countdown begins. The key is to keep an eye on the item until it goes on sale. Then liftoff! Combine the coupon and sale prices for the best possible deal.

Get Organized

Internet users can rely on online coupon directories and don't need to cut out and organize every coupon every week. I call it the No-Clip System, and it requires as little at 15 minutes a week to use. However, many of us still prefer to have coupons literally at our fingertips, so I'll review easy ways of keeping coupons manually organized. And for the ultimate in coupon savings, I'll show you how to combine coupons, in keeping with store and manufacturer policies. Most shoppers do not realize it is possible to "stack" coupons, or to use more than one coupon per item. As long as they are different types of coupons, this can be perfectly fine. I'll teach you how to do it.

Read the Fine Print: Understanding Coupons

Go by the words, not the pictures: Grocery coupons typically include an image of the item and a written description. In many cases, the coupon will apply to several sizes and varieties of the same item, although the picture may feature one particular variety (often the most expensive). Strategic Shoppers know to study the wording rather than just picking up the item that matches the picture. Here's an example. You might have a coupon offering $1 off a certain brand of toothpaste. But that brand comes in multiple varieties, ranging from the $1 basic item to the $3.49 premium product. If you simply grab the item pictured on the coupon, you'll save $1 off the $3.49 version. If you pay close attention to the wording, you'll know to select the $1 item and get it for nothing. Discounted prices are great, but nothing beats free!

The smallest size can offer the biggest savings: In general, the largest size of an item is usually the best deal when you buy it at regular price, since the unit cost tends to be lower. (This isn't always true, of course.) When you're using coupons, the smaller size can actually be the bigger bargain. Take the time to figure the unit cost and then figure your savings on the various sizes that are available. You might find that downsizing is in order. If the 26-ounce jar of pasta sauce is on sale for $1.50 and the larger 45-ounce jar costs $2.50, then a $1 coupon would bring the cost of the small jar to 50 cents, or a cost of about 1.9 cents per ounce. Use the same $1 coupon on the larger jar and it's about 3.3 cents per ounce. Naturally, you want to grab the smaller jar, and if you have more than one coupon, you can purchase the equivalent of the larger jar at the same discount as the smaller one.

Consider trial sizes: In some cases, a coupon will say "any variety" rather than saying "for 12-ounce size or larger." "Any variety" means trial sizes are included, so check to see if your grocery store, drugstore, or discount stores have trial-size aisles. Because prices are lower for trial sizes (although the unit cost is usually not) a $1 coupon can translate into a free item.

The Different Types of Coupons, and Where to Find Them

There are two types of grocery coupons—store coupons and manufacturers' coupons—and both are distributed in numerous ways. You'll find them in your Sunday newspaper's grocery coupon circulars. They might arrive in your mailbox via direct mail. You can print them from the Internet and find them on product packages and in store displays. It is important to know how to tell the difference between store and manufacturers' coupons, because you can usually combine a store and a manufacturer's coupon on the same item. It's easy to know which is which, because coupons are labeled at the top as either "manufacturer coupon" or "store coupon." Many store coupons are redeemable only at that store, and are labeled as such.

In general, manufacturers' coupons are eligible to be doubled based on the store's coupon policy, unless it says "do not double" across the top. In that case, it's still up to the store whether to double the coupon or not. Be sure to ask.

Store coupons are not doubled or tripled and are deducted at face value. When you learn your stores' savings programs, you'll want to find out if they have store coupons and, if so, where they are distributed. Once you have a store coupon for an item you need, you should look for a manufacturer's coupon for the same item. Combining the store's and manufacturer's coupon for an item allows you to "double" the face value.

This example illustrates the power of "stacking" store and manufacturers' coupons:

Item: Brand X Toothpaste, Full Price	$3.00
sale savings realized using loyalty card	-$1.00 (for sale price of $2.00)
store coupon found in store flier for $1	-$1.00
manufacturer's coupon found in newspaper	-$1.00
final price	**$0, or FREE!**

The Sunday Newspaper: Your Primary Source of Grocery Coupons

Nearly 90 percent of the 315 billion grocery coupons distributed in 2008 were issued via the Sunday newspaper circulars available in most cities' daily newspapers.[4] There are generally two coupon circulars each week, one from each of the two newspaper coupon companies: RedPlum and SmartSource. Manufacturers like Procter & Gamble traditionally issue their own coupon circular called BrandSaver at least once per month. Other manufacturers, such as General Mills, Unilever, and Campbell's, may also issue their own circulars a few weeks each year.

According to a 2008 coupon study by Scarborough Research, newspaper circulars are still the main source of grocery coupons for 53 percent of households, although the Internet is a rapidly growing source for many shoppers.

I surveyed the members of CouponMom.com to find out their primary sources of grocery coupons. These members are truly Strategic Shoppers, so I was not surprised that 96 percent of them use Sunday newspaper coupons, as compared to only 53 percent of shoppers questioned for the Scarborough Research study. More than half of CouponMom.com members buy the paper in the store, a quarter of them subscribe to the paper, and nearly a quarter subscribe to the paper *and* buy extra copies of the newspaper in the store.[5]

Coupons vary by newspaper, even within the same city or state. There are more than 250 versions of the Sunday grocery coupon circular, depending on the newspaper that carries it. If you live in an area with more than one newspaper, be aware that papers in larger cities with more readers generally have more coupon offers. If you live in a suburb of a large city and subscribe to the smaller suburban paper, you are not likely to get as many coupon offers in your newspaper's circular as in the larger city newspaper. You should consider comparing the two papers' circulars to see if you would get more coupons if you bought the larger metro area newspaper on Sun-

---

4. NCH Marketing Services study (March 2009).
5. CouponMom.com member poll (April 2009).

days. Most newspapers offer Sunday-only subscriptions. As a Strategic Shopper, it is smart to get at least two or three copies of the Sunday coupon circulars, and even more if possible. You should subscribe to the paper to make sure you do not miss a week, and you can get a discounted subscription through your newspaper's website or by calling your newspaper's circulation number and requesting the "new subscriber" rate or the lowest rate available. Check www.discountednewspapers.com to find your newspaper's rates. In addition to your subscription, you can buy extra copies of the Sunday paper at stores on Sundays. Some stores will sell individual papers or bundled sets of two newspapers at a discount on Sundays. In my area, an early version of the Sunday paper is available on Saturday. (It's known as the "bulldog" edition.) That's a way to get a jump on the week's coupons.

If you do buy extra copies of the Sunday paper in stores to get more coupons, be sure to look through the inserts before buying the paper to be certain that grocery coupon circulars were included in that paper. If there aren't enough coupon circulars printed for all the newspapers printed, then the home-delivered papers sent to subscribers will get the coupons first, and the remainder of the coupon circulars will be included in alternating copies of the newspaper. Also, there are usually no grocery coupon circulars in newspapers during holiday weekends, such as Thanksgiving, Christmas, the Fourth of July, Labor Day, and Memorial Day. CouponMom.com's Grocery Coupon Database is updated every Saturday with details about the following Sunday's coupons. No new listings means there will be no grocery coupons in that Sunday's paper.

In some cities, the grocery coupon companies are testing the idea of mailing the coupon circular to homes rather than including it in the newspaper. In other cities, shoppers may get a coupon circular in their newspaper and also receive the same circular in the mail during the week. Mailing coupon circulars may be a growing trend, as direct mail can reach more households as newspaper circulation declines.

Coupons on Online Website Directories, such as CouponMom.com

When I first began using grocery coupons in 1993, the only way to use newspaper coupons effectively was to clip and organize them all each week.

This about drove me nuts! Because a typical week's circulars may have one hundred coupons, it would take about an hour to cut out, file, and organize coupons for that week's shopping trip. Big coupon weeks have as many as two hundred coupons in the newspaper circulars. Inevitably, I would end up getting frustrated when I couldn't find a coupon I knew I had seen somewhere, or when I discovered that the coupon was expired after spending the time searching for it.

The Internet has changed all that. It's now easy to use newspaper coupons without having to clip and organize them each week. On CouponMom .com I offer a Grocery Coupon Database—an online directory of every coupon issued in the Sunday circulars. Rather than clipping newspaper coupons every week, you can simply enter that Sunday's date on the cover of the circular and save the entire circular. Then the CouponMom.com database points you to the circular containing the particular coupon you need for a given shopping trip. Suddenly your coupon-clipping career becomes a lot less time-consuming, as you're able to quickly "flip and clip." Because the database tells you exactly where to look for the coupon you need, preparing for your shopping trip should take just 10 or 15 minutes instead of several tedious hours. Later in this chapter, we will describe other coupon organization systems you can use if you prefer to cut out and organize all of the coupons each week.

You can learn more details about using the Coupon Mom system to make using newspaper coupons easier in chapter 8: Surf and Save: Using CouponMom.com.

Trading Coupons with Friends

The Sunday newspaper might be full of diaper coupons one week and coupons for first-aid products the next. If you have a busy, "ouchy"-prone four-year-old and your next-door neighbor has a new baby, it's not hard to guess who needs which coupons. If you find you have too many of one sort of coupon and not enough of another, consider trading. You can organize a formal coupon swap or just trade with a friend when you both need coupons you don't have. More than half of the CouponMom.com members say they trade coupons.

Coupons by Mail

Often, the savings will come right to you. Here are some tips for getting store and manufacturers' coupon offers by mail.

The rewards of loyalty: According to the Scarborough study, 35 percent of households use store and manufacturers' coupons received in the mail. (But 65 percent are tossing valuable savings by mistake—don't trash the "cash" that shows up in your mailbox!) More than 97 percent of CouponMom.com poll respondents said they use store coupons received in the mail. These are often more useful than ones you'll find in the newspaper or on store displays. That's because they're often tailored specifically for you. Stores are diligent about tracking consumer choices, and the data they collect when you swipe your customer loyalty card (if your store offers such a program) helps them know which products you like. Because they want to keep you as a customer, it makes sense for stores to send you coupons for items you're likely to buy. In chapter 6, I talked about signing up for your store's loyalty card. By providing your complete mailing information, you've actually enlisted the store as your bargain-hunting ally. I tracked the coupon offers I received from my store over a three-month period. I received $136 in free coupons and used $85 worth of them immediately. That's a 63 percent redemption rate—63 times higher than the national average of 1 percent coupon redemption rate. It's a win for both sides. I've benefited from the savings, and the store has benefited from my loyalty as a shopper.

Requesting coupons from manufacturers directly: Strategic Shoppers know that asking a manufacturer for coupons usually works. They want to sell products, after all, and if you've gone to the effort to ask for coupons, they know you're likely to buy. More than 80 percent of CouponMom.com poll respondents said they had requested and received coupons from manufacturers at no cost. You can request coupons via e-mail by going to the customer service contact link on a manufacturer's website, or by calling the 800 number listed on the website for the customer service department. In either case, you should express your preference for the company's products and politely request coupons, being sure to include your complete mailing address. You can even copy and paste the same e-mail message and send it to several companies at the same time to save time.

Our own study illustrated the positive results that come from simple requests. A team of CouponMom.com researchers sent polite e-mail requests to eighty-one companies and received free coupons in the mail from forty-nine companies. That's a 60 percent success rate. We received 195 coupons with a total face value of $178—and thirteen of the coupons were for $52 worth of totally free items. Response time varied from two to twenty-six days. The average response time was nine days. That's not a lot of effort or waiting for a good amount of savings!

Even better, the companies that responded positively paid the postage to send the coupons, whose value would increase at stores that double coupons. A list of the companies that sent coupons appears in the appendix in the back of this book. Although each company's coupon supply can change and your experience may not be the same as ours, results like these prove that it's worth your time to shoot off an e-mail or two (or eighty-one) to your favorite companies to request free coupons.

Vocalpoint coupons: This Procter & Gamble program sends coupons to members to use themselves or to share with friends. I signed up for Vocalpoint a couple of years ago, and several times a year I receive a packet of coupons for a single product. The first coupon, intended for my own use, has a high value and may even be for a free item. The next ten or so coupons will be for a lesser amount off the same product, and Vocalpoint encourages me to share these coupons with friends. Sometimes I do, and sometimes I use them myself, depending on the item's sale price. You can sign up for free at www.Vocalpoint.com.

Coupons Online

Printable coupons are the fastest-growing source of grocery coupons. The Scarborough study showed that while only 11 percent of households reported using printable coupons in 2007, just 6 percent of households used them in 2005. That's an 83 percent increase in two years. We polled the seasoned Strategic Shoppers who are CouponMom.com members, and 91 percent of respondents use printable grocery coupons. They are easy to print, they are free, and the inventory of printable grocery coupons continues to grow as manufacturers realize that we like to use them.

The number of sources for printable coupons continues to grow as well.

Along with CouponMom.com, you can find them at sites including Coupons.com, SmartSource.com, and RedPlum.com. None of these sites require registration to print coupons. You can also print coupons directly from most grocery-store websites. If you searched the term "printable grocery coupon" on the Web, you would find thousands of listings. However, many of the sites tend to feature the same printable coupons at any given time, so you can choose the sites that don't require registration if you prefer.

Manufacturers' websites are fertile coupon-hunting ground as well. Sign up for e-mail newsletters and you'll likely receive them regularly. The CouponMom.com research team has done some legwork for you here, too. A list of manufacturer sites with printable coupons appears in the appendix.

Some stores do not accept printable grocery coupons because of concerns that they might be counterfeit, but we've found that this isn't much of an issue. Just 1.3 percent of the respondents to our CouponMom.com member poll said that their stores did not accept printable coupons, a very low number, considering that 91 percent of the respondents said they use printable coupons.

It goes without saying that you should never use fake coupons. Using a counterfeit coupon is a serious offense, even if you use it accidentally. Never buy printable coupons from an auction site or other website, since legitimate printable coupons are free. If you see high-value printable coupons for sale online, you can be sure they are counterfeit. And printable coupons for free items are cause for scrutiny, too. If it seems too good to be true, it probably is.

E-coupons

When was the last time you showed up at the airport with an actual paper ticket? Chances are, the last flight you took involved an electronic ticket. It's a faster, easier way to get passengers moving. Electronic grocery coupons are somewhat similar in that there is no paper to keep up with as you prepare for your trip. This is a relatively new effort by manufacturers, but I'm guessing we'll see this trend continue to grow. As of this writing, elec-

tronic coupons sites include Shortcuts.com, Upromise.com, and Cellfire
.com. Some individual grocery store websites have their own electronic coupons, such as GiantEagle.com and Kroger.com.

Electronic coupons are not paper coupons that you print. Instead, their
value is added to your store loyalty card. When you buy the item and swipe
your card, the discount is automatically applied. It's hard to think of a
more convenient way to save money! This method of coupon use does require registration, since your loyalty card is how the store issues the discount. Signing up is free, though, and does not require a credit card. Once
you register, you can view a selection of coupon offers and click on the ones
you like.

Since electronic coupons are new to many shoppers, take note of the
following guidelines regarding their use.

- Read the item description very carefully and buy the exact size
  and variety described by the coupon offer. If it isn't an exact
  match, the coupon will not work.
- Electronic coupons are deducted only at face value—even if
  the store doubles traditional coupons.
- You can select only one coupon per offer.
- Coupons do expire and will disappear from your card automatically after their expiration date.
- After you select your coupons, it's a good idea print a list of
  your e-coupons so you don't forget about them or overlook
  their expiration dates.
- Electronic coupons are available only at participating stores,
  although new stores are continually joining the programs. To
  find out if your store participates, check your store's website in
  the coupon and/or savings section.
- The sites add coupon offers on a regular basis, so you should
  check the sites to add new coupons at least twice a month.
  Subscribing to the electronic coupon site's e-mail newsletter
  is the best way to find out about new coupons as soon as they
  are added. Because each manufacturer may limit the total

number of coupons that can be downloaded, check the site as soon as new coupons are available. You need to "act fast while supplies last" to make sure you get the savings before they are gone.

- Upromise eCoupons work slightly differently than the other electronic coupons. Rather than having the coupon value deducted at the register, the coupon value is actually credited toward your Upromise account. At any time, you can have your Upromise account balance directed toward a college savings plan, or, if you prefer, you can request that it be sent to you in cash.

Depending on the store and the particular electronic coupon site, you may be able to stack electronic and paper coupons for the same item. A $1 newspaper coupon combined with a $1 e-coupon doubles your savings.

Where to Find Store Coupons

One place to look for store coupons is, well, the store. Store coupons can be a Strategic Shopper's best find. They may offer discounts on items that manufacturers' coupons generally don't cover, such as fresh produce or meat. But don't stop looking for coupons at the store! Once you've rounded them up, store coupons combined with manufacturers' coupons can give you maximum savings.

Look for store coupons in your store's weekly ad. Some stores routinely have coupons in their ad every week.

Look in the Sunday newspaper coupon circular for store coupons. Local supermarkets and Target will occasionally place their own store coupons in those circulars.

Check the newspaper to see if your store places a regular ad with their coupons on Sundays or in the Food section during the week.

Look for special flier and coupon-booklet racks at your store that may have store coupons.

Make sure you have provided your full mailing information when you signed up for your store's loyalty card. If you aren't sure if you did, get a new card at the store and fill out the mailing information completely. My Kroger sends me one or two coupon mailers per month that have many coupons for products I buy, as well as free-item coupons. As I mentioned earlier, I received $136 worth of coupons from my store mailers in three months. That's an average of $45 per month of free money, or $540 per year just for checking the mail. Because the store knows what I buy, I used at least 63 percent of the coupons immediately and would be likely to use more of the coupons as the items went on sale before the coupons expired.

Check the store's website to print coupons. Many stores provide printable grocery coupons on their sites, and the first coupons listed are their own store coupons. For example, on one of my store's websites I can print a $5-off coupon for their own brand of diapers. Store coupons for private-label items are particularly attractive, because the after-coupon price is generally less than name-brand items with manufacturers' coupons. Large chains like Safeway, Kroger, and CVS/Pharmacy have added store coupons within their printable grocery coupon sections.

Store websites may also have dedicated sections for their own coupons. For example, Meijer stores have a Meijer MealBox coupon section with new coupons each week, and so does SuperTarget's website.

Remember to ask your store if they accept competitors' store coupons that you can use along with the coupons you already have for your store. If they do, you can use multiple stores' coupons at your one store. You can also use drugstore coupons such as "$5 off a $25 order" that you receive via e-mail at your grocery store if it accepts competitor coupons.

Subscribe to free store magazines. You can pick up a free copy at your store if they have one, and if it includes a subscription card, fill it out and send it in. Some store magazines may feature coupons that will be delivered right to you.

Where to Find In-Store Manufacturers' Coupons

Look for SmartSource boxes containing coupons (regular coupon users call these "Blinkies"). They're located in boxes attached to the store shelves, conveniently right next to the item they're promoting. If the coupon is for an item you use but it isn't on sale and you don't need it immediately, take one or two coupons to use when the item goes on sale in a future week.

Check your receipt and any paperwork that comes with it. Many stores print coupons along with receipts at the cash register, and the coupons printed for you will typically be guided by what you've just purchased. This instant marketing program can save you money on your next shopping trip. If you are brand-flexible, you can save every week using last week's coupons, even if they are for different brands than the ones you usually use. Regular coupon users call these "Catalina" coupons, referring to the company that operates the program, Catalina Marketing.

Look for shelf tags next to products that describe promotion requirements for getting coupons for cash off a future order. For example, the tag may say "Buy Two of Brand X items and get $1 off your next order." (These are "Catalina" coupons.) If you also have a coupon to buy the item, you could end up with a net profit. For example, if the product costs $1.25, you have two $1 coupons for the item, and you get a $1 coupon off your next order when you buy two items, you are netting a "profit" of 50 cents in the form of store credit for your next purchase. Saving money with coupons is great. Did you ever imagine that you could actually make money by using them?

Look for coupons on the package. Logically, coupons on packages have the highest redemption rate of any type of coupons (about 40 percent). Although that is high for coupon redemption, I am amazed that 60 percent of shoppers do not use the coupons that are right on the package! They most likely did not notice them, or else they expected the cashier to take the coupon off. Keep your eyes open and take the coupon off for the cashier and hand it to him or her.

Organizing Your Coupons Easily with My "No-Clip" System

I have a recurring nightmare. In my dream, I am standing in the grocery store, in front of an item that's on sale. There's only one left, and it looks like such a great bargain! And yet, I know that somewhere—in the back of a kitchen drawer, under the car seat, or stuck in a book—there is a coupon that would make the item free. I stand there in agony, unable to move, as another shopper grabs it off the shelf. As I watch my would-be free item roll away in someone else's cart, I wake up, screaming, "If only my coupons had been organized!"

All right, that's actually not true. But this "nightmare" scenario probably plays itself out in grocery stores every day. If you'll get organized, you'll sleep well knowing you've saved every possible penny on your grocery shopping.

Getting your coupons together does not have to take a lot of time. Believe me, trying to use coupons without organizing them will end up taking far more time—and can frustrate you as you search for coupons scattered all hither and yon. My No-Clip System will take just 15 minutes a week, and this chapter will also describe other popular systems available depending on how much time you have.

If you don't like the idea of spending hours a month cutting out and organizing coupons, I recommend that you give my No-Clip System a try. The No-Clip System doesn't mean you'll never touch the scissors again. It simply means that instead of snipping away every Sunday afternoon, you can save the entire coupon circular and pull out those scissors only when you plan to shop. It is the best way to organize coupons that are specifically from the weekly Sunday circulars.

Here's how it works:

Each week, get the Sunday newspaper and pull out the grocery-coupon circulars. Write that Sunday's date on the front covers.

Save the coupon circulars in a file folder, shoe box—whatever works for you. Even if you don't use grocery coupons every week, as long as you pull the coupon circulars out of the Sunday newspaper every week and write that Sunday's date on the covers, you will have a full supply of coupons available when you decide to use them.

When you are ready to shop, consult the Grocery Deals list for your store at CouponMom.com. These will show you what the best grocery deals are each week, and whether or not there is a coupon available for the sale items. Select your items on the list, and print your customized shopping list.

Use the shopping list you print on CouponMom.com to reference the coupons you need by the date they came out and the specific coupon company names. There are two coupon circulars, SmartSource and RedPlum. So coupons that came out on April 5 would be noted as 4/5S or 4/5RP. Each time you use the site, you'll be able to print a list of the newspaper coupons that fit your shopping needs. Your list of coupons will print in order of the date the coupons came out (see the chart on page 87). You'll have to cut out only the coupons you need from your stack of coupon circulars, organized by date.

To find other coupons you need on CouponMom.com, you can also reference the site's Grocery Coupon Database, which will also reference the coupon date. Select the coupons you need, print your list, and also find those in your coupon circulars. In the next chapter, I'll explain this feature and the other features of CouponMom.com in more detail.

One system I do not recommend is one I see all the time: clipping coupons and then tossing them into a plastic bag in no particular order. While this is certainly a quick way of handling your coupons, you're sure to spend quite a bit of time fishing for the right coupon when it's time to check out. And I doubt users of this "method" are saving hundreds of dollars a year with coupons. If you want to save real money, you need a system that makes it easy to find the coupon you need when you need it.

Effective organizing can be easy. A CouponMom.com member poll found that the most popular coupon organization system, used by 29 percent of respondents, is the checkbook-size accordion organizer that you can find at most discount or office-supply stores for $5 or less. Another 23 percent exclusively use the No-Clip System, which is absolutely free. The third most popular system was the binder system, used by 19 percent of respondents, which I'll describe in detail later in this chapter. You can also set this up for $5 or less. The final 29 percent of respondents admitted that they did not have a coupon organization system at all.

I prefer the No-Clip System I just described for my coupon organization. I save the entire circular and write that Sunday's date on the cover. Guided by the CouponMom.com Grocery Deals store lists, I know where to look for the coupons I need, and clip only those which I keep in the front pocket of my coupon organizer to pull out easily when I pay for my groceries. For coupons that do not appear in the Sunday circulars, I also have a plastic accordion checkbook-size organizer that I bought in 2001 for $3 at a discount store, so it has cost me about 38 cents a year so far. It is still as good as new, although it has some miles on it! I use that to hold the coupons that I cut out, receive in the mail, find in store displays, get in magazines, or pick up at the register. I always take that organizer with me when I shop, and I have my name and phone number inside so I can claim it if I ever accidentally leave it in a shopping cart. I've done that more than once. Each time I've gone to collect my missing coupon organizer I've noticed a drawer full of other people's unclaimed coupon organizers. To me this would be like leaving a wallet full of cash lying around without bothering to claim it!

If you are a Busy Shopper, you may not have time to clip coupons at all, but coupons can still help you. As I described earlier, many stores' websites feature electronic coupons you can automatically load onto your store loyalty card. Log on, click on the coupon offers you like, and their value is transferred to your card. If you have a few minutes while surfing, you can print many coupons off the Internet. Keep the printouts in your wallet or with your grocery list so you won't forget to use them at the register.

If you are a Rookie Shopper, my No-Clip System will make it easy for you to quickly access many sources of coupons as you make your shopping list. You may also want to get a small accordion-style checkbook-size organizer to keep loose coupons from mailers, register tapes, and in-store displays separated and neatly organized.

Varsity Shoppers may prefer having coupon boxes or baseball-card binders to take to the store so they will be able to have access to all of their coupons while they are shopping. There are actually many unadvertised sale prices in the supermarket each week, and Varsity Shoppers know that it makes sense to bring their full coupon collection to the store. You never know what you might find on sale—and when you may be able to cash in on *big* savings. To keep the collection current, once a week they can cut out and organize the newspaper and printable coupons to make it easy to find them when they need them in the store.

If you're ready to move into the Coupon Big Leagues, it's time to consider the Binder System. This method is popular with Varsity Shopper CouponMom.com members. If you're interested, visit the CouponMom.com Forum and search for the word "binder." You'll find very helpful discussions about how to set one up, as well as helpful step-by-step pictures. Experienced members will be happy to help you get started.

This method entails using a large three-ring binder with plastic baseball-card holders for coupons. Pages may be organized by section of the store, with each compartment designated for a specific category of coupons. For example, the entire page may be coupons for the baking aisle, and one compartment may hold cake-mix coupons, while another may hold coupons for cooking oils. You can view the coupons with a flip of a page rather than having to take out a stack of coupons to search through every time you spot an unadvertised sale price during your shopping trip.

Some companies sell binder coupon systems for $25 or more. However, it's very easy to make your own binder system inexpensively, for $5 or less. You can recycle a large binder you already have, check thrift stores for used binders, or buy one at a discount store. You can start with a 1-inch binder and transfer to a larger 2- or 3-inch binder as your collection grows, if necessary. Some coupon users get binders that zip so they can avoid having any coupons fall out if the binder is accidentally dropped.

Because larger coupons need to be folded to fit into the card-holder slots, consider buying a few "currency protection" insert pages, which have larger slots. Or look in the photo-album section of your discount store and buy pages that hold 4x6-inch photos. The pages are more expensive but may be easier to manage. And if you're using a binder to organize, you're likely such a coupon rock star that you're racking up serious savings—surely enough to spring for a few specialty binder pages.

A Final Word

Pretend you and I are going shopping together. Just before we check out, I offer to pay half of your grocery bill. My generous offer is not going to cost me a penny and will help you get the most out of your grocery dollar. Surely you're not going to turn me down! Using coupons is the next best thing to having someone pay for half (or more!) of your groceries. I hope that among clipping, surfing, clicking, printing, and swiping, you will make coupon use a part of your Strategic Shopping plan.

Eight

Surf and Save:
Using CouponMom.com

I developed CouponMom.com to help to take the headache out of organizing coupons and to make it far easier to use them effectively. These days, with the power of the Internet, surfing to find coupons is the wave of the future. Sites like mine make saving money a snap!

In this chapter we're going to discuss:

- how my website, CouponMom.com, can help you find easy ways to trim your own grocery bill and use the savings to give back to others
- features such as a coupon database, deal alert, and grocery deals by state to make sure that wherever you are, the website can help you
- the newest site feature, the CouponMom.com Forum

The Year Was 1993 BC (Before CouponMom.com) . . .

I have been using the Strategic Shopping method since the dawn of time. Which is to say, before everyone was on the Internet. Back in those primitive days—the early 1990s—I would spend a couple of hours each Sunday afternoon scanning sales circulars and clipping grocery-store coupons from the newspaper. It was time-consuming but well worth it.

Today, as I've already shown you in the previous chapter, the Web makes it much quicker to find the best grocery deals. Between Internet pages and blogs that list individual stores' prices matched with newspaper coupon savings, printable coupon sites, and electronic coupon sites, it's never been easier to find ways to save. Even if you aren't an experienced Strategic Shopper, it's a snap to find the best grocery deals simply by clicking on grocery websites.

I love hearing from members of the CouponMom.com community, who report that their bills are down while giving is up. And members often learn from one another. One member told me that she was encouraged to give CouponMom.com a try after she saw a fellow shopper put the program to work.

"A lady in line at the grocery store in front of me saved $104 on her bill," this member told me. "I knew then I had to try it!"

I'm always interested to know how people make CouponMom.com best work for them, so I poll users from time to time to get a sense of where people are when they find the site and which features are helping them the most. An April 2009 CouponMom.com member poll yielded some interesting information.

- 42 percent said they were *not* Strategic Shoppers at all before joining the site.
- 48 percent said they knew of some Strategic Shopping methods before joining the site but learned more and saved more after joining the site.
- 45 percent save more than $200 per month on groceries as a result of CouponMom.com.
- 21 percent save more than $300 per month on groceries.
- 84 percent reported donating items to local charities, food drives, friends, or family members in need.

I think that last number—representing the largest percentage of CouponMom.com users—is the most exciting.

. . .

As I explained in the previous chapter, CouponMom.com tells you where to find coupons you need and when to use them to maximize your savings. Cutting out only the coupons you need when you make your shopping list will take 15 minutes or less per week, compared to the hours it can take to figure out each store's grocery deals and to cut out and organize all of the newspaper coupons. And you'll probably save more money than you would simply by searching for deals yourself. By the time you're ready to go shopping, CouponMom.com's expert members have already scanned your stores' deals for you. It's like having a budget butler just ready to guide you to the best possible savings week after week!

Coupon Use as a Way of Life

"I used to be the shopper who went to the store and paid retail for every item in my cart. I've never been able to hold on to my money. I love to shop. But now I'm trying to make my dollar go further. I've saved over $3,000 since I started using coupons. That's not just what I'm not paying, that's cash in a bank account that I'm not spending. Each time I go to the store, I check my receipt and tally up the totals, and whatever savings I had from each store I put into my son's savings account. It's a way of knowing that in the future I'm going to be all right.

I use the CouponMom.com Forum five or more times a day to see where the latest deals are. I always print my coupons through the Coupon Mom website. The Grocery Deals database and drugstore lists help me to choose the items I want and compare prices. It also helps with compiling a grocery list. I've never been a person to stick by a list until now. I've also learned to shop at stores that I never shopped at before to get awesome deals.

This is not just about now. It's about my future. I have been teaching my sister, mom, and sister-in-law. I've also educated the girls at work. They call me the 'coupon queen.' Couponing has taught me several things in life, par-

ticularly the value of a dollar. I didn't realize how wasteful I was with my money until now."

—Janet Reed, Baltimore, Maryland

Main Features of CouponMom.com

I traded a career in sales and marketing to become the full-time, at-home CEO of the Nelson Family Inc. I don't regret for a minute leaving the corporate world to stay at home with my sons, but I put my professional skills to use all the time with CouponMom.com.

Other websites provide detailed grocery deals lists, but they require members to pay a subscription fee. My site is free to use. CouponMom.com is an easy online tool for planning ways to save money on the food and household products that your family needs. It is easily searchable, is regularly updated, and allows members to select and print their own customized shopping lists. Each store list is updated by 10:00 a.m. on the day prices change to give shoppers access to their stores' information seven days a week.

I've showed you how you can use the site to start your own No-Clip System of organizing your coupons. It doesn't take long at all once you've signed up (that's free, by the way!) to feel at ease scrolling through the rest of the website's features. But here's a more extensive overview of everything the site offers, to help you feel familiar the first time you log on.

Grocery Deals by State

No matter where you live, consider me your virtual neighbor, eager to give you the best tips on saving money in your area. Now consider the two million website users, and you get a sense of the savings community ready to welcome you! The Grocery Deals by State section is the most popular feature on CouponMom.com, used regularly by 91 percent of members. Because the key to Strategic Shopping is matching store sale prices with available coupons, this section makes it easy for members to save. It provides detailed lists of individual retailers' sale items matched with coupons available in each state. In addition to providing lists of great deals for thousands of the largest grocery stores across the country, the site also lists three national drugstore chains' deals (CVS/Pharmacy, Walgreens, and Rite Aid), as well as two national discount stores' grocery deals (Super Wal-Mart and SuperTarget).

Deals by Store Each Week

Although this book will teach you how to figure out the best grocery deals at any store on your own using Strategic Shopping concepts, you can rely on CouponMom.com to do the legwork for your stores listed on the site. I think once you give the site a try, you'll find it's a fun, caring community to be a part of. We're all here to help one another!

Although each store list has one hundred or more deals listed each week, this snapshot of sample deals at one store during one week illustrates how to use these lists.

Date the Coupon Came Out	Kroger Best Deals Item Description Sale Dates 4/12 to 4/18	Total Coupon Value	Quantity	Sale Price	Final Price After Coupon	% Saved
3/29S	Barilla Piccolini pasta, 16 oz.—charity!	$1.00	1	$0.75	**FREE**	100%
3/29S	Barilla Whole Grain pasta, 13.25 oz.—charity!	$1.00	1	$0.75	**FREE**	100%
3/29 RP	Quaker Rice Cakes, 3-4 oz.—charity!	$1.00	1	$1.00	**FREE**	100%
3/29 RP	Suave deodorant, 2.5 oz.—charity!	$1.00	1	$1.00	**FREE**	100%
3/8 RP	Johnson's Buddies bar soap—charity!	$1.00	1	$1.09	$0 .09	92%
3/1 RP	Mahatma Long Grain rice, 16 oz.—charity!	$1.00	1	$1.09	$0.09	94%

3/1S	Melitta coffee filters, assorted sizes	$1.00	1	$1.25	$0.25	84%
3/29S	Softsoap liquid soap, 7.5 oz.	$0.70	1	$1.00	$0.30	84%
4/5S1	Brut deodorant	$0.55	1	$1.00	$0.45	77%

Here's What Each Column Heading Means

- **Date the Coupon Came Out:** The first column refers to the date that the coupon needed for that particular grocery deal came out in the Sunday newspaper grocery coupon circular.
- **Item Description:** The sale items include details such as the brand name, variety, and possibly the specific weight of the item. The term "charity" after the item description means that it is a good item to buy and donate to local food pantries and shelters because it is nonperishable, nutritious, and inexpensive.
- **Total Coupon Value:** The value of the coupon after the store's double- or triple-coupon policy is applied, if available. For example, a 50-cent coupon becomes a $1 coupon if the listed store doubles coupons.
- **Qty. (Stands for Quantity Required for the Final Price):** If the store sale requires the purchase of more than one item or if the coupon requires a multiple purchase, the quantity column will clarify the required number of items to get the discount shown.
- **Sale Price:** The featured sale price before the coupon value is deducted.
- **Final Price After Coupon:** The final price of the item, per item, after the coupon is deducted. Even if the quantity shown is more than one, the final price shown here is per item.
- **% Saved:** The percentage difference between the item's full price and its final price. The full price is not shown on the list due to space restrictions.

Printable Grocery Coupons

If I gave you a license to print money in your basement legally and morally, you'd take me up on that offer in a snap. Here's the next best thing! The second most popular feature of CouponMom.com site is the Free Printable Coupon section. It has dozens of grocery coupons representing major brands, such as General Mills, Yoplait, Kellogg's, Huggies, Betty Crocker, Pillsbury, and many more. Some 83 percent of members report printing coupons from the site regularly to increase their savings. And if your busy life doesn't allow you the 60 seconds it might take to register on CouponMom.com, this section should be extra-appealing. Site visitors can print grocery coupons without having to register. You will need to download a coupon printer, which is perfectly safe for your computer. CouponMom.com provides the most updated offers and alerts members via the weekly newsletter when new printable coupons are available.

The Grocery Coupon Database

You don't read every newspaper in the country, do you? Don't worry—we do! Well, we're scanning the coupons, anyway. The Grocery Coupon Database, used by 76 percent of CouponMom.com members, pulls data from all across the country and organizes it neatly and efficiently. Because newspaper coupons vary by region of the country, as manufacturers offer different coupons to selected markets based on their marketing objectives, the site currently provides seventeen different versions of the Grocery Coupon Database, based on state or region of the country. Our staff members enter the individual newspapers' coupon information into the database for members to reference and find coupons easily.

Although members aren't able to print the newspaper coupons from the database, users can put the Coupon Mom system to use here. That means putting a specific Sunday's date on the cover of the coupon circular and saving the entire circular. When you need to find a coupon, you can go to the Grocery Coupon Database and enter the name of the coupon you need in the search box. It will tell you the coupon details and the date the coupon came out, so you'll know where to look.

The Grocery Deals list will also reference the coupon date so you can spend just a few minutes cutting out the coupons you need. If you keep your coupon circulars in a box or a file in order of date, it becomes very easy to take advantage of your share of the 315 billion grocery coupons issued each year!

The Grocery Coupon Database also helps you keep track of printable and electronic grocery coupons from various sources. For example, if Colgate toothpaste is on sale at your store and you searched the Grocery Coupon Database to find a Colgate coupon, you may see a newspaper coupon referenced from last month's newspaper, as well as an electronic coupon, as well as a coupon you can print. By having access to this comprehensive database, you would be able to triple your savings and stock up by getting three bargain tubes instead of one.

COUPON DATABASE COUPON CODES EXPLAINED

The coupons are noted by date and the first initial of the circular's name in the Grocery Coupon Database. For example, a coupon that came out on February 12 from the RedPlum circular would be labeled 2-12RP. A coupon that came out on the same date from SmartSource would be labeled 2-12S. If two circulars from the same company are issued in the same week, which happens a few weeks a year, we number the circulars. You would see 2-12 S1 and 2-12 S2. During some weeks, there may be extra circulars from specific companies, such as Procter & Gamble, Unilever, General Mills, and others. The site's Coupon Database section will explain what the current coupon circulars' codes are. For example:

Sample Codes

S : SmartSource

RP: RedPlum

PG: Procter & Gamble

GM: General Mills

UN: Unilever

S1 or S2 or RP1 or RP2: SmartSource 1, SmartSource 2, RedPlum 1, RedPlum 2. When there is more than one circular from the same company during the same week, we will assign a number to it. By checking the Grocery Coupon Database, you can tell what the specific numbers are for each circular based on the coupons referenced.

COUPON DATABASE SAMPLE

Issue Date	Expires	Coupon	Value	Qty.
2-08S	4-30	Blistex Lip Care product, any	$0.35	1
4-05PG	4-30	Bounty paper towels	$0.25	1
3-29S	4-29	Breakstone's cottage cheese, 4-pack	$0.60	1
3-29S	4-29	Breakstone's sour cream, 16 oz. or larger	$0.55	1
4-05S2	6-28	Breyers yogurt, 6-oz. cups	$1.00	6
4-05UN	5-31	Breyers ice cream, 1.5 qt. or larger	$0.55	1
2-22S	5-31	Bumble Bee Premium Tuna Pouch, 2.5 oz.	$0.55	1

Here's What Each Column Heading Means

- **Issue Date:** This is the date the coupon came out in the Sunday paper, as well as the code for the specific coupon circular.
- **Expires:** The expiration date of the coupon.
- **Coupon:** Brand names, specific varieties and sizes, or other details.
- **Value:** The face value of the coupon.
- **Qty.:** The purchase requirement of the coupon.

THE COUPON AND DEAL ALERT

If you're an AOL user, you're familiar with the friendly greeting that alerts you to new e-mail in your inbox: "You've got mail!" We don't actually speak to you through the website, but we'll let you know when "You've got deals" with our Coupon and Deal Alert feature.

Because there are literally hundreds of coupons and grocery deals available in each city every week, we created a way to automatically let members know when their favorite items are deals at their specific stores or have coupons available. Even if you are a CouponMom.com member, you need to register again for the Coupon and Deal Alert to be able to list your preferred items. Signing up for this particular feature will help tailor a savings plan just for your family.

To get started, specify the stores and specific items you would like to track. There's no limit. For example, if you would like to know when tooth-paste is a deal or has a coupon, you could specify "toothpaste" as an alert item. If you shop at Kroger, Wal-Mart, and CVS/Pharmacy, you could spec-ify all three stores. Then whenever a coupon comes out in the Sunday paper for any brand of toothpaste, it would be included in your alert. Whenever any brand of toothpaste is listed as a deal on your state's Kroger, Wal-Mart, or CVS/Pharmacy list, that information would also be listed in your alert. You can also specify specific brands, such as "Crest" or "Colgate," to limit your results.

Alerts go out twice a week (Sunday and Thursday) to make sure you don't miss a deal. You can find the link to sign up for the Coupon and Deal Alert in the Grocery Coupon Database section of the website. Think about it. This feature literally puts us to work for you, at no cost to you, to help you save money. Can you think of a better offer?

THE COUPON MOM FORUM

There's a reason social media sites are red-hot in our society right now. They allow people to keep in touch and share information and ideas—not to mention lots of cute pictures of their kids and pets. The CouponMom .com Forum isn't the place to post your vacation photos, but it just might be the place where you'll learn to perfect savings strategies in order to pay for that vacation.

We launched the CouponMom.com Forum in August 2008 to give members a place to share ideas, tip one another off to specific unadvertised deals, and brainstorm creative strategies at their stores with other members. It also gives beginning Strategic Shoppers a fun and easy way to learn from the pros. The great thing about using CouponMom.com is that the better members get at shrinking their own grocery budgets, the more excited they are to help others perfect saving strategies of their own.

The Forum has sections dedicated to specific deals for each grocery store, drugstore, and discount store listed on the site. Members can post information about coupon deals, rebate offers, unadvertised sales, and budget-friendly recipes. And we can all share the happy results we've expe-rienced at the checkout line in the Success Stories section.

Forum membership is separate from CouponMom.com membership, so it requires its own registration and password. In order to post messages, you will need to join the Forum. But anyone can read the tips and strategies on the Forum without having to join the Forum or the site.

In addition to our most popular features, CouponMom.com offers restaurant coupons, free-sample offers, online coupon codes, and printable coupons that can be redeemed at businesses in your community. And as we'll discuss in greater detail in chapter 21, the site offers ways to help you put your savings to use beyond your own family's needs, by aiding organizations such as food pantries in your area.

A Final Word

As much as I love talking about saving money and using my website, sometimes I think members say it best.

A CouponMom.com member from Virginia wrote to say, "This site has really changed the way I shop and has helped me change my attitude about spending. I have always tried to be as thrifty as possible but apparently didn't really know how to do it right. Now, thanks to this site and this forum of great people, I have cut my grocery bill in half."

Nine

Think Inside the (Big) Box: Saving at Supercenters

Buying in bulk is typically the ticket to bargains. In other chapters, we've talked about how buying food in larger, non-convenience sizes lowers your cost. When huge national retailers buy in bulk from their suppliers and set up shop in buildings the size of airport hangars, they can pass their lower costs on to consumers. But big-box buyer beware: Big stores can mean big savings, but you'll need to keep applying Strategic Shopping methods to make sure bigger truly is better when it comes to your grocery budget.

In this chapter we're going to discuss:

- a review of some of the most widespread big-box players
- how big-box stores differ in pricing and policies from traditional grocery stores
- how each shopping personality can benefit from shopping at supercenters

Big Savings, Big Temptations

Grocery supercenters can offer just about anything you need to keep everyone in your family fed, clothed, and entertained. You can pick up snacks for a pool party or cleaning supplies for the pool, steaks for the grill or the grill itself, and pet food or even, in some cases, the pets themselves! These emporiums of food, fashion, and furnishings typically cover about 170,000 square feet, or about four times the size of the typical large supermarket.

Big-box shopping can save time, gas, and money, since you're able to buy food as well as clothing, electronics, furniture, lawn-care supplies, school supplies, gifts, pet food, prescriptions, and more. But in a store that sells virtually everything, a wide variety of impulse purchases lurk in every aisle. A rock-bottom price on a gallon of milk is great, but picking up a new set of patio furniture that catches your eye can undermine your frugal intentions in a hurry!

The Major Supercenters

Super Wal-Mart: Wal-Mart operates 2,630 Supercenters that average 187,000 square feet. Most are open twenty-four hours a day, seven days a week. According to Nielsen research, approximately two hundred million people shop at Wal-Mart each year.[6] Supercenters carry a full array of groceries, including meat, produce, frozen and refrigerated foods, dairy products, in-store delis, and in-store bakeries. In addition to the large Supercenters, Wal-Mart operates 883 smaller Wal-Mart discount stores with smaller grocery sections and 150 Neighborhood Markets that offer a full range of groceries in a smaller supermarket format. Wal-Mart also owns the 598 Sam's Club wholesale clubs, which require membership.

SuperTarget: Target operates 1,699 stores in 49 states, 245 of which are SuperTargets. These stores each typically have a complete grocery store, including a produce section, deli, and in-store bakery, as well as refrigerated and frozen foods and general groceries. Most Target stores have a general grocery department, without a produce department, deli, or bakery, even if they are not SuperTargets.[7]

Kmart: Kmart operates 1,368 stores in 49 states, 47 of which are Kmart Super Centers with a full selection of groceries, including meat, frozen and refrigerated food, dairy products, and in-store delis and bakeries.[8]

---

6. According to company background information at Walmartstores.com.
7. According to company background information at Target.com.
8. According to company background information at Kmart.com.

What's the Difference? Comparing Supercenters and Traditional Supermarkets

Pricing: Supercenters generally employ "everyday low price" strategies. Most items are typically advertised at prices that remain constant. This is helpful for the time-pressed shopper who needs to stock the pantry without waiting for a sale. While some items are featured in sales promotions, the pricing in supercenters usually does not fluctuate as much as that in traditional grocery stores. Once you've tracked prices in your local grocery store over time, you'll be able to recognize when big-box pricing really is a deal. Not every item will be cheaper at the supercenter, so it's worth your time to discover which products are consistently sold for less there. If the price difference is significant on many of your key items, it may be worth it to split your shopping. Purchase on-sale items with coupons at your supermarket, then cherry-pick the best deals at the supercenter.

Coupon policies: Supercenters accept grocery coupons, and some will double coupons. In the past, Kmart has featured promotion periods during which coupon values were doubled during a certain period of time. Be sure to ask about coupon policies so you'll have accurate pricing information for comparison purposes.

Store coupons: SuperTarget occasionally offers its own store coupons in Sunday newspaper inserts. Shoppers can also print coupons from its website, Target.com. Combining store coupons with manufacturers' coupons (as explained in chapter 7) often produces rock-bottom deals. For example, if you have a $1 coupon for Brand X cereal printed from Target.com and a $1 coupon for Brand X cereal from the Sunday newspaper circular, you can use both coupons on one box of Brand X cereal to save $2 per box. If Brand X is on sale for $2, your breakfast is free! Even a "regular" Target may offer these sorts of bargains. CouponMom.com points you to deals like this every week.

Price comparison: There's a reason Wal-Mart is the world's largest retailer and the nation's largest grocery chain. According to retail analysts, grocery items at Wal-Mart are often priced anywhere from 10 to 20 percent lower than at its competitors. Because prices on individual items on your shopping list may vary, it's still important to check prices. Combining sales, promotions, and coupons at your smaller local grocery store can frequently beat a Wal-Mart price.

Price matching: As if its generally lower prices weren't enough, Wal-Mart is willing to match competitors' advertised prices if you find someone else offering a better deal. If you find a lower advertised price on an item stocked at Wal-Mart, present the competing store's ad showing the lower price and ask the store to match it. Don't be bashful about asking for a price match! Remember, you'll need to actually produce the competing store's advertisement, not just declare that you've seen the item priced lower elsewhere. So be sure to review all local stores' weekly ad circulars to find the best prices, then compare them against Wal-Mart's. If Wal-Mart doesn't beat them, they'll match them.

By the Numbers: Comparing Supermarkets and Super Wal-Mart

To see for myself how the numbers stacked up, I decided to check the prices of forty-one of my regular grocery items at a major supermarket in my area and the local Super Wal-Mart. The Wal-Mart didn't carry three of the items I was looking for, so I scratched them from the list. In most cases I compared prices for the store-brand variety of an item rather than the name brand when I did not have a specific preference. Of the forty items on my list, twelve were name-brand items and twenty-eight were store-brand items. Keep in mind that prices vary by week at the supermarket and everyone's list of regular grocery items varies, too. But the lesson here is simple. It's worth it to check prices of key items at supercenters.

This price comparison did not take into account how grocery coupons would have changed the prices. Wal-Mart does accept grocery coupons but does not double the face value of coupons as some supermarkets do. But the retail analysts and the Coupon Mom agree: Based on my cost comparison of key items, it's clear that Wal-Mart Supercenter prices are indeed 10 to 20 percent lower.

PRICE COMPARISON OF 43 KEY ITEMS
SUPERMARKET COMPARED TO WAL-MART SUPERCENTER

Percentage of 43 key items carried by Supercenter	93% (3 items not available)
Overall price difference, all 40 items carried by Wal-Mart	12% lower at Wal-Mart

WAL-MART AND SUPERMARKET PRICE COMPARISON OF 40 ITEMS (JUNE 2009)

Item	Wal-Mart Price	Supermarket Price	Brand
bananas, per lb.	$0.53	$0.45	store brand
beef, ground, 80% lean, per lb., fresh	$2.38	$2.66	store brand
Birds Eye Steamfresh frozen broccoli cuts	$1.25	$1.39	store brand
Blue Bonnet margarine spread, 16-oz. tub	$0.93	$0.88	name brand
Butterball ground turkey, fresh, per lb.	$2.42	$2.69	name brand
Celestial Seasonings tea, 20 ct.	$2.32	$3.19	name brand
cereal, crispy rice, 12 oz.	$1.49	$1.89	store brand
cheese, American, slices, 12 oz.	$2.08	$1.59	store brand
cheese, mozzarella, 8 oz. chunk	$1.89	$1.33	store brand
chicken breasts, frozen, 3 lb.	$6.97	$7.19	store brand
cookies, chocolate sandwich	$2.00	$2.35	store brand
cookies, fig bar, 16 oz.	$1.27	$0.99	store brand
eggs, large, 1 dozen	$0.97	$1.00	store brand
Eight O'Clock Coffee, 12 oz.	$3.58	$4.89	name brand
flour, 5-lb. bag	$1.25	$1.39	store brand
Green Giant romaine lettuce hearts, 3 ct. bag	$2.67	$3.29	name brand
Hunt's ketchup, 24 oz.	$1.23	$1.50	name brand
Hunt's pasta sauce, 26-oz. can	$0.84	$1.00	name brand

jam, strawberry, 32 oz.	$1.88	$2.19	store brand
Jiffy corn muffin mix, 8.5 oz. box	$0.42	$0.43	name brand
Kraft Lite mayonnaise, 30-oz. jar	$2.68	$3.54	name brand
milk, 1 gallon	$1.98	$1.99	store brand
Nature's Own Double Fiber bread, 20 oz.	$2.84	$2.99	name brand
oatmeal, 42 oz.	$2.28	$2.49	store brand
orange juice concentrate, 12 oz.	$1.42	$1.46	store brand
oranges, mandarin, 11 oz.	$0.62	$0.69	store brand
oranges, navel, 4 lb. bag	$2.75	$3.99	store brand
peanut butter, 18 oz.	$1.36	$1.27	store brand
pinto beans, dry, 2-lb. bag	$1.62	$1.95	store brand
rice, white, long-grain, 5-lb. bag	$3.12	$3.69	store brand
sugar, white, 5-lb. bag	$1.98	$2.49	store brand
sweetener, aspartame, 100-ct. packets	$1.07	$1.88	store brand
syrup, pancake, 24 oz.	$1.88	$1.86	store brand
tomatoes, canned, 14.5 oz.	$0.54	$0.56	store brand
tortillas, corn, 30 ct.	$1.44	$1.50	store brand
tortillas, flour, 10 ct., burrito size	$1.92	$1.19	store brand
tuna, chunk light, 5-oz. can	$0.72	$0.75	store brand
Tyson whole fryer chicken, per lb.	$0.88	$1.08	name brand
vegetables, frozen, 16 oz.	$0.88	$1.00	store brand
yogurt, 32-oz. tub	$1.57	$1.79	store brand
Total: 40 items (12 name brand, 28 store brand)	**$71.92**	**$80.45**	**-12%**

Wal-Mart's everyday prices during this sample week averaged 12 percent less than the supermarket's lowest price available (sale price or regular price). Wal-Mart did not carry three of the items needed: store-brand egg substitute, store-brand rice cakes, and frozen ground turkey.

So, Where Should You Shop?

If every price on every item every day were always lower, all the time, at Wal-Mart, regardless of sales, coupons, or promotions at your local supermarket, I would be writing a very short book. The first page would also be the last, and it would read like this: "Shop only at Wal-Mart. The end."

I suppose my friends at Wal-Mart would declare that the must-read title of the year, but there's a little more to the story. Because I am a heavy coupon user, I will continue to buy and stock up on items when they are selling for 50 percent off or more, with coupons, at my local supermarket. Combining sales and coupons often means I can buy name-brand items for less than their store-brand counterparts. But my pricing comparison justifies making at least one weekly shopping trip a month to Wal-Mart to stock up on many items that are not typical coupon deals. Because my Wal-Mart Supercenter also sells most of the other grocery items I use, I can occasionally skip the supermarket altogether and get what I need for the week at Wal-Mart.

Every Shopping Personality Can Save

The Busy Shopper will probably most appreciate shopping at supercenters, since it's literally one-stop shopping for much of what a household needs each week. Particularly if you don't have time to clip coupons or pore over sales circulars, supercenter shopping gives you some assurance that you're making the most of your grocery dollars. As my price comparison confirmed, shoppers can expect to save 10 to 20 percent off the typical supermarket prices for their grocery items, with no other effort. If you have no time whatsoever to plan, at least plan to shop at a big-box store.

If you are a Rookie Shopper, you will find it worthwhile to check the prices at supercenters to see which items there are the best deals. You may find it helpful to schedule a monthly stop to stock up on the best big-box bargains. Combine coupons with sale prices at supercenters for the best possible deals.

Varsity Shoppers probably know all the Wal-Mart greeters in their towns by name! You enjoy the challenge of combining supercenter store coupons or price-matching policies with manufacturers' coupons to purchase items at their lowest prices, or even to get them for free. Be sure to apply Strategic Shopping methods at the supercenter just as you would at the supermarket.

A Final Word

As mentioned earlier, the great thing about supercenters is their large volume of inventory, which means lower prices. But all these choices, all offered at fabulous prices, can tempt you to veer from your budget. Strategic shopping doesn't end at the supercenter's door. Be sure to stick to your list and the amount you intend to spend, even when surrounded by acres of seemingly irresistible bargains.

Ten

— —

Is Bigger Always Better?
Saving at Wholesale Clubs

If there is a Costco, Sam's Club, or BJ's Wholesale Club in your area, it's worth your time to check out these bargain-boasting behemoths. You could fit about three regular-size supermarkets into the average wholesale club, and once inside, you can find just about everything. The typical makeup is 60 to 70 percent general merchandise, with the grocery department generally consisting of large sizes and bulk sales.[9] With such voluminous inventories, wholesalers are able to offer lower prices—their merchandise markup ranges from about 8 to 13 percent, compared to the 50 percent markup found at traditional retailers.[10]

Wholesale clubs can be great for shoppers whose local supermarkets don't double coupons, who prefer products that aren't often discounted with coupons, or whose large households make large quantities a necessity. But it's important nonetheless to apply the principles of Strategic Shopping when cruising the huge aisles of these mega-stores.

In this chapter we're going to discuss:

9. Food Marketing Institute: www.fmi.org.
10. SmartMoney.com, quote from Michael Clayman, editor of trade publication *Warehouse Club Focus.*

- factors to consider when deciding whether to join a wholesale club, and details that can help you decide which club best fits your household's shopping needs
- the coupon policies at the major wholesalers
- the best bargains you'll find at wholesale clubs, and what to be wary of when shopping there

Beware of Impulse Purchases

It's time for a Coupon Mom confession. Even I have fallen victim to the siren call of "bargains" I didn't know I needed until I saw them.

A friend and I went to a Costco in my area, purely for research. That was the plan, anyway. She grabbed a cart just in case we spotted any irresistible prices too good to pass up. I carried just my clipboard, ready to scour the aisles for information, not purchases.

Well, guess how this story ends? When we finished our fact-finding mission, my friend's cart groaned with $315 worth of merchandise—even though she had said she didn't actually need anything when we got there. "Good thing you didn't need anything," I mused. "Can you imagine what you would have paid if you did?" Of course, I got a little off track myself. I almost made it out without straying from my goal of collecting only intelligence, but then a large jar of basil marked at just $2.79—a 75 percent savings from my supermarket—caught my eye. And as for the new bathrobe and fleece vest I grabbed, well, what can I say? Even the Coupon Mom caves sometimes.

The key to shopping in a wholesale club is discipline. Learn to master the club's savings programs, know which prices are the best deals, devise a plan that brings home the best bargains, stick to your list and stay within your budget. Fall off the wagon, and you could end up with a loaded-down cart.

Sizing Up Potential Deals

Buying a huge container of anything is always a better deal, right? Not always. Just as you need to resist the lure of impulse purchases when shopping at wholesale clubs, you also need to resist the assumption that a giant size is automatically a giant bargain. While wholesalers are known for low prices, Strategic Shopping can uncover better buys at the supermarket, drugstore, or discount store. By using strategies we've discussed throughout this book, such as stacking coupons and combing them with sales and promotions, you can regularly find ways to beat wholesale clubs at traditional retailers.

Comparing unit cost is key to knowing whether the item you're buying at a wholesale club is a tremendous deal or just tremendous. Before you snap up that hefty $22 container of laundry detergent, in other words, put your calculator to work and run the numbers. Smaller sizes—and smaller prices— might work better for you when you have a very tight budget.

And even if the unit cost is lower, super-size shopping has other potential pitfalls, such as "consumption inflation," or the natural tendency to eat or use more of a product when we have plenty. In his book *Mindless Eating*, Brian Wansink writes about a hilarious and telling experiment he and his graduate students performed. They handed out big buckets of popcorn for free at a cinema, and most patrons plowed through it, even though it was stale, five-day-old popcorn. It didn't matter that the product was crummy— it was there, and that was good enough for the movie munchers. "Give them a lot, and they eat a lot," Wansink concluded.[11]

I wouldn't mind if my kids ate more salad because I bought a big container at the wholesale club, but we all know that it's not just salad they would graze on. Purchasing extra-large bags of chips or cookies is an invitation to overdoing it at snack time.

Try Before You Buy

Most wholesale clubs will let you take a test drive before joining, by shopping with a one-day pass. It makes sense to check out a few clubs in your area to see which one would best fit your shopping needs. Not every club carries every brand as a supermarket would, and you'll likely find that

---

11. Wansink, Brian. *Mindless Eating: Why We Eat More Than We Think* (Bantam, 2006).

one club carries more of your MVPs, or Most Valuable Products, than others.

When I compared wholesale clubs in my area, I quickly realized that only one club carried my favorite brand of sandwich bread for 27 percent less than my supermarket. If I purchased my bread at that club, I'd save $83.20 per year on that one item alone. Since membership cost $40, the savings on just that one MVP would justify the fee. When deciding which club to join, take a clipboard or a notebook and compare prices by using one-day passes at a number of clubs. It'll soon be evident which one makes the most sense for you.

How to Choose: What to Consider Before Joining a Club

Sam's Club has a nifty feature called Click 'n' Pull, where shoppers can order items on the website and pick them up at the store. This is also helpful for comparing prices online. It's a great convenience, but this program alone probably won't be the deciding factor in which club you join. The following are some other factors to guide you as you consider signing up.

Proximity

You're not going to find wholesale clubs on every corner. If the nearest one is far from you, it may be practical to go a few times a year to stock up on bargains, but it probably doesn't make sense to trek there weekly to save $1 on milk. If you do live near a wholesale club, it makes sense to consider weekly shopping trips for dairy products and produce. If our club was nearby and I bought my family's dairy products at the wholesale club each week, I would save an average of $20 per month on dairy products such as eggs, cheese, milk, and egg substitute.

Bulk Packaging

Even when wholesale clubs' unit costs are lower than supermarkets' costs, the large sizes might not work for you. If so, you might divide and conquer. Pair up with a friend who needs similar quantities and wants similar savings. Many nonperishable items are packaged in sets of two, perfectly suited for the buddy shopping system. Ideally, you and your friend can alternate shopping trips to save time as well as gas money.

Membership Fees

Wholesale club membership generally costs $40 to $50 for a household annually. Check the stores' websites and ask about special promotions. BJ's Wholesale Club has offered free short-term memberships in the past, and Sam's Club has offered short-term seasonal membership promotions when shoppers could sign up for the summer for $15. Sam's also offers a Collegiate Membership. It costs $40, the same as a household membership, but comes with a $15 gift card and an extra card for a parent or roommate to use.

Deals on Non-Grocery Items

Even if you never buy anything to eat at a wholesale club, its prices on electronics, tires, travel packages, or other major purchases could make membership worthwhile. At the time of this writing, Costco offered a two-year membership to a national fitness center for $300, or 60 percent lower than the center's own advertised special of $750. If you regularly used the health club, that $450 savings alone would more than justify Costco's $50 annual membership fee.

Non-Member Bargains

As required by law in most states,[12] wholesale clubs must provide selected services to non-members. Chief among these is pharmacy prescriptions. Costco and Sam's Clubs are known for low prices on prescriptions, and non-members can take advantage of these savings. (BJ's Wholesale Clubs do not offer pharmacies.) You can search Costco's prescription prices on the chain's website, but you'll need to call your local Sam's Club pharmacy for pricing. Costco also has a Member Prescription Program that gives additional discounts to members who do not

---

12. According to corporate headquarters' representatives of wholesale clubs (June 2009).

have insurance coverage. It is free to members, and specific savings vary by prescription. Sam's Club has a price-matching and price-guarantee policy that will match any other pharmacy's lower prices as well as give an additional 2 percent discount where allowed by law.

Budget Booze

In my comparisons, major brands of beer cost at least 10 percent less at wholesale clubs than they do at traditional retailers, and savings can be as high as 35 percent on higher-end wines.[13] In some states, non-members can also take advantage of wholesalers' competitive prices on beer and wine. Check with your local club on your state's policy.

Limited Brand Selection

Call it a big paradox. As big as they are, hulking wholesale clubs actually carry fewer brands, sizes, and varieties than supermarkets do. A typical supermarket may stock 35,000 products, while a wholesale club stocks 5,000 to 7,000 products. With many items, you're limited to one name-brand option in one size. Some items will also have a private store-label option, but you will find fewer private-label options in wholesale clubs than in supermarkets. If you are flexible on which brands you buy, your supermarket or discount store will have a wider variety of brands that will be less expensive than the premium name-brand option at the wholesale club. Wholesale-club pricing does benefit shoppers who are loyal to that particular premium brand.

Store Savings Policies

If you are a Busy Shopper, the bulk savings at wholesale clubs offer great value with very little effort. If you are a Rookie or Varsity Shopper, don't assume that buying in bulk is the end of the potential savings at wholesale clubs. With extra savings programs, you'll pay even less. All three clubs have programs offering rewards points with special store loyalty cards or credit cards to redeem for free merchandise at the club.

---

13. "The Best and Worst Warehouse Club Deals," SmartMoney.com (Sept. 17, 2008).

Coupon Policies

The three clubs have significantly different coupon policies, as follows.

About once a month, **Costco** members receive mailed booklets that offer store coupons for general merchandise, personal-care products, and many grocery items. A recent Costco booklet had $143 worth of coupons for food and household items. The coupon values are as big as the store's product sizes and can save you as much as 30 percent. For example, my mailer had a $10 coupon for a 48-pound bag of name-brand dog food, which cut the $37 price tag down to $27 and its cost per pound to one-third less than any other store's price. Costco does not accept manufacturers' coupons.

BJ's Wholesale Club is the only club that takes manufacturers' coupons. You can use one per item, even when the item is sold in a multi-pack. For example, if BJ's Wholesale Club sells a twelve-pack of Brand X beans, you can use up to twelve coupons for Brand X beans. BJ's Wholesale Club members also receive the quarterly magazine *BJ's Journal*, which features coupons for both grocery items and general merchandise, including electronics. I counted fifty grocery coupons worth $200 in a recent *BJ's Journal*. Register your membership card at bjs.com and you can access printable, high-value coupons. At the time of this writing, I counted forty-four printable grocery item coupons worth $108 on the BJ's Wholesale Club website. Selected members also receive a monthly Member Savings Book with even more coupons. For example, the July 2009 issue offered $219 worth of grocery coupons to use at BJ's Wholesale Club.

Sam's Club does not accept manufacturers' coupons and recently began offering its own store coupons on a limited basis to selected members. The stores do accept baby-formula vouchers. Check with the store in your area for details.

WHOLESALE CLUB POLICY COMPARISON[14]

Policy	Costco	Sam's Club (a division of Wal-Mart stores)	BJ's Wholesale Club
annual fee	$50 household	$40 household	$45 household
coupon policy	accepts Costco store coupons	accepts only manufacturers' vouchers for Similac	accepts BJ's store coupons and manufacturers' coupons
in-store coupons	available at product demo stations	not available	available at customer service desk or demo tables
manufacturers' coupons	does not accept	does not accept	accepts one per item, even in multipacks
manufacturers' rebates	rebate section at Costco.com; can print rebate forms	not available on website	rebate section at BJs.com, can print rebate forms
number of items	4,000[15]	5,000	7,000
number of members	45 million	47 million	confidential
number of private-label items	330	400	confidential
number of U.S. locations	407 in 40 states	598 in 49 states	180 in 15 states[16]
printable coupons	not available	not available	print store coupons from www.bjs.com

---

14. As verified by corporate headquarters' representatives of each club in June 2009.
15. From "Costco: A Bulk Buyer's Playground." ABCNews.com (April 2008).
16. BJ's Wholesale Clubs are located only in Connecticut, Delaware, Florida, Georgia, Maine, Maryland, Massachusetts, New Hampshire, New Jersey, New York, North Carolina, Ohio, Pennsylvania, Rhode Island, and Virginia, while the other clubs have broader national coverage in 40 (Sam's) to 49 (Costco) states.

rebate program that earns store credit	2% rebate on purchases with $100 membership level (max $500 per year)	2% rebate, but requires having Sam's Club Discover Card with $100 membership level; 2% rebate also applies to Wal-Mart purchases	2% rebate on purchases with $80 membership level (max $500 per year)
store coupon booklet	mailed 8 to 10 times a year to all members	Digital coupons available through eValues program to premium members	quarterly *BJ's Journal* with coupons mailed to all members; additional coupon books mailed to selected members
store magazine	*The Costco Connection,* mailed monthly	not available	*BJ's Journal,* mailed quarterly and includes coupons
surcharge on non-member shopping	5%	10%	15%

Where the Deals Are: The Best Wholesale Club Bargains

A team of CouponMom.com researchers fanned out to help determine your best bets for bargains when shopping at wholesalers. According to their findings, here's a list of items you're most likely to buy at their lowest costs by club shopping.

Dairy products: Although it can be a challenge to stock up on perishable dairy products, expect to pay about 30 percent less than your supermarket's price on eggs, butter, cream, half-and-half, individually wrapped cheese sticks, egg substitute, and both block and grated cheeses. Milk is generally cheaper at the wholesale club, depending on how low your supermarket's milk price is that week. Gourmet cheeses sell for half the supermarket's price. If you use coupons and combine them with sale prices or buy the store brand, you will have greater success at the supermarket buying sour cream, margarine, individual yogurt cups, ice cream, cottage cheese, and cream cheese there. If you don't use coupons, you will fare better shopping for these items at wholesale clubs.

Fresh produce: You'll pay less per pound for top-quality produce at a wholesale club, but you're going to have a lot of food on your hands. I bought a 4-pound package of fresh strawberries for $6 at a wholesale club in my area. The same amount would have cost $10 at the supermarket. But in a typical week I generally need only half that amount, for which I would pay $5. My wholesale club's prices per pound for apples, bananas, oranges, carrots, and lettuce are also less than they are at the supermarket, but those items came in similarly large quantities. You'll find some organic items at the wholesale club as well. I found a 5-pound bag of organic baby carrots at Costco for $5.29, a 58 percent savings off the supermarket's 1-pound bag priced at $2.49. If you don't eat enough produce to justify the larger quantities, BJ's Wholesale Club might work for you. There you can find smaller, supermarket-size packages in the produce department. We don't all need 20 pounds of potatoes or six heads of lettuce at a time. At BJ's Wholesale Club, you'll be able to find produce in more manageable quantities.

Baking ingredients: Even if you don't want to buy a 25-pound bag of flour, the savings potential can be significant on other baking items for those of us who bake regularly. You'll find name-brand chocolate chips, real vanilla extract, yeast, basic spices, evaporated milk, vegetable oils, and nuts for 40 to 60 percent less than supermarket name-brand options. If you don't mind buying a large quantity, the savings are significant. I bought a 16-ounce bottle of store-brand vanilla extract for $5.99 at Costco, a 79 percent savings over the 4-ounce store-brand option my supermarket sells for $6.99. CouponMom.com member Suzanne Taylor of Atlanta loves the wholesale price on yeast. "I bake pizzas, rolls, and breads almost every week," she says. "I am able to buy a 32-ounce bag of name-brand yeast for around $4. Considering the 4-ounce jars of the store brand at the grocery store can run almost $3, or $6 for the name-brand 4-ounce jar, this is a great deal. One bag lasts about six months, and they store well in the freezer."

I found yeast at Sam's or Costco for 80 percent less than at the supermarket, making it an excellent bargain. I can store yeast in the freezer, and homemade pizza crusts, rolls, and breads are much less expensive than prepared options. I have a time-saving bread machine, so the yeast is a great bargain for me.

Fresh and frozen meat, chicken, and fish: Not only is the club price lower, but the grade is also higher. I've noticed that the cost of USDA Choice at my area wholesaler is lower than that of USDA Select at my supermarket. The USDA grades beef according to the degree of marbling and the age of the animal, which determines the tenderness of the beef. The higher the degree of marbling, the more tender and flavorful the beef will be, which also has a direct impact on its cost. The most expensive grade is called Prime and is usually only available in fine restaurants or meat markets, as only 2 to 3 percent of the beef supply is categorized as Prime. About 50 percent of graded beef is the next Choice grade, which is more common. About one-third of graded beef falls in the Select category, which has less marbling and therefore is leaner but may not be as tender as Choice, so it is generally the least expensive of these three grades.

A comparison of meat, chicken, pork, and fish prices between local clubs and my supermarket found that club prices averaged 25 percent less, even when the club beef had a higher Choice grade. Packages are larger, so unless you're feeding an army, you'll want to store or freeze smaller quantities of ground beef, steaks, roasts, and chops for future meals. Some items, such as chicken, are sold in larger packages but are individually vacuum-packed in meal-size portions to make freezing easier. Frozen 1-pound rolls of 91 percent lean ground beef have been the very best bargain I've found. They sell for 40 percent less than the most comparable fresh 93 percent lean ground beef at my supermarket.

Bakery and deli items: Wholesale clubs feature super-size baked goods, rotisserie chickens, and "take and bake" extra-large pizzas for the same price as smaller supermarket alternatives. These are perfect sizes for entertaining. One of the most popular items at the clubs in my area is the large 3-pound rotisserie chicken priced at about $5. The same bird would be $8 in my supermarket's deli. The clubs' $16 sheet cakes will feed more than twice as many people as my supermarket's $16 cake. And they are high-end, delicious cakes with fillings and real buttercream frosting. They also offer extra-large pies, muffins, pastries, and bagels, all at lower prices than you'd pay at a supermarket bakery for the same quantity.

Plastic bags, garbage bags, foils, and plastic wraps: If your family wraps, bags, and trashes a good bit, buying these goods at wholesale prices is a good bet for you. Stocking up on these items makes sense, because they last forever and you'll always need them. Varsity Shoppers in the CouponMom .com community say that even with sales and coupons, it's hard for supermarkets to beat the wholesalers here. I compared the cost of Ziploc quart-size freezer bags at various stores and found that Costco's box of 216 bags, the equivalent of about eleven regular-size supermarket boxes, cost $6.39 after using a $2 coupon offered in Costco's monthly mailer. That's about 3 cents per bag. To beat that price, you'd have to find the same bags priced at 60 cents or less for a twenty-count box at the supermarket. (And even without the Costco coupon, the supermarket would have to sell the twenty-bag box for 78 cents to be competitive.) Not even the dollar store, selling twenty-bag boxes for $1, could touch the wholesale club price. I also found the lowest unit costs on name-brand aluminum foil and store-brand trash bags at wholesale clubs.

Batteries: If there's ever been a product to stock up on, it's batteries. Between your digital camera, the television remote control, flashlights, your kids' toys, and various electronics, you're always going to need them. Since they last forever, you definitely want to load up when you find a great deal. Without a doubt, the best price on batteries is at the wholesale club. Costco's Kirkland brand of AA batteries sold in forty-eight-count packs work out to the equivalent of 92 cents for a four-pack. The best supermarket store-brand price I was able to find was at least $1 for a four-pack.

Frozen juice, fruits, and vegetables: Wholesaler prices are hard to beat here, too. At a club in my area, the private-label frozen orange juice concentrate cost 42 percent less than the price of my supermarket's store brand and lower than any coupon bargain I've seen. Large bags of frozen vegetables and fruit were also a bargain. Organic name-brand frozen mixed vegetables at Costco came in at less than half the cost of the same brand at my supermarket.

Private-label household and paper supplies: Name-brand bath tissue and laundry detergent are generally no cheaper than supermarket sale prices, but you can save at wholesale clubs by buying store brands. Name brands and store brands sometimes come from the same manufacturer, by the way. Georgia-Pacific, for example, makes Quilted Northern and Angel Soft, as well as most of Costco's Kirkland brands of bath tissue. Kirkland bath tissue is one of Costco's top-ten best-selling items, so its quality meets their shoppers' standards at up to half the price of other name brands.[17]

Snacks and quick meals: Small food courts inside wholesale clubs are great places for a quick—and cheap—bite. My neighbor's family of six enjoys lunch of beef hot dogs and soft drinks for less than $10 at the Sam's Club near us. Other inexpensive options include frozen drinks, pizza by the slice, wrap sandwiches, pretzels, and frozen yogurt.

A Final Word

Everything about wholesale clubs is big. The buildings are big, the containers are big, the savings can be big—and the temptation to load up on things you don't really need can be big. Fortunately, Strategic Shopping fits all budgets and all store sizes. By applying the principles I've noted throughout this book, you can make sure wholesale clubs are a perfect fit for your family.

---

17. As verified by Georgia-Pacific and Costco public relations representatives (June 2009).

Eleven

- - - -

The Frill Is Gone:
Bag the Savings Yourself at
Bare-Bones Stores

News flash: The grocery store isn't your only option for groceries. It's worth your time to check out various sources of items on your list each week. Remaining open to new places to shop can produce savings in places you may never have considered.

In this chapter we're going to discuss:

- what you can expect at a no-frills grocery store, and what you'll have to give up
- the surprising finds at dollar stores
- how to work outlet, specialty, and natural-food stores into your shopping schedule in order to save

Scale Down to Save Big

Some of the grocery stores in my area are starting to resemble upscale hotel lobbies, with wood-paneled sitting areas furnished with plush chairs, along with complimentary coffee and even snacks. A few even have play areas where children can run around while their parents shop.

Those luxurious amenities, of course, are not free. They're meant to lure shoppers who are driven by comfort and convenience, and are therefore not as concerned with scoring the greatest bargains. This does not describe me. I have discovered that no-frills stores, which offer limited service and typically carry fewer than two thousand items and few perishables, are great sources of bargains.

If you are a Rookie or Varsity Shopper, you'll be able to enjoy rock-bottom prices and even free items at traditional supermarkets by combining sales and coupons. Because supermarkets use the "high-low" price strategy by marking popular items down by up to 50 percent each week, it's not hard to get grocery items for pennies when you combine a coupon with the supermarket sale price. But this doesn't work with everything on your list. It can be hard to find sales or coupons offering discounts on some items—often staples, such as flour, sugar, salt, eggs, and other basics. That's when it is time to join the 35 percent of Coupon Mom shoppers who also shop at more bare-bones alternatives to supermarkets.

These include the following.

Bakery outlets: These shops are fairly common and easy to find. You can expect to save more than 50 percent on popular name-brand baked goods that are near their sell-by date. The selection varies, and these stores typically don't accept manufacturers' coupons. Some local bakery outlets print their own coupon booklets, so ask the staff if one is available. Bakery outlets often run promotions or discounts on top of their already lower prices, because they'd rather sell at a huge price reduction than have to discard unsold products. On Mondays, my local bakery outlet sells loaves of bread for $1, as compared to $2.99 for the same brand at the grocery store. I am perfectly happy to use day-old bread when it sells at a 67 percent savings, particularly when I buy it to make toast! My price comparison of two local bakery outlets found that all breads sold for at least 50 percent off the retail price, and pastries and doughnuts sold for 75 percent off their retail price. If you have room in your freezer, stocking up on breads, muffins, doughnuts, or pastries gives you a consistently cheap source of baked goods. You can use these websites to see if there is a bakery outlet near you, or you can always check Google.

- www.bakeryoutlets.com/storelocator.asp
- www.gwbakeries.com/outlet.cfm
- www.bimbobakeriesusa.com/our_brands/outlet_stores.html

Dollar stores: Stores like Dollar Tree, Family Dollar, and Dollar General provide a limited selection of interesting grocery bargains. Some of them accept coupons, resulting in huge bargains. Since the number of dollar-store locations has increased 50 percent since 2001, from about thirteen thousand stores to nearly twenty thousand across the country,[18] you shouldn't have trouble finding one near you. In general, dollar stores stock limited selections of nonperishable dry goods, paper products, and spices. Larger stores, such as those in the 99-Cents Only chain, are more likely to have produce and refrigerated and frozen grocery items as well. Inventory varies based on shipments, but the price is predictably 99 cents. If you show up at the right time, you can score serious deals. CouponMom.com member L. S. Wheatly reports snapping up name-brand items like Hot Pockets Paninis, Oscar Mayer hot dogs, Rold Gold pretzels, or Sunny Delight drinks, all at 99 cents. Better yet, she finds fresh vegetables there, 3 pounds for 99 cents. Don't assume that everything at a dollar store is the best deal, though. An MSN Money report comparing dollar-store prices to other stores found that items such as vegetables, plastic storage and trash bags, and bottled water were priced higher there than at traditional supermarkets.

Grocery salvage outlets: You've probably shopped for clothing at retailer outlets, which offer unsold skirts, suits, or shoes at a discount. A similar principle applies with grocery outlets. These small, individually owned stores, sometimes called "bent-and-dent" stores, carry merchandise that has not sold at a traditional supermarket but is still suitable for sale. (Be sure to check expiration dates.) Often, mussed packaging alone results in bargains. Say a brand of canned food is sold packaged in a carton. If the carton is torn or bent, the cans inside are still as good as they ever were, but they may seem less appealing because of the exterior damage. It's sort of like buying a car after a hailstorm. So what if the roof has been pinged up some

---

18. Fulmer, Melinda. "Dollar Stores: Where the Deals Are." MSN Money (April 2009).

if everything else works? The smart shopper is able to overlook a few super-ficial imperfections to save, but finding these bargain emporiums can be a bit of a challenge. Because most outlets do not have websites, you may need to do a Google search, or try www.andersonsmarket.info/directory.

Meat markets and specialty butchers: Prices at these stores may be equal to or lower than your supermarket, and specialty markets may carry higher-quality cuts of meat. Some markets smoke their own meat, make their own sausage, and provide custom services. Even if you have to make a special trip to get to the market, the savings you realize by stocking up on a month's supply of meats for the freezer can be worth the trip.

Military commissaries: These establishments offer very competitive prices for active and retired members of the military and their families. The website www.commissaries.com says commissary prices are, on average, 31 percent lower than traditional supermarkets. Commissaries do accept gro-cery coupons, although they do not double them and generally adopt an "everyday low price" strategy rather than offering periodic sales.

Amazon.com: The huge online retailer stocks a vast array of items—not just books. Amazon also offers a number of name-brand nonperishable items. If you buy them by the case, the cost per unit rivals many supermar-kets, even with sales and coupons. It isn't hard to qualify for free shipping, and Amazon offers several coupon codes each month. Although its regular grocery prices are comparable to regular prices at the supermarket, coupon offers such as "get $20 off when you buy $49 worth of Kellogg's products" often result in a lower priced item that you can have delivered to your door with no additional shipping costs. This is an especially attractive option if stores in your area do not double coupons.

Health-food stores and natural markets: Even if you don't buy organic and natural foods routinely, your nearest natural market could be a good source for bargains, particularly if you buy in bulk. Natural markets sell dry goods, such as grains, nuts, legumes, oatmeal, and various types of flour, sugar, baking yeast, and dried fruits. Sold by the pound, they may be less expensive than supermarket alternatives. Liquid products, such as olive oil, honey, and maple syrup, may be offered for sale minus packaging, meaning you can bring in your own reusable containers to save on cost (and limit items that may end up in the landfill). My favorite bargains at the local natural market are spices sold by the ounce. You can buy just the amount you need at prices far below supermarket prices and save up to 90 percent. A recent price comparison of spices sold at my local natural-foods store compared to the supermarket spice aisle found dramatic differences. This table shows a small sample of common spices I use that cost an average of 84 percent less when I buy them in bulk at the local natural market.

Spice	Supermarket Price per Jar	Bulk Price for Equivalent Amount	Bulk Savings
basil leaves, .62 oz.	$4.38	$0.62	86%
bay leaves, .12 oz.	$3.52	$0.12	97%
cream of tartar, 1.5 oz.	$2.52	$0.68	73%
ground ginger, .8 oz.	$2.17	$0.30	86%
nutmeg, 1.1 oz.	$3.76	$0.94	75%
		average bulk spice savings	**84%**

If I needed only a tablespoon of a spice I use just a few times a year, it would cost me pennies rather than $3 or $4 for a full jar from the supermarket that could sit in my cabinet for ten years or more. When you buy a smaller amount, the spices are also at their peak of freshness, so they taste better, too.

Frill-Free Shopping

Shopping at these types of stores means trading ambience for savings, so get ready for warehouse-style buildings with cement floors, products stacked in their packing boxes, and limited signage. On the plus side, there are no membership fees and items are sold in regular-size packages.

Aldi and Save-A-Lot are two of the largest national no-frills discount-store chains. Aldi currently has 1,000 stores in twenty-nine states and carries 1,400 items, mostly store brand. Save-A-Lot has 1,200 stores in thirty-nine states and carries 1,250 items, including store and name brands.

(A large major-chain grocery store carries 35,000 items or more.) Both stores carry items in every major grocery category, including frozen, dairy, meat, and produce, as well as canned and nonperishable food items. I do not have a Save-A-Lot in my area, but a CouponMom.com member with the screen name Ameeker in Hastings, Michigan, reports that her Save-A-Lot store boasts a clean interior and friendly cashiers. She says the store accepts coupons and has great prices on produce, and notes that their inventory is divided fairly evenly between name-brand and store-brand items. Featured sale prices change monthly, meaning you have a little more time to scoop up bargains. I have shopped at Aldi several times and recommend it as a good source of bargains. Non–coupon users who are flexible about which brands they buy will find it easy to save by buying common grocery items at Aldi. Many CouponMom.com members raved about their Aldi shopping experiences as well.

In general, what you're going to find at no-frills discounters includes the following.

Limited selection: You'll find one or two options per product, which is a drawback if you like lots of choices, or an advantage if you want to simplify your shopping. The Aldi store in my area carries one size of each type of item. For example, if I want to buy flour, they offer two choices: a 5-pound bag of all-purpose flour or a 5-pound bag of self-rising flour. My local supermarket would sell more than two dozen varieties of flour in different sizes and, different varieties, and would offer at least a few different brands. But if I need only all-purpose flour and Aldi's brand meets my expectations, I save 10 percent by buying it at Aldi when compared to my supermarket's store brand. Other items have much more dramatic price differences, such as snack crackers and cookies. I like Aldi's 12-ounce box of vanilla wafer cookies, and they are 56 percent less expensive than my supermarket's store brand.

Product guarantee policy: Some outlet and discount stores have a no-returns policy, so be sure to familiarize yourself with the rules of the store where you're shopping. Aldi's policy is an extra-generous "double guarantee," which means if for any reason the customer isn't satisfied with the quality of an item, they will replace the item and refund the customer's money (with the exception of non-food special-purchase items and alcohol). I haven't had to use that yet, as I've been satisfied with the items I've purchased, but I wouldn't hesitate to use it if I needed to.

Discount prices that stay put for a while: With the exception of a handful of featured sale items, most of the items at a discount store have the same price each week. This makes it easier to compare prices with other stores each week. For example, a CouponMom.com member in Atlanta said she created a list of her grocery items' prices at Aldi. She uses that list as a comparison tool when she reviews prices at the other local supermarkets each week. If the items' sale prices or sale-plus-coupon prices are higher than Aldi's, she'll add that item to her Aldi list. She still gets the benefit of supermarket bargains when their prices are lower than Aldi's price but will not pay more than Aldi's prices for non-sale items at her supermarket. Because I use coupons, I stop at Aldi only once every month or so to buy grocery items for which I don't have coupons. Non–coupon users can expect to save more at Aldi, because they'd buy a wider variety of items on a more frequent basis. Overall, I found that my basic non-coupon grocery items at Aldi cost 32 percent less than the store-brand option at my supermarket, or a savings of $35 on my cart of items. In my case, stopping at Aldi just once a month still saves about $420 per year.

Limited customer service: Part of the reason no-frills stores are able to offer such low prices is lower staffing levels. Don't expect to be welcomed by "greeters" whose only job is to say hello, and prepare for possible lines when waiting to check out. It's not unusual to see the cashier doing tasks like sweeping or cleaning when there are no customers to check out. No-frills discount stores generally do not have full-service bakeries, delis, meat service counters, or pharmacies, and don't expect a free coffee station or free cookies at the bakery. (Who's complaining here, though? With the money you save, you can probably afford to host a coffee hour for your neighbors at your home!) Aldi customers also bag their own groceries, and you can either BYOB or pay 5 cents per bag. Aldi even figured out a way to avoid having to collect grocery carts in the parking lot. Their grocery carts are locked at the front of the store, and in order to unlock one you need to insert a quarter into a slot on the cart. When you return the cart, your quarter is returned. Because most shoppers figure walking the cart back is worth a quarter, the store rarely needs to send staffers to collect carts. That's pretty smart, I think.

Varying coupon policies: Aldi and Big Lots do not accept grocery coupons, while some discount stores, including Dollar General, Save-A-Lot, and Bottom Dollar Food, do. Some stores print their own coupons, so watch store fliers and be sure to read the fine print on the store's ad or website to verify their coupon policy.

Limited payment methods: Many outlet and dollar stores will accept only cash or debit cards, although some take credit cards. I don't mind the idea of cash-only shopping, especially for those on a tight budget. Paying in cash forces you to closely monitor your spending, since you can't spend what you don't have.

Is It Worth It?

Yes, shopping at alternative locations can be a bit of a hassle. They might not take coupons. They might "put you to work" bagging your own groceries or putting up your own cart. The décor in many of them is about as chic as a military barracks. So is it worth it to save a few bucks? You decide. I have found that dozens of items were less expensive than my supermarket's store brands and were dramatically less expensive than name-brand options. For example, individually frozen brand chicken breasts sell for only $5.49 for a 3-pound bag at my Aldi store. That compares very favorably to my supermarket's price of $8.99 for a 3-pound bag, and is even lower than the supermarket's sale price of $6.99 per bag. Aldi's everyday low price on frozen chicken breasts averages out to $1.83 per pound, which is less than my supermarket's lowest sale price on fresh chicken breasts of $1.99 per pound. Frozen ground turkey at $1.19 a pound is also a great bargain as compared to $1.75 per pound at my supermarket, and an even better bargain when you consider that I'm substituting the ground turkey for ground beef at $2.69 per pound. Buying a few weeks' supply of chicken and ground turkey saves more than enough for my household to justify a monthly stop at Aldi.

Here's a sampling of items I compared for price. As you can see, the Aldi prices are significantly lower than my supermarket's store-brand price, and I've found that all of these items meet my quality standards.

Department	Price Comparison of Aldi to National Supermarket Chain's Store-Brand Items, April 2009	Aldi Price	Supermarket Store Brand Price	Savings
produce	apples, Golden Delicious, 3-lb. bag	$2.69	$3.49	23%
grocery	carrots, 2-lb. bag	$0.99	$1.39	29%
dairy	cheese, chunk, 8 oz.	$1.29	$1.99	35%
frozen	chicken breasts, 3 lb.	$5.49	$8.99	39%
grocery	cookies, chocolate sandwich	$1.39	$2.39	42%
grocery	cookies, fig bar	$0.99	$1.79	45%
dairy	eggs, 1 dozen	$0.89	$1.29	31%
grocery	garlic, minced, 8-oz. jar	$1.19	$1.99	40%
grocery	jam, strawberry, 18 oz.	$1.29	$2.69	52%
produce	lettuce, romaine hearts, 2 lb.	$1.99	$3.29	40%
dairy	margarine spread, 16-oz. tub	$0.99	$1.39	29%
grocery	mayonnaise, 32 oz.	$1.99	$3.05	35%
dairy	milk, 1 gallon	$1.89	$2.58	27%
frozen	orange juice concentrate, 12 oz.	$1.25	$1.59	21%
produce	oranges, navel, 4-lb. bag	$2.49	$3.99	38%
grocery	pinto beans, dry, 2 lb.	$1.59	$2.15	26%
grocery	rice cakes	$1.29	$1.99	35%
grocery	rice, white, long-grain, 3 lb.	$1.79	$2.40	25%
household	sponges, kitchen, 6 ct.	$0.99	$2.54	61%
grocery	sugar, white, 5-lb. bag	$1.99	$2.36	16%
grocery	sweetener, aspartame, 100-ct. packets	$1.19	$1.99	40%
grocery	syrup, pancake, 24 oz.	$1.39	$2.49	44%
grocery	tortillas, flour, 10 ct., burrito-size	$0.99	$1.59	38%
grocery	tuna, chunk light, 5-oz. can	$0.62	$0.75	17%
frozen	turkey, ground, 1 lb.	$1.19	$1.75	32%

frozen	vegetables, 16 oz.	$0.99	$1.25	21%
dairy	yogurt, 32 oz.	$1.59	$2.49	36%
	Total	**$42.42**	**$65.65**	**35%**

Because most of the items are nonperishable items that can be stock-piled in my pantry or put in the freezer, I'd be likely to buy two or three of each of the items during my monthly trip, saving $50 or more by stocking up on my bargain items.

Many CouponMom.com members are big Aldi fans. Kelly Snyder, from Lenexa, Kansas, loves getting staples, produce, and chips there. She finds that Aldi's oil, sugar, and flour are cheaper than any corresponding brand-name or store-name product, even with a coupon, and her family loves Aldi's 99-cent tortilla chips. "I don't mind bringing my own bags, because I do that anyway when I shop," she added. "And taking only cash helps me stay on budget—extras are rarely thrown in the cart."

A Final Word

If you've been used to luxurious shopping surroundings, switching to a bare-bones grocery store or bagging your own items might take a little getting used to. You can do it! The grocery store is a means to an end, not the end itself. And rethinking discount stores to fit into your weekly shopping needs can turn you on to bargains you never knew were there. Think of it as a savings treasure hunt!

Twelve

Trim the Fat from Your Grocery Budget: Savings Strategies for Buying Meat

Many of us plan menus around which meat, poultry, pork, or seafood item we're going to be serving as an entrée. Because meat generally serves as the "main event" at dinnertime, it can represent a significant slice of our grocery budget. It's important, then, to learn savings strategies. Trimming what you spend on meat can have a major impact on what you spend overall.

In this chapter we're going to discuss:

- timing purchases to coincide with sales, so that despite price fluctuations at the store, the price you pay remains consistently low
- finding ways to "stretch" the meat you buy to get several meals out of one item
- striking up a friendship with the butcher and making the most out of your freezer, so that you know when the best prices are coming and can stock up when prices fall

Don't Let High Meat Prices Take You for a Ride

I'll make a deal with you. Test-drive my ideas for saving money on meat, and I'll make your car payment next month. Agreed?

Okay, so I'm exaggerating—but not entirely. I stock the freezer with boneless chicken breasts when I find them at their lowest prices. When chicken breasts aren't on sale, they aren't on my list. In my area, this means buying them at $2 per pound rather than $5.49 per pound, a price difference of 63 percent. For my family of four, this strategy alone adds up to a yearly cost savings of $468, or a little more than the average monthly payment on a new car.

In other words, timing is key when buying meat. Track numbers for a few weeks and pricing trends will jump out at you. Once you're familiar with the sales cycles in your area, you'll know when it's time to load your cart, and your freezer. When prices inch back up, you can stroll past the butcher, knowing that your freezer is stocked with meat you bought on sale.

The days following holidays are often prime times for the best prices. On the day after Thanksgiving, as people crowd the malls for bargains or fight in the electronics-store aisles over the season's hot toy, consider a less frenzied outing. Turkey prices that day are incredible, and there's usually no one throwing elbows to snag those bargain birds. You'll find similar savings on ham in the days right after Easter. Again, in times like these, the freezer is your friend, allowing you to stock up when prices drop. This way, you essentially pay the same low price for meat at all times.

I start the weekly shopping list by reading supermarket sales sections in the newspaper. At least one type of main-dish ingredient is the featured front-page sale item in the store ad, and that's what I plan to load up on. Whether it's boneless chicken breasts, pork loin, ground beef, or ham, the featured item typically costs half of its regular price, and by paying attention week after week, it's quickly apparent what tends to go on sale when. My store has boneless chicken breasts on sale every other week, so I buy two weeks' worth and freeze what I won't use right away. Pork tenderloin hits its lowest price about once a month, so I buy enough for four weeks.

Of course, even the best sale probably won't turn pricey steaks into great buys. The cost of rib eyes, T-bones, or New York strip steaks can fall by half and still remain too expensive for the bargain shopper's pocketbook. Learn to plan the majority of your meals around less-expensive items, saving those high-cost cuts for special occasions.

But that doesn't necessarily mean giving up the steak dinner your family enjoys once in a while. Paying $10 per pound for a high-end steak is obviously more expensive than the $2 per pound London broil on sale, but it's still more budget-friendly than dining out at a swank steak house. A steak dinner at home will cost you 75 percent less than a steak dinner at a fancy restaurant. Turn that $468 chicken breast payday into a fine steak dinner at home—especially if your car is already paid off!

The Not-So-Super-Size Meal

Back in the Dark Ages—when fast-food chains were just catching on—a typical order of fries for an adult resembled what we'd find in a kid's meal today. Grabbing a soft drink back then meant popping the top off a 6-ounce bottle that would be dwarfed by today's massive soda vessels. The super-size theory of portion control has left the drive-through and followed us home or into higher-end restaurants. USDA guidelines say that a proper portion of beef or chicken is about 4 ounces—about the size of a deck of cards—but a generous hamburger or grilled chicken breast we serve could easily be twice that size. As a result, we're blowing our diets and budgets at the same time. Cutting back on portion size is a quick and simple way to eat better and less expensively, immediately.

If you fear cutting back on portions will sacrifice nutrition, check out nutritiondata.com, which offers detailed calorie and nutritional information. Enter your gender, age, weight, height, and exercise level, and the site's nutrition calculator will tell you how many calories and grams of protein, fiber, and other nutrients you need. Chances are you're consuming more than your body needs, and those super-size portions are draining your wallet while potentially packing on pounds.

Dining Drama: A Tale of Two Kitchens

Two neighbors, Cathy and Chrissy, purchase the same amount of chicken or beef to feed their families for a week, with very different results. Here's an example of how strategic menu planning can stretch entrée ingredients.

Cathy uses ground beef to make four burgers for dinner one night. The next night, Cathy serves whole grilled chicken breasts. By the third night, it's back to the grocery store, since she's run out of main-dish ingredients.

Chrissy gets a lot more mileage out of her items, using the ground beef in chili, sloppy joes, tacos, and a hamburger casserole. Similarly, she uses the chicken in a vegetable stir-fry, and later in healthy wrap sandwiches and a delightful chicken salad.

Chrissy knows side items are the key to success. Wheat bread, lettuce, beans, vegetables, and rice in the stir-fry make up at least half the meal, rather than serving a side dish with a large portion of chicken. These side items add nutritional value without the demanding price tags of the main entrées.

Act Fast for Last-Minute Bargains

Many supermarket meat departments will mark down meat that is about to expire. Be sure to cook or freeze it immediately. Your store's butcher is a great resource for figuring out when meat is about to be marked down, and if you're willing to spend a few minutes scanning expiration dates yourself, stores sometimes offer unadvertised discounts. If you find packages with expiration dates within a day or two and ask for a discount, often the department's meat manager will mark them down for you. It's in the store's interest to sell it to you at a discount rather than risk having to throw it out and lose the sale altogether.

Buy Low, Freeze High

Buying in bulk is almost always cheaper, because it's less convenient. But paying more for the same amount of food just because it's packaged in single or double servings is a ridiculous waste of money. Instead, divide and conquer! With a little time and a few plastic containers or freezer bags, you can create your own conveniently sized portions at tremendous savings.

One CouponMom.com member buys 5-pound packages of ground beef, which is of course more than she can use at one time. But she divides the large package into seven smaller ones, at roughly ¾ pound apiece. Now she's ready to grab just the right amount for sauce, chili, soup, casserole, or taco recipes that call for a pound of ground beef. The quarter-pound difference isn't noticeable to her family of four, and she finds this system results in two extra meals.

Not only does buying food in bulk and separating it into smaller sizes at home save money, but it also helps avoid wasted food, since you're going to thaw only what you need for any one particular recipe. Also, since you've divvied the item up into correct portions, you're able to make it go further. If you prefer buying meat one small package at a time, pay close attention to labels. I've noticed that when I need only a pound of ground beef, the smaller packages at my store are usually closer to 1¼ pounds or more. That rounded-up system of packaging cleverly gets you to spend more at the store and might entice you to eat more at home. Save the extra if you are forced to buy more than you want, and use it on another day.

The Frozen Chosen: Finding Deals in the Freezer Aisle

Individually frozen chicken pieces, fish fillets, and ground-beef patties often cost less than their fresh counterparts. Frozen versions also can be more convenient, since they do not have to be thawed before cooking. And because you're going to thaw just what you need for a particular meal, frozen items can help you avoid waste.

I compared fresh and frozen ground beef, chicken, and fish, and found savings in the freezer.

Chicken: Because stores discount often at 50 percent off, the fresh version is usually the least expensive option during sale weeks. However, if you need chicken and fresh is not on sale, the bagged individually frozen chicken pieces in 2.5- to 5-pound bags (depending on the cut) cost at least 10 percent less per pound than the full-priced fresh versions. For example, at my store one name brand of fresh boneless chicken breasts sells for $4.49 per pound at regular price. That same brand's individually frozen chicken breasts sold in a 2.5-pound bag cost 11 percent less at $3.99 per pound. The store brand of frozen chicken breasts costs $2.99 per pound at full price, which is much better than paying $4.49 per pound for the fresh version if it's not on sale.

Fish: I buy fish when it's on sale and look for frozen fillets when it's not. In an interview with NPR, Mark Bittman, author of the cookbook *How to Cook Everything,* said that frozen fish is actually fresher than fish that is sold as fresh in supermarkets. Unless fresh fish is on sale, the cost per pound of frozen fish fillets is generally less, and you can cook just the amount you need. Exact portion control is a real advantage of frozen fillets, because fish is relatively expensive and isn't a great leftover item.

Ground beef: The price of ground beef can vary based on whether you buy it fresh, frozen, prepackaged, or as patties. Ground beef can come in individual packages ground at the store, or it can be sold by weight from the butcher's case or sold fresh prepackaged in a roll, frozen in a roll, or sold as fresh or frozen ground-beef patties. The price per pound will vary as weekly prices change, so there isn't a hard-and-fast rule about which form is least expensive. It is worth taking the time to compare a few options to make sure you are getting the lowest price for the type of ground beef you prefer. For example, one week at my store the highest-grade fresh ground beef was "on sale" prepackaged for $3.69 per pound, while the same type and grade of ground beef was selling at "regular price" for $3.25 per pound from the butcher's case. It pays to compare!

Ground turkey: The same brand of ground turkey may sell in a foam package in the fresh poultry section and also sell in a 1-pound frozen package in the frozen poultry section. At my store, the price of fresh ground turkey (85 percent lean) is $2.69 per pound and the price of frozen ground turkey in a roll (also 85 percent lean) is $1.75 per pound when I buy four rolls in a package. In this case, buying the frozen version saves 35 percent for the same product.

Lower Your Price with a Little Do-It-Yourself Effort

Trimmed chicken breasts are the front-row concert seats of the grocery store. Convenient and appealing, they cost far more than their cheap-seats cousins sold in bulk, fat and all.

Brand-name fresh chicken sold in perfectly trimmed portion sizes costs $4.67 per pound at my store. But I can purchase the same brand's boneless chicken on sale for $1.99 per pound, then take the time to trim the fat myself. By weighing the trimmed chicken on my food scale, I calculated that the net cost per pound of the actual chicken used was still only $2.10. That's less than half the cost of the prepackaged version. If I needed convenient individual portions, I could easily weigh out individual portions with my food scale (or guess serving sizes pretty accurately if I didn't have a scale) and repackage them for the freezer in just a few minutes.

Similarly, at my supermarket I can buy ground beef that is 73 percent lean for about $2 per pound, but 93 percent extra-lean ground beef is $5 per pound. There's a way to eat lighter without paying more, though. Rather than pay more than twice as much for the extra-lean option, I'll buy the 73 percent lean variety, brown it, and rinse it with hot water in a colander. In essence, I'm creating a healthier package of meat just by taking the time to get rid of some of the fat. I take the same approach when browning the less-expensive, higher-fat ground turkey.

Turning Low-Price Cuts into Tender Morsels

Cheaper cuts of beef, such as chuck roast, skirt steak, top round, or London broil, have less fat and are therefore less tender than rib eye and New York strip steaks. But don't think that the budget cuts can't show a little tenderness. The low-fat choices in the meat department are healthier choices that you can soften up with a little preparation TLC.

Cook slowly at a low temperature: There are a number of ways to make inexpensive cuts of meat tender and flavorful, such as cooking roasts slowly in the oven or in a slow cooker. Inexpensive pork roasts and even the least

expensive pork butt become tender and perfect for barbecue pork sandwiches when cooked in a slow cooker.

Use marinades and rubs: You can also marinate steaks like skirt steak
for several hours to make them tender, or use a seasoning rub. You can buy
marinades and seasonings for pennies when you use coupons, or you can
make your own. Bottled salad dressings purchased for pennies with coupons
also make good marinades. I make a large batch of a favorite chicken marinade with bargain ingredients and keep it in my refrigerator for convenience. I always get compliments. I also use delicious homemade rubs for
meat that are easy to make. You'll find recipes in chapter 20.

The Butcher as Bargain Broker

Buying in bulk from the butcher is a serious no-brainer. Ask to have a whole
pork loin cut into chops or have a ham cut into slices, and you'll benefit
from bulk savings while having someone else create convenient portion
sizes for you. You'll need to buy the full pork loin or ham, but you'll get
nearly twice as much meat for the same cost as you would buying it in
smaller sizes.

In a recent price check, my store's full price for boneless pork loin was
$2.99 per pound, and boneless pork loin chops were $4.99 per pound. I ask
the butcher to slice the pork loin into thick chops while I shop and save $2
per pound with no extra effort on my part. The butcher is also willing to
slice large hams while I shop. When I get home, I can use some of the pork
for dinner that night, freeze the sliced ham for sandwiches, use a few chunks
for various recipes, and even use the ham bone for soup.

Buy Whole for a Whole Lot of Savings

If you're buying chicken only in parts, you're cheating yourself out of bargains. If you buy chicken parts for $1.49 per pound and whole chickens
are 99 cents per pound, you'll probably get more meat for your money by
baking a whole chicken. You can learn to cut a whole chicken if you need
to have chicken parts for a specific dish. Search online to find a video on
how to cut up a whole chicken, or find instructions in a cookbook. If your

family of four eats two chicken dinners a week, buying the whole chicken instead of parts will save you more than $200 per year without any change to your menu.

Deli Meat Discounts

Even the Coupon Mom herself can find cheaper alternatives to coupons sometimes. For us, the discovery happened at lunch. Our family frequently eats sandwiches for lunch at home. For years I bought packaged lunchmeat with coupons because it was convenient and inexpensive. My store sells the 9-ounce tub of packaged deli lunchmeat at a full price of $7.45 per pound. Even a 5-ounce package of lunchmeat selling at sale price of $2 is still $6.40 per pound. We preferred deli lunchmeat to the packaged lunchmeat, so when packaged lunchmeat was not a bargain, I bought the featured sale-priced deli lunchmeat each week at about $6–$8 per pound, depending on the brand.

To cut our grocery costs and make healthier meals, last year I started baking extra chicken breasts, whole chicken, and turkey breast, and slicing my own ham from half a ham purchased in the meat department, for sand-wiches. Not only did it save a lot of money over the course of a month, but everyone in our family also preferred having "real" chicken, turkey, or ham for sandwiches. Now I just take a small package of sliced ham out of the freezer or throw an extra couple of chicken breasts in the oven, slice them, and keep the meat in a container in the refrigerator for convenience. The do-it-yourself route is especially handy if your store doesn't staff a butcher position. I have bought spiral-sliced ham and cut it into smaller portions myself at home very easily. If I can do it, you can do it.

To compare costs, the $1.99 sale-priced chicken breasts cost only $2.67 per pound after trimming and cooking, which is less than half the price of either the packaged lunchmeat or the deli meat. Other economical and healthy alternatives to lunchmeat include chicken salad, tuna salad, egg salad, leftover meatloaf, grilled cheese, and, of course, peanut-butter-and-jelly sandwiches.

When frozen bone-in turkey breasts are on sale, I buy at least one for the freezer and one to thaw in the refrigerator. It's easy to make a roasted turkey breast for dinner, and the leftover turkey is excellent for turkey sandwiches. You'd pay a premium for real turkey breast at an authentic delicatessen, but it is a bargain when you bake it yourself. After cooking the 5.5-pound turkey breast I purchased on sale for 99 cents per pound, it yielded 2 pounds of fully cooked turkey (trimmed of all fat and skin) for an average cost of $2.75 per pound for high-quality sliced deli turkey.

Not only is that cost 66 percent lower than the deli turkey sold at the store for $7.99 per pound, but it also took less time to prepare the turkey breast for baking than waiting at the deli counter.

Avoid the High Cost of Small-Serving Packaging

Buy pre-cooked strips of packaged chicken and you'll pay up to 70 percent more than you would for raw chicken that you cooked yourself. If you need the convenience of cooked chicken, take the same approach as I described earlier by slicing your own cooked chicken to use in sandwiches instead of expensive packaged lunchmeat. Simply bake extra chicken in the oven and keep the fully cooked chicken in the refrigerator to make the next nights' dinners easier. Food safety guidelines suggest that you can keep cooked chicken in the refrigerator for up to four days, and you can avoid the preservatives that packaged chicken has. At a price of $4.99 for a 9-ounce package of cooked chicken breast, you'll pay $8.87 per pound as compared to the $2.67 per pound cost for cooked-at-home sale-priced chicken breast, a savings of 70 percent.

You'll pay the same premium for tubs of pre-cooked barbecue pork, shredded barbecue chicken, or sloppy-joe meat sold in the refrigerated packaged meat section. If time is an issue, give the slow cooker a try to make barbecued pork, beef, or chicken with less effort. You'll also be able to make a much healthier version of these entrées, because you can trim the fat more closely and use less sugary sauce than the packaged versions.

Time Is Money, and It's Worth It to Check Out Several Stores

It takes time and a bit of a hassle, but it really is worthwhile to cruise various grocery stores to determine who has the best sales, prices, and quality when it comes to meat. Especially since it is a higher-priced, main-entrée item, your annual savings will justify investing time in finding the least expensive source.

Check out supermarkets, discount stores, and even wholesale clubs to compare. If you don't belong to a wholesale club, you can call your nearest store to ask if you can have a free one-day pass. That will allow you to note prices and decide if it is worth joining to save money on your key items.

I compared prices for several types of chicken, meat, and fish at my supermarket, two discount stores, and a wholesale club. I was surprised to find that the very least expensive option of boneless chicken breasts was the individually frozen chicken breasts sold in a 3-pound bag at Aldi. Its regular everyday price was actually 9 percent lower than my supermarket's lowest sale price on fresh boneless chicken breasts, $1.83 per pound as compared to $1.99 per pound at my supermarket during sale weeks. Because I wanted to be sure the 3-pound weight shown on the bag was accurate, I weighed the chicken after thawing on my digital food scale, and it was a couple of ounces over 3 pounds. Aldi's frozen ground turkey sold for $1.19 per frozen roll, which is 32 percent less than my supermarket's price on frozen ground turkey. Needless to say, I stock up on those on my Aldi trips.

Consider Wholesale Clubs for Main-Dish Ingredients

You say you have no time to track sales? Or that you have a huge family? Or maybe you buy items that never seem to go on sale. If any of these describes you, it might be worthwhile to consider buying your meats at a wholesale club. I compared meat and poultry prices at a local wholesale club to two local supermarkets' prices. In every case, the wholesale club had the lowest price per pound for the twenty-two items in my analysis. Some items' prices were lower than my supermarket's *sale* prices. In terms of overall value, the wholesale club's main-dish ingredients are also known for their restaurant quality and freshness due to high sales volume and turnover. You will have to buy larger quantities at wholesale clubs, which is fine if you are cooking for a large group or if you have freezer space. I liked the chicken packaging at Costco because the 6-pound package had six individual vacuum-packed packages of chicken, so I didn't have to come home and divide the chicken and repackage it into smaller packages myself.

If you stocked up on meat and poultry when it was at its rock-bottom sale price at your supermarket, you will most likely pay prices that are equal to or in some cases less than wholesale clubs' prices.

WHOLESALE CLUB PRICE PER POUND: COMPARISON TO SUPERMARKET
REGULAR PRICES

Item—Price Comparison May 2009; All Prices Are Listed as per Pound	Costco Price	Supermarket Regular Price	Price Difference
beef, boneless brisket	$3.99	$4.99	20%
beef, boneless chuck roast	$2.49	$4.29	42%
beef, boneless eye of round roast	$2.69	$4.99	46%
beef, boneless top sirloin	$4.49	$5.99	25%
beef, flank steak	$4.89	$6.99	30%
beef, ground round, 85% lean (Costco 88% lean)	$2.69	$3.69	27%
beef, rib eye steak	$6.89	$7.99	14%
beef, stew meat	$2.99	$3.89	23%
beef, T-bone steak	$6.99	$9.99	30%
beef, top round steak	$3.49	$4.79	27%
chicken breasts, fresh boneless, reg. price	$2.99	$ 3.99	25%
chicken breasts, individually frozen, name brand	$2.49	$4.50	45%
chicken breasts, individually frozen, store brand	$1.99	$2.99	33%
chicken, drumsticks or thighs	$0.99	$1.19	17%
chicken, rotisserie, fully cooked, 3 lb.	$4.99	$7.99	38%
chicken, whole frying chicken	$0.89	$0.99	10%
lamb, leg of	$3.99	$5.99	33%

pork, boneless pork loin	$1.89	$2.99	37%
pork, boneless pork loin chops	$2.69	$4.99	46%
pork spareribs	$1.89	$1.99	5%
pork tenderloin	$2.79	$3.99	30%
turkey, fresh ground	$2.29	$2.69	15%
average savings at wholesale club			**30%**

Let's Talk Turkey

Fact one: Lower-fat ground turkey can stand in for ground beef in some pasta sauces, soups, chilis, and casseroles.

Fact two: My family isn't exactly crazy about the way turkey tastes compared to ground beef.

To get the benefit of the first while addressing the second, I use ground turkey in recipes that include a tasty sauce, and the cost savings is even more delicious. Using frozen ground turkey is up to half the cost of using fresh ground beef, and saves calories as well as dollars.

The Meatless Meal: Go Green, Save Green

A meat-free dinner will likely save an average of $5. Take the meat, poultry, pork, or fish off the menu just one night a week, and you've saved $260 in a year. Consider main-dish salads with beans and cheese, pastas, vegetable stir-fries, meatless casseroles, bean-and-cheese enchiladas, vegetarian chilis, soups, and egg dishes. Dried beans are inexpensive and provide a complete source of protein when combined with grains, such as rice or tortillas. I also like to use lentils in many different kinds of dishes because they are very inexpensive, high in protein and fiber, and cook quickly without having to pre-soak like dried beans. Check our recipe chapter and your favorite recipe websites to find good meatless recipes that your family will like.

Going meatless once in a while saves money, improves your health, and gives the planet a break. Bringing beans and pasta to your table consumes far less energy and natural resources than chicken or beef. Michael Pollan, the author of *The Omnivore's Dilemma* and *In Defense of Food*, calculated an interesting effect of meat-free living. The environmental impact of every American household eating one meatless dinner per week would be comparable to taking thirty to forty million cars off the road for a year, he found, because of decreased emissions created by meat production. Eating chicken instead of beef is also eco-friendlier. Beef production generates eleven times the emissions as chicken production. The production of one pound of beef requires 2,500 gallons of water, whereas a 10-minute shower requires 42 gallons of water. I found it very interesting to read that Dr. Rajendra K. Pachauri, a global expert on climate change, suggests that people can have a greater positive impact on the environment by reducing their meat consumption than they would by switching to hybrid cars. It's certainly less expensive to have a Meatless Monday than it is to buy a new set of eco-friendly wheels!

A Final Word

Remember that because the beef, chicken, poultry, or pork you serve usually represents the largest portion of your grocery budget, it also represents the largest possible savings. Stay on the lookout for sales, make the butcher your partner in bargain hunting, and prepare to do a little bit of butchering yourself to create your own convenient portion sizes. And consider the occasional meat-free meal. The total result will feel like someone took a nice, sharp cleaver and trimmed off a huge chunk of your grocery bill!

Thirteen

Save Green in the Produce Department

Would you pay someone a six-figure salary to wash your lettuce? Is eating an apple a day instead of a banana worth $1,000 to you? It sounds extreme, but simple strategies in the produce department can dramatically cut your grocery bill, whereas letting habit and convenience guide your decisions can needlessly drain your wallet. Items in the produce department are brimming with nutrients that belong in your diet, but this section of the grocery store is also full of savings opportunities, if you'll use some easy tactics.

In this chapter we're going to talk about:

- how the type of produce you buy can drastically alter your overall grocery bill
- why remaining flexible about the items you pack in your lunch or toss in your salad is key to sticking to your budget
- why the way your fruits and vegetables are packaged matters, and how a little extra time spent in the kitchen can add up to tremendous savings

Do It Yourself!

I'm not sure when we all got too busy to wash lettuce. When I was growing up, grocery stores sold heads or bunches of lettuce rather than the pre-washed, pre-chopped convenience packages we see today. Today it seems the bagged varieties have a much more dedicated following than the lowly heads or bunches that need to be washed and chopped, judging from the amount of space each takes up in the typical produce section.

I used to buy bagged salads, either on sale or with a coupon, but found I didn't like the funny preservative taste. So I've gone back to buying lettuce that needs some attention. A salad spinner and lettuce crisper make it easy to wash the lettuce once and have it ready to go for several days, with no preservatives.

Curious, I decided to research to determine the value of all that spinning and crisping. It takes me 5 minutes to wash a 2-pound bunch of romaine. Because the 10-ounce bag of romaine salad cost $2.50, and my 2.2-pound bunch of romaine costs $1.68, I saved $6.32 by washing my lettuce instead of buying the equivalent amount of about three bags of washed romaine. Some quick calculations show that works out to a "salary" of $76 per hour, $3,040 per week, or more than $158,000 per year. If you'd like to hire me at that rate, I'll be happy to come wash your lettuce for you!

Coupons don't really make much of a dent in the exorbitant lopsided cost of bagged lettuce. Even with a $1-off coupon, I still would have paid more per pound for the bagged lettuce than I would if I'd washed it myself. Using three bags of salad per week, I'm saving $302 annually just by washing lettuce myself.

Similarly, buying pre-cut produce instead of bagged is like taking a toll road instead of a freeway. It might save time, but you're going to pay for that convenience. Pre-cut celery sticks, apple slices, and containers of cut fruit command premium prices, and even less-prepared items such as celery hearts, baby peeled carrots, or romaine lettuce hearts are going to cost far more than the same items in a less-readied state.

Try the 5-Minute Rule: This is not to be confused with the 5-Second

Rule, which claims that if you eat food off the floor it's A-okay as long as it doesn't sit there for more than five seconds. (I don't agree, by the way.) If it takes you 5 minutes or less to prepare an item instead of buying it pre-cooked, pre-washed, or pre-cut, then it is well worth your time to save the money by doing it yourself. As with our six-figure lettuce example above, I thought it would be fun to calculate the "wage" of preparing items yourself. Every item on this list took 5 minutes or less to prepare. Take a look at the steep cost of convenience.

Save with the "Do-It-Yourself Approach"	Savings per Item	Percentage Saved	Hourly wage
apples; buy a 3-lb. bag instead of 14 oz. slices	$3.26	82%	$39
cantaloupe; buy a whole melon instead of cut-up melon	$5.00	71%	$60
carrots; buy a 1-lb. bag instead of baby peeled carrots	$1.09	55%	$13
carrots; buy a 1-lb. bag instead of shredded carrots	$2.28	72%	$27
celery; buy a bunch instead of celery sticks	$6.93	86%	$83
iceberg lettuce; buy a head instead of shredded lettuce	$5.86	87%	$70
romaine lettuce; buy a bunch instead of bagged lettuce	$6.32	79%	$76
strawberries; buy a pint instead of cut-up berries	$2.66	62%	$32

The next time you're cruising through the produce department and are tempted to grab those cute pre-sliced cantaloupe cubes to toss into a dessert or salad, ask yourself one question: *Can I afford to pay someone a yearly "salary" of more than $124,000 for that small convenience?* I could win the lottery tomorrow and the answer would still be no!

Produce Selection Strategies

Now that we've demonstrated the high cost of saving a little time, let's look more carefully at the importance of choosing wisely when determining which items to buy in the produce department. By shopping with a strategic eye, it's easy to make simple choices that result in a much lower overall bill.

Stick to the basics: Perhaps even more than a handsome cut of steak, out-of-season, imported—and therefore more expensive—fruits and veggies can tempt us with their come-hither appeal.

Those out-of-season raspberries would make such a lovely addition to your cereal in the morning, even though traveling halfway around the world results in a $5 price tag for a half-pint container. That tousled mass of imported arugula would make for such an artfully arranged salad, especially if we sautéed a few portobello mushrooms and tossed them in. And they seem so wholesome in those gleaming bins, perhaps freshly misted, that surely it couldn't hurt, right? Wrong! Unsexy choices like lettuce, carrots, celery, cabbage, apples, bananas, oranges, green beans, asparagus, or broccoli deliver the same nutrients at far less cost. The humble—and versatile—potato is your partner on the path to a smaller grocery-store bill. There is no high-rent district in my fridge. You're not going to find exotic fruits or vegetables in there—unless they're on major sale, of course.

Buy in season: The farm-to-table trend cropping up in hip restaurants makes fashionable use of a pretty basic concept. Produce tastes better when it's fresh! Even better, in-season items are far less expensive, since it costs less to deliver them to the store where you shop. Keep a close eye on what's in season, and plan dishes around those items. Nothing's more delicious than a bargain.

Bag those frozen deals: Frozen vegetables are just as good for you as fresh because they are frozen immediately after harvest, when nutrients are at their peak. If the quality suits you, there's no reason to pay more for fresh. Plus, you can hang on to frozen veggies and cook just what you need for any given recipe, lessening the chance of waste. A strategy to consider: Don't wait until you actually need vegetables to buy them. Stock up in advance when prices are at their best. Coupons used in conjunction with store sales can result in incredible savings. My freezer is loaded with bags of brand-name broccoli or green beans purchased for just 30 cents. In some cases they've actually been free!

Know your serving sizes and substitutions: We tend to think of produce in terms of its cost per pound or unit, when we should instead consider its cost per serving. By figuring out how much of an item you need for a particular meal, you're able to better assess its cost per serving—and choose the most economical ingredients. For example, if red potatoes cost $1.69 per pound and russet potatoes cost $3 for a 5-pound bag, it's not easy to tell how much it would cost to serve each type of potato for dinner. When you count the number of potatoes per pound and do the math, you'd find out that the cost per medium red potato is 79 cents per person and the cost of a medium russet potato is 27 cents per person. In other words, a family of five would save $2.60 per dinner simply by choosing to serve russet potatoes instead of red potatoes. Then again, if the family had brown rice at 8 cents a serving instead of potatoes, they'd end up saving $3.55 on one dinner as compared to the cost of serving red potatoes. It pays to do a little math!

An apple a day might cost you dearly: Is there any more virtuous practice than eating an apple a day? Maybe not—unless it's eating a banana instead. Don't fall into the trap of buying the same fruits week after week just because you're in the habit of always packing an apple for lunch, for example. A large Red Delicious might cost as much as $1, depending on the season, when an orange might cost half as much and a banana only a fourth. If that's the case, take a minute to ask yourself: *Is having an apple really worth four times as much as having a banana instead?* Put another way, if your family of four substituted a less-expensive banana for apples, you'd save $1,100 in a year without making any other changes to your budget and without shopping around. It's important to note that the prices in this example are from the same supermarket. Shopping at numerous stores isn't necessary when you know what the costs of simple substitutions are in terms of variety and size.

Bulk up: I'm not telling you never to eat another apple. I just want you to consider how you're buying them. Just as buying meat in bulk translates into savings, buying bagged fruits or vegetables can cost much less. With potatoes, for example, you'll generally pay less per pound if you buy the 10-pound bag of potatoes rather than the 5-pound bag, or the 5-pound bag of carrots rather than the 1-pound bag. I buy the 5-pound bag of carrots at 70 cents per pound rather than paying 89 cents for a 1-pound bag. That's a good value if you can use that amount in two weeks, but it makes sense to buy larger bags only if you are sure you'll use the larger quantities. Back to our apple example: When I compare the price of apples either sold individually or sold in 3- or 5-pound bags, I am amazed at the cost difference. If each person in a family of four ate one apple per day, that single item could cost as much as $1,470 per year or as little as $303 per year, depending on *how you buy* apples.

Apple Variety	Weight per Serving	Cost per lb.	Cost per Serving	Annual Cost of Apples at One Serving per Day per Person, for a Family of Four
large Golden Delicious, sold individually	9 oz.	$1.79	$1.00	$1,470.00
medium Golden Delicious, sold individually	6 oz.	$1.49	$0.56	$816.00
medium Golden Delicious, sold in 3-lb. bag ($3.49, 8 apples)	6 oz.	$1.16	$0.44	$637.00
small Red Delicious apples, sold in 3-lb. bag ($2.49, 12 apples)	4 oz.	$0.83	$0.21	$303.00

The blemished bargain: Part of the appeal of selecting fruits or vegetables individually is the opportunity to inspect every inch. After all, buying cheap potatoes or onions isn't a bargain if they turn out to be imperfect, right? Not so fast. Produce sold by the bag may be 20 to 50 percent less expensive than buying individual pieces by the pound. It's handy to use your calculator to compare the per-pound cost of each option, but you'll likely find that even if you discover a problem and have to toss a bruised piece or two, you've still saved money by purchasing the bag.

Weigh and compare flat rates with per-pound prices: Heads of iceberg are a little like snowflakes: Each one's a bit different. If the item is being sold at a flat rate instead of by the pound, you've basically been given a shot at free food. When I buy lettuce by the bunch, I pick out a few bunches that look the largest. I weigh each of them on the produce scale and buy the heaviest one, which is usually 10 to 20 percent heavier than the smallest one. Similarly, when I compared the largest head of lettuce to the smallest one in the display, I discovered a 50 percent difference in weight. The shopper who purchases the smallest head at 1½ pounds would pay 50 percent more per pound than the shopper who ended up buying the largest head at 2¼ pounds. The same principal applies when buying items like bagged celery, carrots, potatoes, apples, or onions. A few moments at the scale is definitely worth your time.

Waste not: It is worth repeating that the USDA estimates that households waste between 10 and 40 percent of their grocery dollars, depending on their grocery spending level. Apart from the moral and environmental implications of wasting food, tossing unused items you just didn't get around to eating makes zero sense when you're trying to whittle your grocery bill. The keys to avoiding waste are planning ahead and taking careful stock of what you have before you hit the grocery store. Try these tips:

- Think through the number of apples, bananas, heads of lettuce, etc., that you will need for the week's meals and snacks as you make your weekly list.
- Buying bagged items often means buying smaller fruits or vegetables, which can cut down on waste. How many times have you seen a family member throw away a partially eaten apple?
- Clean out your produce drawers each week when you make your shopping list. Plan your next meals to include the produce you already have on hand.
- Leftover vegetables can be used to make soup. Get creative!
- If you don't have time to make a soup, cut the vegetables up and put them in a freezer container. When the container is full, make a soup out of veggies that would have otherwise gone to waste.

- When bananas are on the ripe side, peel and cut them into chunks and keep them in a freezer dish to use in blended drinks or banana bread.
- Cut bruises out of apples and serve the remaining sections in pretty slices.

Don't fall for pricey add-ons: Those fresh, lovely strawberries are just begging to jump in your cart. And look, they're on sale! Right next to them, the store's employees might have helpfully arranged a stack of full-priced sponge cake and whipped topping, knowing visions of strawberry shortcake will be dancing in shoppers' heads. Again, resist the temptation to pay premium prices for convenience. Flip through your coupon organizer until you can buy white cake mix at a steep bargain and serve the same dessert for far less.

Shop around: Check discount stores, wholesale clubs, and even dollar stores to see if they can beat your supermarket's produce prices. Many CouponMom.com members report that they find the lowest prices on produce at no-frills discount stores, such as Aldi or Save-A-Lot, as well as dollar stores with produce sections. Trader Joe's, if you have one in your area, sells produce on a per-piece basis rather than a per-pound basis. A recent Trader Joe's discovery: bananas for 19 cents each, as compared to 25 cents or more at the supermarket. Wholesale clubs also offer bargain prices on most produce, but size can be an issue if you aren't shopping for a large family. If that's the case, then you might consider shopping with a friend or neighbor. BJ's Wholesale Clubs package produce in smaller sizes than some other wholesalers, so it's worth comparing prices if a BJ's is convenient for you.

Homemade dressings: By combining sales and coupons, you can sometimes buy salad dressing for close to nothing. Free, of course, is good. But it's almost always going to be much less expensive to make your own dressing—and the homemade variety often tastes better, too. Check cookbooks or recipe websites for ideas. (If that's too much work, whisk a dollop of olive oil, a splash of balsamic vinegar, and a pinch of salt and pepper for a cheap, easy, and tasty dressing.) But before you pay $3 for a 3-ounce packet of salad toppings or toasted nuts, you can save 70 percent on a per-ounce basis by topping your salads with roasted sunflower seeds (sold in the popcorn aisle) or by toasting chopped nuts you buy in bulk for half the price.

Speaking of nuts, the pricing can be downright nutty: Sometimes a grocery store can actually beat its own price, just depending on where an item is placed. I compared the price of pecans, walnuts, and almonds sold in 1-pound bags in the produce department to the same type of nuts sold in 1-pound bags in the baking aisle at the same store. Almonds were 27 percent less expensive and walnuts were 14 percent less expensive in the baking aisle as compared to the produce department. However, pecans were 29 percent less expensive in the produce section as compared to the baking aisle. Store prices will vary, but it pays to compare when different brands of the same item are sold in more than one department of the store. Nuts are a real bargain at wholesale clubs. My comparison found that the wholesale club's nut prices are about 50 percent less expensive than the lowest supermarket prices. You'll have to buy a larger quantity at the wholesale club to get the savings. Again, consider splitting with a friend or freezing what you won't use right away.

Timing is everything: Early-morning shoppers might be able to buy yesterday's produce at half-price, but you won't know unless you ask. Make friends with your grocery stores' produce managers to see if they'll consider such a markdown. The store would rather sell it to you for less than have to toss it at a complete loss.

Get the most nutrition for your dollar: Pound for pound, iceberg and romaine lettuce at my supermarket are pretty comparable. But they part ways in terms of nutrition. Romaine lettuce has much more vitamin A and vitamin C than iceberg, and the full bunch of romaine has more of these vitamins than the more expensive romaine hearts, which have been stripped of their darker outer leaves. Now think about that for a minute: A smaller, less nutritious product costs more than the larger, healthier option. Guess which one I recommend?

Consider substituting less-expensive produce options that have comparable nutrition for your standard choices: An orange will provide all the vitamin C you need in a day. So will two cups of chopped green cabbage. And the cabbage costs about two-thirds less than the orange. I understand you might not want to substitute steamed cabbage for a sliced orange at breakfast or with your lunch, but consider tossing finely chopped cabbage into soups or salads, or use it in coleslaw or stir-fries.

Buy local produce: Locally grown produce is more than a passing trend. It's a great way to eat less expensively, since the cost of transporting produce a few miles is far less than trucking it across the country. Look for "locally grown" signs in stores, and ask your produce manager where the store gets its produce, if this option appeals to you.

Find a farmers' market: For the absolute freshest produce, it's hard to beat a farmers' market, unless you want to dig in the dirt yourself and wait a few months to eat. A trip to the farmers' market is a great way to support your local economy and take advantage of items unique to your community. Plus, it's fun! Especially if you have children, a food-shopping trip can become an adventure and learning experience, and there will be no candy racks tempting them as you wait to make your purchases. Depending on the size of your local farmers' market, you might be able to buy produce, eggs, home-made soaps or breads, fresh-cut flowers, or potted herbs. Prices vary, but since the farmer doesn't pay for marketing, shopping carts, lighting, or employees, as a large grocery store does, you're able to realize those savings.

The USDA estimates that there are more than 4,600 farmers' markets across the country, and its data show that more shoppers are buying directly from farmers. Direct sales of food from farmers to consumers grew by 49 percent from 2002 to 2007, the USDA reports. Although this category accounts for less than 1 percent of food sold in the United States, total sales in this category grew to $1.2 billion in 2007.

If you aren't aware of a local farmers' market near you, try the online directory of farmers' markets on the USDA's Agricultural Marketing Service's website (www.ams.usda.gov) and look for the Farmers' Markets and Local Food Marketing link on the left side of the page. I used this directory and found a large market 10 miles from my home with fifty-six participating farmers, open Saturday mornings from May to September. The USDA directory does a good job of listing information about these large farmers' markets, but I found far more small and medium-size farmers' markets by going to Google and entering the name of my suburb and the term "farmers' markets." I found a few good local websites with long lists of farms that sell directly to consumers, as well as lists of weekly farmers' markets.

Shopping at a farmers' market is somewhat akin to shopping at yard sales. For the best selection, get there early. For the best price, show up around closing time. Chances are the farmer would much prefer sending you home with a half-priced bushel than lugging it home, unsure if it'll be able to be sold at all. If you become a "regular" at your area farmers' market, the participants may work with you on getting the best price or selection.

And if you're really into cutting out middleman markup but lack the time or space to dedicate a patch of your yard for vegetable gardening, consider visiting "pick-your-own" farms.

Search Google for local "pick-your-own" farms, or visit a fun site I discovered, www.pickyourown.org. This might not necessarily rival the cheapest bargain at the wholesale club, but think of it as a low-priced outing. If at the end of the day your family has fresh produce and worn-out kids ready for bed soon after devouring the fruits (or vegetables) of their labor, you've discovered a bargain indeed.

A Final Word

Yes, chopping your own lettuce takes a few minutes. Planning meals around in-season produce might require a little creativity. And washing, peeling, and chopping carrots from a bag isn't quite as convenient as chomping ready-to-eat baby carrots (which, by the way, are just regular carrots whittled down to a cute size). But with some effort on your part, savings in the produce department is about the closest thing you'll find to money growing on trees!

Fourteen

— — — —

Dear Dairy: Savings Strategies on Milk, Yogurt, Cheese, and Eggs

Dairy items play an important role in daily nutrition, adding important calcium and protein to our diet. This is important for building strong teeth and bones in children and keeping them strong and healthy in adults. USDA guidelines recommend that adults consume 1,000 milligrams of calcium daily.

In this chapter we're going to discuss:

- the significance of milk prices on your overall grocery bill
- ways to cut the cost of dairy products by skipping convenience packaging
- do-it-yourself measures for saving money on dairy items (No, I'm not going to suggest you get a cow or churn butter.)

Got (a Deal on) Milk?

Years ago, the first President Bush took a little heat when, during a photo op at a grocery store, he had no idea what a gallon of milk cost. As political "controversies" go, this might seem pretty mild, but the fact that it resonated with people illustrates what a bellwether the price of a gallon of milk is in our society. Some shoppers will actually switch stores if they find milk at a significant savings from their regular market, and when grocers put milk on sale, they often trumpet that fact by featuring it in their weekly fliers.

While it clearly catches people's attention (and sometimes grabs national headlines), I don't think the price of milk alone should have a major influence on how you shop. You won't find many people more keen than me on stretching dollars at the grocery store, but believe it or not, I met a woman who even I thought was a little intense about price. Her obsession: milk. She was making extra trips to the wholesale club to buy two weeks' worth of milk to freeze. I asked why she didn't just pick it up at the grocery store, and she looked at me like I was nuts! Surely, she figured, buying in bulk at this big-box wholesaler and then putting her savings on ice was the path to cutting her grocery bill. Turns out her regular supermarket was selling milk for the same price. She was wasting time, if not money, by making the extra trip to the wholesale club without even checking prices.

Even if she was saving a few bucks, it's questionable whether she would have been making much impact on her overall grocery bill. Her family went through 2 gallons of milk per week. Over the past few years, I've seen the price of a gallon of store-brand milk range from $1.99–$4.39, but even at the high point, 2 gallons of milk would represent just 6 percent of a weekly $150 grocery bill. Say this super-zealous milk shopper saved a dollar on each gallon by trekking to the wholesaler and freezing milk. She's still peeled just 1.3 percent off her total grocery spending. If you ask me, she was focused a little too intently on this one product.

Still, some people are cutting back on dairy products as a way to save money. An April 2009 study published by the Midwest Dairy Council showed that a third of respondents said they were buying fewer dairy products to save money. And 43 percent of those shoppers said they felt they could get the nutrition benefits of dairy items from other foods.

I would argue that even when dairy products are at their highest price, they are still a nutritional bargain. Even at $3 per gallon, a 1-cup serving of skim milk costs 19 cents and packs a nutritional wallop. That 19-cent glass gives you 8 grams of protein, or 17 percent of an adult's daily requirement, along with 30 percent of the calcium and 20 percent of the vitamin D you need in a day. By comparison, 1 ounce of cooked chicken breast provides those same 8 grams of protein, but at a 32 percent higher cost.

Rather than taking nutritious dairy products off your menu or wasting time hitting store after store on a bargain-seeking milk run, consider the following effective savings strategies.

Look for loss leaders: The products featured on the cover of supermarket sales fliers are sometimes known as "loss leaders." The store knows it will lose money on this super-cheap item but figures once they hook you with a bargain, they can reel you in to potentially spend money elsewhere. Loss leaders tend to be perishable items that are not easy to stockpile. Popular loss-leader items often include staples such as milk, bread, eggs, chicken, or beef.

I met the president of a large grocery store chain several years ago and asked him the best strategies to save money on milk. There wasn't much to it, really. He said his stores typically put milk on sale every other week, so clearly the thing to do was stock up when prices fell. Since milk is perishable, it's obviously smart to purchase gallons with the longest sell-by dates on the labels.

Try store brands: Brand-name and store-brand milk, cheese, or butter all have to meet USDA requirements. Why spend extra money for corporate marketing and advertising when the product is virtually identical? I compared the name-brand prices for popular dairy products at my store and found a significant difference in price but not much difference in quality. The store-brand items' prices were an average of 39 percent lower than the name brands, so unless I'm scoring a serious deal with sales or coupons, it's store-brand dairy for my family.

Look for markdowns: The time to pounce for possible deals is when the clock is ticking on a dairy product's expiration date. Experts say that it's safe to eat dairy products for a week after their sell-by date when the product hasn't been opened yet, and the savings could be significant. Ask store managers for a deal on dairy that's about to hit its expiration date. Chances are, they'd rather charge you less for it than have to chuck it. If that doesn't work, ask the department manager when items are going to be marked down.

Store properly to avoid waste: If that giant bulk container of sour cream becomes a science project before you can use it, you haven't really saved much money. It does make sense to buy a larger quantity if the price per serving works out to be less, but be sure to keep those savings from spoiling, literally. Store your dairy products in the back of the refrigerator to keep them as cold as possible. Don't put milk, eggs, and other dairy products in the refrigerator door, where the temperature fluctuates the most. If you buy a large block of cheese, cut it into smaller pieces and wrap them tightly in plastic wrap or foil, or put them in airtight containers in the refrigerator. The unused cheese will be exposed to air less frequently and will last longer. Buy items such as cream cheese or cottage cheese when you know you'll use them, to avoid turning the fridge into a penicillin lab.

Bigger is not always better: Resist the siren song of a 5-pound block of cheese on sale at the wholesale club if there's no reasonable chance you're actually going to use it. And don't assume that the larger package is always the better deal. Compare the unit cost of various sizes of dairy products, such as 16-ounce tubs of cottage cheese to 24-ounce tubs, or individual 6-ounce yogurt cups to larger 24-ounce tubs. It may turn out that the smaller size is the better deal, especially when you throw in sales and coupons.

Here's a "grate" idea for saving money: Block cheese is often less expensive than shredded cheese per pound, and it takes only a few minutes to shred cheese. Because shredded cheese can cost up to twice what a block of the same cheese can, my $5 hand grater paid for itself a long time ago. It's quicker to grab and easier to clean than a food processor, and it saves the unneeded expense of convenience packaging.

Strong flavors, strong savings: If you buy cheeses with stronger flavors, such as sharp cheddar, you can use less of it in recipes while still adding flavor. Or add flavor with seasoning. I find that with cheese grits, you can use a dash of hot sauce or a pinch of cayenne pepper and get away with using less cheese. This saves money and trims fat and calories from the dish.

Shop in your store's "low-rent" district: When you're on a beach vacation, an oceanfront room costs more than a room with no view. It's essentially the same product, but the location jacks up the price. The same principle can apply at the grocery store, where the price of similar items can vary significantly just because of the aisle they're found in. You may find that feta, blue cheese, goat cheese, Vermont cheddar, Parmesan, and Romano cheeses sold in the deli or gourmet section of your market have lower-priced counterparts in the humble dairy case. I compared costs at my supermarket for the same types of cheese sold under different brand names in these two departments and found that the dairy-case versions cost as much as 63 percent less than the gourmet-cheese options. If you ask me, saving that much money is worth trading down from the deli-department to the dairy-case view!

COMPARISON OF CHEESE PURCHASED IN THE DAIRY DEPARTMENT RATHER THAN THE DELI DEPARTMENT AT THE SAME SUPERMARKET

Cheese Variety	Cost in Supermarket Deli Department	Cost in Supermarket Dairy Department	Savings
blue cheese, chunk, per lb.	$15.99	$5.98	63%
cheddar, sharp Vermont, per lb.	$11.99	$5.98	50%
feta, per lb.	$15.97	$8.76	45%
goat cheese crumbles, per lb.	$19.96	$13.96	30%
Parmesan, chunk, per lb.	$15.99	$5.98	63%
Parmesan, shaved, per lb.	$15.97	$6.67	58%

The deli department vs. the deli counter: At my grocery store, you can grab prepackaged cheese in the deli or ask to have it sliced at the counter. It's the exact same product, but just taking the time to have it sliced for you can save money. For example, an 8-ounce package of deli sliced American cheese sold next to the deli counter costs $4.99, which is $9.98 per pound. I can buy the same cheese if I'm willing to wait to have it sliced for $5.99 per pound, a 40 percent savings. When the deli counter puts sliced American cheese on sale, it may be as low as $2.99 per pound, which is typically less expensive than other brands' wrapped American cheese slices sold in the dairy case at their regular prices.

Discount-store dairy: Some of the best bargains at wholesale clubs and discount grocery stores are in the dairy department. For example, my local wholesale club sells eggs, milk, cheese, egg substitute, whipping cream, cream cheese, and half-and-half at lower prices than the store-brand options at supermarkets. My local Aldi also has lower dairy prices than the supermarket and doesn't require the large bulk purchases of the wholesale club. If your household goes through a lot of dairy products, it may be worth a trip or two each month to area discount stores to save. Our family of four uses a moderate amount of dairy items, and the savings potential of buying them at the wholesale club or Aldi's would be $20 per month. An extra $240 per year is worth working discount-store shopping into my routine.

Stock up and freeze cheese: Cheese keeps longer than other dairy items, so load up when the price is attractive. When cheese is on sale with a coupon, or when your store brand is selling at a rock-bottom sale price, you can stock up for a few weeks and freeze it. (Unlike meat, it doesn't need to be frozen right away, even if you aren't going to use it immediately.) The consistency of block cheese can change after freezing and thawing, making it crumbly and harder to shred afterward, so consider shredding it before freezing. If you buy a large bag of shredded cheese, divide it into smaller bags before freezing to make it easy to thaw just the amount you need each week. It is generally not a good idea to freeze cream cheese, cottage cheese, or ricotta cheeses, since freezing dramatically changes their consistency.

Here's a little trick to keep your shredded cheese in top form after freezing: Add a spoonful of flour to the bag and shake it up so that the cheese shreds come apart easily after thawing. Fillers are added to commercial shredded cheese, which is why it does not stick together after being thawed.

Use coupons: Name-brand prices can occasionally beat the store brand when you have coupons. Companies regularly run coupons for yogurt, cheese, eggs, ice cream, sour cream, refrigerated fruit juices, margarine, butter, and canned whipped cream. Margarine and butter can be frozen, so if you are able to buy them practically free with a coupon, be sure to stock up.

Do-It-Yourself Strategies

The cheapest source of dairy products, short of owning a cow, is your own effort. You can further trim your dairy bill if you're willing to employ a few do-it-yourself strategies.

Make your own yogurt: Cultured milk products have been around for thousands of years, and the first batches of yogurt probably happened by chance, when milk happened to ferment. The point is it's really not that hard to whip up your own yogurt, if you're willing to invest a little time. If you bought milk at $3 per gallon to make the yogurt, you'd save 73 percent over the store brand or sale-priced yogurt at 50 cents per 6-ounce cup. If you buy your milk at a discount store or on sale, you'd save more than that. The $3 milk price translates to an annual savings of $533 for a family of four, assuming each family member eats one 6-ounce serving of yogurt per day. Think of it this way: If you made your own yogurt from the time a child is born until his or her eighteenth birthday, you'd bank more than $9,500 in savings. That money might come in handy when he or she heads off to college! I found helpful yogurt-making guidance at www.makeyourown yogurt.com. You can also buy a highly rated yogurt maker on Amazon.com for about $25, or check a local thrift store for an even cheaper model. Someone with less patience than you might have parted with his or her yogurt maker.

Make your own milk with nonfat dry milk: Powdered milk can help you stretch the most out of your grocery dollar if times are tight. For the best bargains, compare costs at discount stores or wholesale clubs to your local supermarket's price. If you're going to try this option, I recommend serving it in cereal, in recipes, or in blended drinks first, to give your family a chance to get used to the taste gradually. If you're going to serve it straight up, mix the milk the night before and keep it very cold in the back of the refrigerator.

A Final Word

From the cream in your coffee in the morning to the (occasional) bowl of ice cream at night, dairy products likely make up a significant portion of the food your family eats each day. By keeping a sharp eye out for sales, employing Strategic Shopping methods, including stocking up when prices drop and making sure to keep your unit prices under control, you can keep dairy from taking up too significant a portion of your food budget.

Fifteen

Attack Your Snack Bill: Saving on Treats

There's nothing wrong with sensible snacking between meals, so long as you don't let the cost of chips and pretzels muscle in and take over a large portion of your overall food bill. Because snacks sometimes feel like treats, it can be easy to let our guard down when checking prices. After all, if we're going to indulge in something sweet and blow a few calories, we can forget about watching pennies, right? Wrong!

In this chapter we're going to talk about:

- considering a wider, healthier range of food items for snacking
- paying attention to packaging so you're not paying extra just for convenient serving sizes
- learning to compare store-brand and name-brand snack items
- bargain beverages

Don't Let Snack Food Wreck Your Budget

Grab the store-brand tissues. I have one tearjerker of a story for you. I once went shopping with a woman who left the grocery store with her wallet $100 lighter but with practically nothing to eat. And she was *happy* about it!

The woman seemed sincerely interested in learning how to use grocery coupons in order to improve her bottom line, and I was glad to help. I love this type of challenge, so we made a date to meet at the market with the goal of hacking $100 from her monthly food bill.

Things started out well, since she'd made a list of specific items she needed. I'm very big on shopping with a list—I would no sooner hit the store with no list than I would set out on a trip without knowing which road to take. But soon after our shopping trip began, she started deviating from the list quite a bit. First she decided to swing by the bakery to order a special cake. Then it was on to the snack aisle for her children's favorite name-brand cookies and chips. Then she picked up a bag of chocolate-covered pretzels. Finally, she grabbed a box of frozen pastries on a lark, saying she liked trying new products.

Before long this shopping trip started to feel like a car trip when the map blew out the window and no one bothered to stop for directions—we had gotten way off track. By the time we got to the register, my friend had about $100 of items in her cart, including $40 worth of these special treats. I thought I might faint, but she was thrilled! To her credit, she had done a pretty good job of saving money. She had used some of my savings strategies, saving $78 off full price. But her cart had almost no "real food" in it, just junk food and few basic staples from the list. Moving forward, I advised her to keep up the good work using coupons but to focus on sticking to her shopping plan and avoiding unnecessary snacks.

Avoid the Snack Tax!

Data from the Food Marketing Institute show that the average household spends 4.4 cents of every grocery dollar on snack foods and 8.6 cents per grocery dollar on beverages. That's like turning every dollar you spend at the supermarket into 87 cents and incurring a 13 percent "snack tax." I'm willing to bet that many households, especially busy ones with children, pay an even higher "snack tax."

You say your kids want something to eat after school? I hear you. After-school snack time has been a sacred rite at my house for years. But resist the urge to let your kids fill up on pricey nibbles because it's convenient. With childhood obesity and juvenile diabetes on the rise, we could all stand to consider healthier options for snack time. And it just so happens that healthier munching is often less expensive.

Keep a bowl of washed fruit on the kitchen table, where it's easy to grab. Slice carrots or celery, and keep them in the refrigerator with homemade low-fat dressing or dip. Stock the pantry with pretzels, popcorn, crackers, or rice cakes that you buy on sale or with coupons. And if you want to indulge your family's sweet tooth, take the time to bake your own cookies or brownies from scratch once in a while or from mixes you've bought at a bargain. Ice pops are less expensive and healthier for you than ice cream, and they take longer to eat than ice cream or a cookie. Most kids love them, and the store-brand varieties are inexpensive. Or make your own, with your kids' help. Turning snack time into a fun family project gets the youngest members of your household in on the calorie-conscious, budget-minded decisions.

Comparing Brand Names to Generic Labels

Yes, in some cases, brand-name items taste better. But how much is that worth to you?

Store-brand chips, pretzels, crackers, graham crackers, vanilla wafers, and packaged cookies can be half the cost of their name-brand counterparts. If your favorite brands are on sale or you have a valuable coupon, go for it. If not, I think it's silly not to at least consider trading down to the store-brand variety every once in a while. Chances are your kids won't turn down a cookie just because the box lacks a name brand, and you can put your savings to use elsewhere. Here's an example: Our family loves vanilla wafers. Nabisco Nilla wafers at full price with no coupon can cost 72 percent more than no-name versions, meaning I can save $2.80 by choosing the store brand. The information on the package says there are eleven servings in a box of Nilla Wafers, so I've saved a little more than 25 cents per serving by going with the store brand. Buying the name brand would be sort of like throwing a quarter away each time you had a serving of cookies. Are you okay with that? I'm not.

Read the Fine Print

Since I have a marketing background, I do feel a sort of professional kinship with people whose jobs depend on you paying more for an item just because it looks appealing. But I don't let that collegial goodwill turn into needless spending. At my supermarket, one bag of name-brand tortilla chips cost $3.49, while the different-shaped "scoops" variety of the same brand of tortilla chips costs $3.99 per bag. The bags are about the same size, so at a quick glance it seems like you're getting the same amount of chips and just paying 50 cents more for the "scoop" shape. As if paying an additional 50 cents for a cute "scoop" chip wasn't bad enough, you're actually getting fewer chips. It's all there on the side of the packages, if you'll take a moment to read them. The bag of traditional tortilla chips weighs twice as much, costing 18 cents per ounce, while those "scoops" cost 40 cents per ounce. The lesson here: Read the detailed information to make sure you don't get "scooped."

Similarly, a 10-ounce box of name-brand cheese crackers might cost the same as a different-shaped "crisps" variety of the same brand. The difference is that you're getting only 7.5 ounces of the "crisps," or paying 32 percent more. Like I said, I have a certain amount of empathy for marketing types, but I'm not going to let them rob me. Sorry, guys!

Homemade Savings

No, homemade chips don't taste exactly like chips from a bag, but I don't necessarily think that's a bad thing. My family has come to prefer the taste of homemade ones!

You also need to quit paying hidden marketing, packaging, and other costs associated with store-bought cookies or crackers. The solution: Do it yourself.

You don't have to be an expert baker to make cookies, cakes, or brownies in your own kitchen, and rattling the pots and pans can mean saving 50 percent or more each time you serve treats. If you happen to be an elementary-school room parent, you know how those baked goods add up.

Your child is going to college someday. Don't fritter away his or her future tuition on lemon bars and cupcakes.

We're all busy, so bake as strategically as you shop. Making bar cookies by pressing dough into a baking pan instead of rolling out individual balls shaves valuable time. And learning to make banana bread gives you a plan for fruit that gets a little too ripe, while providing a healthier breakfast option than processed toaster pastries.

If you're willing to experiment a little, you can discover all sorts of ways to save on snack items. For example, you can save by making your own low-fat baked tortilla chips with inexpensive corn tortillas, and spend 75 percent less than buying chips in a bag.

My homemade chips are a bargain at 10 cents per ounce, compared to name-brand tortilla chips that cost up to 43 cents per ounce. Even the lowest-priced store-brand tortilla chips cost 14 cents per ounce. If I were to buy the 90-count package of corn tortillas at my wholesale club instead of the supermarket, the homemade chips would only cost 5 cents per ounce, and I can freeze the remaining tortillas in smaller quantities. They have lots of crunch and more protein and fiber than packaged chips, and I like being able to vary the seasonings and control the amount of salt added. It's also easy to make other snacks inexpensively, such as pita chips and bagel chips.

Birthday Cake Bargains

I've always made our family's birthday cakes, but one year I bought a bakery cake because I thought that would be a special treat for my son. Afterward he told me he liked it better when I made his cakes! My cakes are simple but clearly special to my family. I use a cake mix and make a buttercream frosting and decorate it. I don't think my son cared about the quality of the baking the year I had a professional make his cake—he just liked the idea that Mom made a special birthday treat just for him. By using ingredients purchased on sale or with coupons, you might spend a couple of dollars on a cake you make yourself, compared to $15 or $20 on a cake from your supermarket's bakery or $50 and up from a high-end specialty shop. (I don't know how rich I'd have to be to spend $50 on a child's birthday cake.) I still have a picture of the butterfly cake that my mother made on one of my birthdays. I'm sure she didn't spend a lot, but it meant a lot.

Cookie cakes are my favorite special treats to make, since all you need to do is make a batch of cookie dough, press it into a large cookie sheet with sides, bake it, and add a message and trim it with frosting when it cools. Ice-cream pie is another super-easy dessert. Simply spread ice cream into a graham-cracker crust. The entire dessert for eight will cost you $2 or less, which is much less than the $10–$15 you would pay at an ice-cream store. It's easy to vary the dessert by simply using different flavors of ice cream or different types of crumb crust, depending on what you have on hand (such as chocolate graham crackers, crushed cookies, or even a cornflake crust). Since it's a bit of a production, consider making more than one and popping one in the freezer for future use. Find specific variations and crust recipes in chapter 20.

Avoid the 100-Calorie Pack Racket

Whoever invented the 100-calorie snack bag idea is a genius. By adding nothing besides portion control, whoever this guru was came up with a way to get people to pay more for the same thing, or in some cases even less of it. We feel virtuous knowing we're going to consume only 100 calories, without stopping to think that we've just spent four times as much for the privilege of having someone else dole out our chips or crackers for us. I'll let you in on a little snack-size secret of my own. You can create your own 100-calorie snack bags for free. Crackers and pretzels certainly don't ruin a plastic bag. I save the bags and reuse them, which eliminates waste while saving money.

In other chapters I've talked about my 5-Minute Rule, which holds that if it takes you less than 5 minutes to prepare a food and saves a significant amount of money as compared to the prepared version, then it's worth it to do it yourself. Bagging your own snacks is a great example of 5-Minute Rule success. It takes less than 5 minutes to split a large bag of pretzels into 100-calorie serving sizes of about twenty-one per bag. At a savings of $2.50 for that 5 minutes of effort, I "earn" $30 an hour by doing it myself.

The next time you're tempted to add a box of 100-calorie snack bags to your cart, ask yourself if you could afford to pay someone an annual salary of $62,400 to count out pretzels for you.

Drink to This: Bargain Beverages

Health experts will tell you that one quick way to trim calories from your diet is to cut out sodas or adult beverages, since they can pack on pounds without filling you up or adding much nutrition. Since we're putting your budget on a diet, let's look at ways to cut the cost of beverages, too.

If you drink a few soft drinks a day, try to cut back to one or two. When you do enjoy soft drinks or sports drinks, buy them on sale at the grocery store or drugstore and bring them from home rather than buying them in vending machines or convenience stores at five times the cost.

Cutting back on fruit juice will not only save money, but it is also good for our children's health. Kids who constantly have juice boxes or sippy cups filled with fruit juice in their mouths are at risk for tooth decay and obesity. Children do not need to drink more than one serving of fruit juice a day to get their full supply of vitamin C, and even less if they are getting vitamin C from other sources. Buy the least expensive form of juice that meets your preferences—the best and cheapest juice is usually the frozen concentrate— and skip the expense of individual packaging of juice boxes.

Packaging can jack up the price of beverages, so always choose the least-expensive vessel. A 2-liter bottle of soda is less expensive than buying a six-pack of 12-ounce cans. Making punch or lemonade from a powdered mix is less expensive than buying it in a 2-liter bottle. As always, the do-it-yourself route stretches your beverage dollar. An inexpensive, healthy, and delicious alternative to carbonated soft drinks is seltzer water with a splash of fruit juice. Instead of buying bottled iced tea at the store, make your own for pennies a glass. If you prefer sweet tea, look for an easy homemade recipe online and make it for pennies as compared to bottled sweet tea from the supermarket.

A Word on Water

I wish there was a more exciting way to say this, but drinking plain old water really is the best way to trim your beverage budget. Water is healthy— actually, essential—and virtually free. And yet we find ways to spend more for the substance that covers most of the planet's surface.

According to Greg Karp, author of *Living Rich by Spending Smart* and weekly personal finance columnist for Tribune, Americans have a love affair with bottled water. Since we spend about $16 billion on bottled water a year, I'd have to agree. I laughed out loud at Greg's observation that Evian spelled backward is "naive," but at least Evian actually comes from a spring.

A Natural Resources Defense Council study found that 40 percent of bottled water actually comes from municipal water supplies (translation: It is tap water). Tap water may even be cleaner than bottled water, since federal regulations require tap water to be tested several times a day, while bottled water needs to be tested only once a month. After reading the Reuters report that noted that both Dasani, a Coca-Cola product, and Aquafina, marketed by Pepsi, are essentially purified tap water, I wondered if people would quit spending money to buy bottled water. The answer, obviously, is no.

Water can cost as much as $10 per gallon when we buy it in individual bottles, as compared to half a cent per gallon when we turn on the tap, conveniently located in our kitchen. Think about the hysteria that would break out if gasoline hit $10 per gallon! And yet we pay these high prices for the sake of convenience or because of an often misguided perception that bottled water is better for us.

If you're unsatisfied with the quality of your tap water (often an issue if you live near the beach), it is less expensive to buy a water pitcher filter such as Brita or PUR than to buy bottled gallons of filtered water. A gallon of water filtered with a pitcher system will end up costing you about 22 cents a gallon when you factor in the cost of the pitcher and filters. A less expensive alternative is to simply fill a pitcher and leave it on the counter or in the refrigerator overnight and you'll find that the chlorine taste will go away. The chlorine in tap water will dissipate after 24 hours if left un-covered or if the pitcher spout is open. I recall doing this with the water to fill the goldfish bowl to get rid of the chlorine—it works!

Drinking tap water is good for us—a May 2009 research report by *Men's Health* magazine found that men who drink at least five glasses of water a day reduce their risk of heart attacks by 54 percent—and it's good for the environment. Two million tons of plastic water bottles are sent to land-fills every year. Even though water bottles are recyclable, only 23 percent of bottles are recycled, and the annual cost of disposing of plastic water bottles is estimated to be about $70 million. That's a huge cost in more ways than one.

SIMPLE SUBSTITUTIONS TO SAVE ON SNACKS AND BEVERAGES*

Instead of This . . .	Cost	Try This . . .	Cost	Savings
microwave popcorn, cost per serving	$0.50	regular popcorn, popped with a popper or on the stove	$0.11 with oil; $0.03 without oil	78% 94%
bottled water, six-pack of 16.9-oz. bottles	$2.00	tap water in reusable plastic bottle or cup	0	100%
name-brand chips and snacks, 13-oz. bag	$3.29	pretzels, store-brand, 15-oz. bag	$1.19	69%
individually packaged pretzels for lunch boxes, cost per bag (store brand)	$0.14	bag your own pretzels (store brand)	$0.11	73%
individually wrapped brownies for lunch boxes, cost per brownie	$0.13	homemade brownies, cost per brownie	$0.05	62%
bottled lemonade, 2 liters	$1.67	lemonade mix, 2 liters	$0.33	80%

100-calorie snack bags, cheese crackers	$11.32 per pound; $0.55 per bag	bag your own 100-calorie portions of the same brand of crackers	$3.03 per pound; $0.18 per bag	73%
ice cream, cost per 1-cup bowl at $4 per carton	$0.43	ice pops, 12 ct. at $2 per box, cost per pop	$0.17	60%
packaged cookies, 18 oz.	$3.50	homemade sugar cookies, 2 dozen	$1.00	71%
bottled filtered water, 1-gallon jug	$1.00	filtered water pitcher (Brita or PUR), cost per gallon	$0.22	78%
bottled iced tea, 1-gallon jug	$2.00	make your own iced tea	$0.10	95%
soft drinks, 2-liter bottle	$1.50	seltzer water, 2-liter bottle	$0.79	47%

*These examples assume regular prices, not including sales/coupons.

A Final Word

The easiest way to save on snacks is to cut them out of our diets entirely. This would be the healthiest thing to do as well. So let's all resolve to never snack again. Do you promise never to touch another chip? Me neither. Be honest with yourself when planning your shopping trip, and make good decisions about including snack items in your diet and in your budget.

Sixteen

Healthy, Beautiful Savings: Deals at the Drugstore

The corner drugstore is a smaller, more convenient shopping destination than the massive supercenter when you need to grab just a few items. It can also be a pricier option—unless you apply Strategic Shopping principles. But by carefully watching for sale items and combining drugstores' best prices and shopper cards with coupons or other promotions, you can turn the drugstore in your neighborhood into a great hunting ground for bargains.

In this chapter we're going to discuss:

- how to keep your medicine cabinet stocked with toiletry supplies for pennies, or even for free, by timing your drugstore purchases correctly
- a detailed look at the most beneficial savings programs drugstores offer, and how to employ several strategies to arrive at incredible deals
- tips for how each shopping personality can reap the best bargains at drugstores

Because national chains operate thousands of locations across the country, finding a drugstore is no problem. Finding a drugstore bargain? That's also no problem, once you learn to apply Strategic Shopping methods. A quick stop at the drugstore on your way to work or while running other errands can become a valuable part of your overall savings plan.

Stores such as CVS/Pharmacy, Rite Aid, and Walgreens all offer their own sales, promotions, coupons, and rebate offers. Learn to combine these strategies and you'll end up with great deals and even free items! Each week I walk out of the drugstore with at least one item I've gotten absolutely free. In some cases I actually earn a "profit" by racking up store credits that can be used on future visits. Mastering drugstore policies to get the best prices on cleaning products, cosmetics, grocery items, vitamins, medications, and toiletries frees up dollars in your budget that can be spent on food items at the grocery store.

CouponMom.com can point you directly to the best deals and offers this week, but we'll go over some tips in this chapter to get you started.

Shop When You Don't Need To

What's the surest way to pay full price at the drugstore? Wait until you run out of something! This very idea makes me cringe, not only because I am averse to paying full price, but also because it's so easy to stock up on drugstore items. Toothpaste, unlike fresh fruit or vegetables, can be stored on the shelf for months until you need it. And believe me, I'd rather find room in my bathroom cabinets for ten tubes I was able to get on deep discount or for free than to have to pay $3 for a tube because I ran out.

As you might guess, I keep a closet brimming with shampoo, conditioner, razors, toothpaste, toothbrushes, lotion, cosmetics, vitamins, deodorant, soap, and other items that I paid pennies or even nothing for. When you find similar bargain bonanzas, I'd urge you to go beyond just stockpiling them for your own family. Drugstore deals make great donations. Charities that serve homeless individuals, families in crisis or rescue situations, and the elderly often request personal-care items, since they can be fairly expensive to buy at full retail price. Saving, then sharing, makes especially good use of Strategic Shopping.

Track Prices, Search for Bargains, and Save 90 Percent

We bathe, brush our teeth, and wash our hair and faces for next to nothing at my house—all thanks to the savings I score at the drugstores in my area. I conducted a two-month test of drugstore pricing and savings opportunities at stores in my area and came away with bargains that might surprise you. Using the Deals lists on CouponMom.com for CVS/Pharmacy, Walgreens, and Rite Aid to find the best prices in each store every week, I wound up with 216 items with a full-price total value of $906. My haul included a year's supply of toothpaste, along with toothbrushes, deodorant, shampoo, razors, and shaving cream. I also found excellent deals on skin-care products, bath soaps, multiple boxes of cereal, crackers, snacks, condiments, household cleaners, air fresheners, candles, feminine-hygiene products, bath tissue, cosmetics, and pet food. The cost, after combining sales, freebies, coupons, and automatic and mail-in rebates, was just $80. That's a savings of more than 90 percent!

I should note that this wasn't exactly effortless, and I get that most shoppers don't have the time or inclination to hit three different drugstores each week. But the lesson is clear: Drugstore coupon and rebate programs can add up to serious savings, allowing you some wiggle room in your food budget.

CouponMom.com member Lisa in New Hampshire has the drugstore routine down to an economic science.

"I bought $765 worth of products from Walgreens and Rite Aid in 2008," said Lisa, who tracked her savings all year and contacted me in early 2009. "After rebates and coupons, I received all the products for free and profited $2.21!"

If you decide to give drugstore savings a try, start with one store to get the hang of it. Choose the store closest to you, because a high percentage of savings at CVS/Pharmacy and Walgreens comes in the form of automatic rebates. In other words, the credits you earn on one shopping trip can be used on your next shopping trip. It makes sense, then, to become a regular customer at one particular store.

After learning drugstore savings strategies, branch out. You'll save the most by shopping at several stores on a regular basis, or at least once a month. A Busy Shopper who can pop into the drugstore once every four weeks can expect to save $10 a month. A Rookie Shopper who can work in a weekly trip can expect to save $40 a month. And Varsity Shoppers who regularly haunt two or three drugstores each week can expect savings as well as hundreds of dollars' worth of personal-care products, cleaning products, cosmetics, and food items for free, by combining various savings strategies.

Discovering Drugstore Deals: An Overview of Savings Policies

Sometimes people who aren't familiar with the drugstores' savings programs sometimes tell me they're afraid that the neighborhood drugstore can be the most expensive source of personal-care and grocery items. I say they're right! But using a Strategic Shopping approach can put those fears to rest. The key to saving at drugstores is an understanding of how to put all possible savings opportunities to the best use. Here's a look at all the ways to save.

Scan weekly sales circulars: All of the drugstores feature sale items, "buy one, get one free" offers, rebate notices, or other promotions in their weekly circular. It's available in the Sunday newspaper, in the mail, or on the stores' websites. This is your first stop to savings. Many stores' circulars include store coupons, which can be combined with manufacturer coupons or other offers.

Use store coupons: Drugstores issue their own coupons for both store-brand and name-brand items. These can be available in the weekly sales circular or may be printed on your receipt, so be sure to hang on to it! Additionally, drugstore coupons may be printed at in-store kiosks, from the store's website, from an in-store catalog, or via the store's e-mail newsletter. The magic of store coupons is that you can combine them with manufacturers' coupons if there are any available for the same item. If so, you can use both coupons on the purchase of the single qualifying item, increasing your chance of getting the item free.

Combine "buy one, get one" offers with coupons: The BOGO coupon combo is where drugstore savings start to pile up. The chains generally offer many "buy one, get one free" or "buy one, get one 50 percent off" deals, and if you have coupons, you start treading into freebie country. Unlike some grocery stores, the drugstores' BOGO offers generally do require shoppers to buy two items in order to realize the BOGO savings, so you want to be ready to pile multiple coupons on top of the purchase. You can collect them by buying more than one copy of the Sunday paper, swapping with friends, printing coupons off websites or promotional e-mails, or looking for in-store manufacturers' coupons.

Send in those rebates: Some shoppers are turned off by the idea of rebates, finding them too time-consuming. I'm not one of them. Time is money, yes, but saving money is always worth my time. And it's not as bad as you might think. Many rebate programs are easier and more efficient now than they were in the past. Both CVS/Pharmacy and Walgreens have automatic programs that essentially provide you with rebates, and Rite Aid's rebate program allows you to submit information online, a much quicker process than snail mail. During my nine-week drugstore deals test, 48 percent of my total savings—nearly half—came from the rebate programs. To me, that's worth giving rebates a try.

Use coupons for trial sizes: Trial sizes can be the bane of the budget shopper, because while they generally cost less than full sizes, their unit cost is often higher. With coupons, however, you can get them for free much of the time. Drugstores, catering to convenience-seeking shoppers, generally stock wide selections of trial-size items. If you have coupons for any of them, you're possibly looking at free goods. Make sure, of course, that the coupon specifies "any size." I had two coupons for $1 off any size of a certain brand-name deodorant. The CVS/Pharmacy in my area stocks a trial size of this deodorant for $1. I used my two coupons on two trial sizes and added two more free items to my closet of toiletries.

Ask about pharmacy prescription-transfer coupons and competitor coupons: Drugstores love it when customers transfer prescriptions there, figuring that if a certain store is your destination for a prescription you regularly take, it will become your one and only drugstore destination. On a local basis, drugstores may mail out prescription transfer offers, such as a

$20 store gift card for customers who bring in new prescriptions or transfer one from another pharmacy. Ask if your drugstore will accept other pharmacies' prescription coupons. If so, keep an eye out for your grocery stores' and other drugstores' prescription coupons to have several opportunities to save on prescriptions at your preferred drugstore. For example, CVS/Pharmacy stores accept competitors' prescription-transfer coupons. I did not use any of these coupons during my nine-week test, but if I had a prescription to transfer, I would have saved more.

Check out special membership savings programs: Drugstores sometimes offer special rewards or discount programs to seniors. Ask about it if you qualify.

The 91 percent savings on the 216 items I tracked during my drugstore shopping test resulted from combining every available savings program. Here's a breakdown of how it all happened.

Savings Strategy	Savings Realized from Strategy
Sale prices	$138.64
Manufacturers' coupons	$260.12
Store coupons	$35.47
Automatic rebates (Extra Bucks rewards at CVS/Pharmacy or Register Rewards at Walgreens)	$216.91
Mail-in rebates	$174.88
total savings	**$825.90 (91% off full price)**

Store by Store: A Look at Various Programs

Each drugstore chain differs, so it's worth your time to study up on the various savings opportunities at each one. Here's an overview of what each program features.

CVS/Pharmacy
With 6,900 stores in forty-four states, CVS/Pharmacy is the largest drugstore chain in the country. (Find one near you with the store locator fea-

ture at www.CVS.com.) Because CVS/Pharmacy is the closest drugstore to my house and I pass it several times a week, it is easy for me to shop there each week. Their savings programs are very easy to use once you understand them.

They include the following.

THE CVS/PHARMACY EXTRACARE CARD

Your first step to saving at CVS/Pharmacy is to get an ExtraCare card at your store. Register it online at www.cvs.com to get special savings offers via e-mail and direct mail on a regular basis. After you register your card you will receive a "Welcome" e-mail message from CVS/Pharmacy. This is by no means spam—open it immediately! It will probably include a printable store coupon, such as $4 off a $20 order at CVS/Pharmacy, along with other coupons and offers to save dramatically on your first trip to the store. If you provide your mailing information, you will also receive coupons and offers by mail. Because using the card allows the store to track what you buy, offers you receive will be guided by your past purchases. In other words, the more you use the card, the more coupons you'll receive and the more closely tailored to your preferences they will be.

The Extra Bucks rewards account offers automatic earnings on all of your CVS/Pharmacy spending. There are two ways to accumulate earnings in your account:

- **2 percent automatic Extra Bucks rewards:** When you shop at CVS/Pharmacy stores or online at CVS.com using your ExtraCare card, you will earn 2 percent of your total nonprescription spending in your Extra Bucks account. At the end of each quarter, you will receive your earnings in the form of an Extra Bucks reward coupon good for in-store or online credit. (You will not get change back if the value of your Extra Bucks reward coupon value exceeds the cost of your order.) The coupon will print on the bottom of your first store receipt in the following quarter, or you can print your Extra Bucks coupon from CVS.com if you have registered your card online. Shoppers who register their cards also may receive special promotion codes to increase rebate earnings. As a registered member, recent offers I have received included a "Triple Extra Bucks" promotion to earn 6 percent on my nonprescription spending for a thirty-day period (rather than the usual 2 percent), a coupon to get a free Mother's Day card when I purchased $30 of merchandise at CVS/Pharmacy, and a coupon for $10 off a $50 purchase.

- **Extra Bucks rewards for prescriptions:** When you use your ExtraCare card when paying for prescriptions, you will receive $1 for every two prescriptions filled.

Each week, specific items qualify for Extra Bucks rewards, which are essentially automatic rebates that you receive in the form of an "Extra Buck" printed on your receipt when you buy the qualifying item. Extra Bucks rewards work like gift certificates good on nonprescription purchases on a future CVS/Pharmacy shopping trip. Extra Bucks rewards expire one month after printing, so keep track of them and don't let your savings disappear. And don't accidentally throw the receipt away—that's like trashing cash! The weekly advertising circulars found in your Sunday paper, online, and in the stores list the details of several Extra Bucks promotions each week.

Read the fine print to understand Extra Bucks rewards promotions: The CVS/Pharmacy weekly ad provides details about each week's promotions, such as "Get a $5 Extra Bucks reward when you buy $15 worth of Maybelline cosmetics." The fine print underneath the ad will tell you how many deals you can get during the promotional period per household. Some deals are limited to one per week, while other promotions allow you to rack up all the deals your cart and medicine chest can handle. Store shelf tags will also tell you the terms and dates of specific offers.

There are two types of Extra Bucks promotions, and both can net you free items:

- **Individual items' Extra Bucks promotions:** CVS/Pharmacy ads feature Extra Bucks rewards available on individual items, and sometimes whittle the cost completely away. Colgate toothpaste at $3.49 could have an Extra Bucks reward for

$3.49. Although you would pay $3.49 at the register, you would get an Extra Bucks reward coupon on your receipt for $3.49 off your next order at CVS/Pharmacy. Essentially, you'd brush your teeth for only the cost of tax on $3.49.

- **Full brand line Extra Bucks promotions:** Many Extra Bucks promotions issue rewards when you buy a minimum number of brand-name products. One week's promotion might offer a $5 Extra Bucks reward for buying three Maybelline items totaling $15. If each item cost $5 and you bought three, one would essentially be free. How beautiful is that?

COUPONS + EXTRA BUCKS = SERIOUS SAVINGS

Stick with me here while I run some numbers for you. You'll never look at the corner drugstore the same way again after you see the effect of combining coupons and Extra Bucks promotions.

Colgate toothpaste Extra Bucks promotion: If you had used a $1 Colgate coupon along with the $3.49 Extra Bucks reward, you would pay only $2.49 at the register and still receive the $3.49 Extra Bucks reward for a future purchase. Not only are you brushing on the house, you've banked a buck in credit.

Maybelline promotion of $5 Extra Bucks with a $15 purchase: Even if you have coupons for all three of the items purchased, the $15 minimum purchase requirement will be counted *prior* to having your coupons deducted. If you have three coupons for $2 off each item, you would pay only $9 at the register and still get the $5 Extra Bucks reward. Your net cost would be only $4 for the three items. That's drop-dead gorgeous!

Timing and combining to using store coupons with Extra Bucks promotions: When you have a CVS/Pharmacy store coupon that requires a minimum purchase amount, present that coupon to the cashier prior to any additional coupons that may lower your total below the minimum purchase requirement. So in the above example, if you have a store coupon good for $5 off a $15 order, along with three manufacturers' coupons good for a total of $6 off, hand over the store coupon first. Then present your manufacturer's coupons after the cashier is done ringing up your order. This way, your net cost is $4 at the register. Because you also receive the $5 Extra Bucks reward, you would essentially be making a $1 profit while getting $15 worth of free items.

Divide your Extra Bucks promotion items into smaller orders to minimize out-of-pocket expenses: An Extra Bucks promotion may have a limit of how many you can buy at one time. Using coupons and Extra Bucks rewards might make the item free. In that case, it may be easier on your cash flow to buy each item individually, using the Extra Bucks reward for your next purchase. Look at the following difference in "out-of-pocket" outlay when you use differing strategies.

Example: Colgate toothpaste, priced at $3.49, with a $3.49 Extra Bucks reward. Limit three per household.

All-at-once strategy: You buy three tubes for $10.47 and receive $10.47 in Extra Bucks rewards for your next order. The net cost is zero, but you've had to shell out $10.47 up front.

Over-time strategy: Buy one tube for $3.49 and receive an Extra Bucks reward for $3.49. Buy the second item for $3.49 and use the first Extra Bucks reward to pay for it (paying nothing at the register), and receive a second $3.49 Extra Bucks reward. Use that to pay for your third item, totaling $3.49 again. The bottom line is the same, but you've had to part with only $3.49.

Rolling, rolling, rolling to use coupons on top of Extra Bucks Rewards: When you pile coupons on top of Extra Bucks rewards, you can strategically "roll" your coupon profits into your total Extra Bucks rewards value. This strategy keeps you from having to spend a lot up front, while allowing you to amass credits for future purchases. Back to our $3.49 Colgate toothpaste example. If you had three $1-off coupons to use on top of the Extra Bucks offer, you're going to pay less and build more store credit savings. Here's how that would work: Buy the first tube for $2.49, using the $1-off coupon, and receive the $3.49 Extra Bucks credit. Buy the next two for $7.98, minus your two other $1-off coupons and the $3.49 credit. Here, your total out-of-pocket expense is $4.98, and you've banked $7.98 in Extra Bucks for a future order. In other words, you've just gotten three free tubes of toothpaste and made a "profit" of $3 in store credit.

Redeeming Extra Bucks rewards: There is no limit to the number of Extra Bucks rewards you can use per order. If you earn four Extra Bucks rewards totaling $20 in store credit, you can use the entire amount on your next order. If that works out to $20, your order is free. (Remember, you won't receive any change.) When you pay at the register, use your manufacturers' coupons and store coupons first, and then use your Extra Bucks one by one, making sure that you do not use too many. Give the cashier the Extra Bucks in order of their value, starting with the highest, to work your way down the total. Keep an eye on the register to make sure you don't waste your store credit. If the final total is less than your final Extra Bucks reward, you will not get change from your final Extra Bucks reward if you use it.

JOIN UPROMISE AND REGISTER YOUR EXTRACARE CARD TO SAVE AUTOMATICALLY

Upromise is a free program that allows you to accumulate cash rewards in an account when you purchase qualifying items at participating retailers. CVS/Pharmacy participates in the Upromise program, so registering your CVS/Pharmacy ExtraCare card with your account at Upromise.com is another way to save. Once you accumulate a meaningful balance, you can transfer it to a college savings account or have it sent directly to you. There are two ways to save automatically with Upromise when you shop at CVS/ Pharmacy:

Automatic rebates: When your CVS/Pharmacy card is registered with Upromise, every time you buy a qualifying Upromise item, a percentage of the purchase price is added to your Upromise account. (The rebate percentage is based on the purchase price before any coupons are used.) Several name brands found at CVS/Pharmacy participate with Upromise, and the program is completely automatic. You will receive your rebates automatically as long as your ExtraCare card is registered in your account.

Electronic coupons: Upromise also has electronic "coupons" for items carried at CVS/Pharmacy. The eCoupons category in the Grocery section of Upromise.com posts new offers on the first day of each month. Select the ones you like, and they will be added electronically to your CVS/Pharmacy ExtraCare card. When you buy the items, the coupon values will be added to your Upromise account.

Save at CVS.com: Although you do not earn Extra Bucks reward coupons for online shopping, you can save by shopping at CVS.com in other ways. If you shop through the CVS/Pharmacy link at Upromise.com, you will earn 5 percent Upromise rebates on your total purchase amount. You will also earn additional Upromise rebates for qualifying items and the 2 percent ExtraCare card earnings on nonprescription spending. CVS.com offers free shipping on orders totaling $49 or more, and you may find attractive discount coupons for online orders at CVS.com, such as $10 off a $50 purchase.

ExtraCare coupon kiosks: Some CVS/Pharmacy locations have in-store coupon kiosks where you can print free coupons. If yours does, scan your ExtraCare card at the kiosk before each shopping trip. I've received coupons for $5 off a $15 purchase this way. If my planned shopping list exceeded $15 before coupons, it's like finding a $5 bill on the way into the store. Other times, coupons for certain items print from the kiosk. Sometimes they apply to that trip's shopping list, and other times they're saved for future trips.

STACKING YOUR SAVINGS: COMBINING OFFERS

Bundling the various savings opportunities is the key to fabulous drugstore deals. For example, the CVS/Pharmacy in my area recently featured Butler Gum toothbrush twin packs, which usually sell for $3.99, for $1.99. In addition, the item offered an Extra Buck reward for $1.99. If you stopped right there, you would essentially have received the item free. But with a $1-off coupon from the newspaper, we go from free to earning a "profit" of store credit. Take a look:

Regular price of twin-pack Butler Gum toothbrushes	$3.99
Sale price with ExtraCare card	$1.99
Less $1 manufacturer's coupon	-$1.00
Price paid at register	**$ .99**
Additional rebate savings	
CVS/Pharmacy Extra Bucks reward	-$1.99
Total sale, coupon, and rebate savings on $3.99 item—2 free toothbrushes and realized a net profit of $1.00	**$4.99**

It should come as no surprise that CouponMom.com features a section called "Best CVS Deals" in the Grocery Deals section!

SO MANY DEALS, SO LITTLE TIME

My CVS/Pharmacy trips take me 15 minutes or less. Creating my list takes about 10 minutes. The key is planning with CouponMom.com to know exactly where the bargains are.

When I tracked the CVS/Pharmacy deals for nine weeks, 111 items worth $406 ended up costing only $44.53, a savings of 89 percent off the full price.

Total Savings at CVS/Pharmacy (Nine-Week Test)	
Cost of 111 items at full price	$406.09
Total savings realized	**$361.56**
Sale price savings	-$77.21
Manufacturers' coupons	-$138.17
Store coupons	-$28.47
Extra Bucks rewards coupons printed at register	-$117.71
Final cost before tax (89% savings)	**$ 44.53**

EVERY SHOPPER CAN SAVE

Once you've mastered all of the CVS/Pharmacy savings programs, it's easy to trim your cost no matter which type of shopper you are.

Busy Shoppers who stop in CVS/Pharmacy occasionally can still expect a few free deals. Check the CVS/Pharmacy ad or the CVS Deals list at CouponMom.com, sort the list by "percentage saved," and you'll get a quick sense of that week's freebies. For example, you may see that Colgate toothpaste is $3.49 with a $3.49 Extra Bucks reward. CouponMom.com might also have a coupon you can print for an even better deal. If you don't think you'll be back in time to use the Extra Bucks reward before it expires, split your order into two purchases. Buy the Extra Bucks freebie by itself in one transaction, and then buy your remaining items in a second transaction, using your Extra Bucks reward to pay for the second order. If you do plan on going just once a month, you may want to wait for a week with multiple Extra Bucks promotions offered, to make the most out of that trip.

Rookie Shoppers can make use of the little more time they have to plan, and can scan newspaper coupons as well as CouponMom.com and the CVS/Pharmacy ad. You may also have the time to make more than one trip in a month. Pick out the best deals at CVS/Pharmacy, make your list, and cut out the coupons to pair with the deals. CouponMom.com makes it easy to find newspaper coupons and any printable coupons that may be available.

Varsity Shoppers plan weekly CVS/Pharmacy trips along with outings to grocery and discount stores. CouponMom.com can help plan your expedition. The site updates each store's prices as early as Sunday morning. Print each store's list of freebies, attach the newspaper and printable coupons, and keep them in your coupon organizer in the car. Because you're organized, it's easy to make the most out of a quick stop while you're running errands that week, and keeping your accordion file of coupons or full binder of coupons with you while you shop will make it easy to take advantage of any unadvertised sales or clearance prices at your store. Over the course of the week, check the CouponMom.com Forum in the drugstore section to learn about other clever sale and coupon combinations from members.

Walgreens Savings Programs

Walgreens operates 6,678 stores in forty-nine states. (Find one near you at www.walgreens.com.) Like CVS/Pharmacy, Walgreens has a weekly sales circular and also features in-ad coupons (CouponMom.com can point you to the best deals). Walgreens does not have a store loyalty card, but its savings programs include Register Rewards. This gives shoppers coupons off future purchases when they buy qualifying items. For example, a recent Register Rewards promotion gave shoppers a $5 Register Rewards coupon with the purchase of $15 worth of Unilever products. Many of the qualifying products were also on sale and had newspaper coupons available, so naturally the thing to do was combine all possible savings opportunities for the best deal. Using $5 worth of newspaper coupons would mean paying $10 at the register and banking a $5 credit for future use, meaning a net cost of $5.

During my nine-week drugstore deals test, I tracked fifty-three items at Walgreens worth $212 at full price for only $11.67, a savings of 94 percent. Here's how the savings added up:

Total Savings at Walgreens (Nine-Week Test)	
Cost of 53 items at full price	$212
Total savings realized	**$200.42**
Sale price savings	-$11.01
Manufacturers' coupons	-$64.22
Store coupons	-$6.00
Register Rewards coupon printed at register	-$99.20
Mail-in rebates	-$19.99
Final cost before tax (94% savings)	**$11.67**

Rite Aid Savings Programs

Rite Aid operates 4,900 stores in thirty-one states and the District of Columbia. (Find one near you at www.riteaid.com.) This chain's savings programs include the weekly circular and in-ad coupons, and it also publishes a monthly coupon and rebate listing called the Single Check Rebate catalog. Available in stores and RiteAid.com, it offers store coupons and rebate offers (available in-store only, not on online sales). For example, one month's catalog had 126 rebate offers with a total value of $797. The weekly sales circular will also point out when a sale item has a qualifying rebate or catalog coupon available.

Single Check Rebates: Rite Aid's rebate program is more convenient than traditional rebate offers. You can list all of your rebates for the month on one form, and you do not need to include UPC bar codes in most cases. It takes only a few minutes to write down the necessary information and put it in the mail. You can also file your rebates online. Maximize your savings by noting rebates for items you like, then check for coupons and wait to see if those items go on sale before the end of the month. You can buy all the rebate-eligible items you like in a month, but only one form per month per household may be submitted. If your coupon and rebate items do go on sale before the end of the rebate period, you are very likely to get the items free. Be sure to keep a copy of the form that you mail in as well as a copy of your receipt. Ask the cashier for a second copy of your receipt if you don't have access to a copier.

"Free-after-rebate" items: Sometimes the Single Check Rebate catalog will feature items that will be free after the rebate. The list of items will be at the top of the rebate form, and store shelf tags will point out items that qualify. If you have coupons for these items, you will receive the coupon savings as well as the full rebate value, up to the actual price of the item in your store.

Savings for seniors with the Living More program: This free program for people 60 and older offers a number of discounts, including 10 percent off purchases every Tuesday and off store-brand products, cash prescriptions, and hearing-aid batteries every day. In addition, there are a number of unadvertised specials throughout the store, and the Living More newsletter offers additional coupon savings. Note that the prescription discount is not valid on any prescriptions covered by insurance, discount cards, Medicaid, Medicare, PACE, PAAD, EPIC, or other government-funded programs. It's also not applicable in California, but cash prescription savings for California residents age sixty-five and older are available through the California Prescription Drug Discount Program for Medicare recipients. (See your pharmacist for details.)

RiteAid.com website for special offers: In addition to the standard savings programs listed here, Rite Aid offers other promotions on its website. For example, the site recently featured two printable prescription-transfer coupons offering new customers $50 in Rite Aid gift cards for transferring two prescriptions. Another offered a $10 gift card with the purchase of $50 worth of an over-the-counter allergy medication.

I tracked Rite Aid's best deals for nine weeks, using sale prices, BOGO offers, store coupons, manufacturers' coupons, and rebates. In the course of a month I tracked 52 items worth $287.80 at a final cost of only $23.88, a savings of 92 percent.

Total Savings at Rite Aid (Nine-Week Test)	
Cost of 52 items at full price	$287.80
Total savings realized	**$264.04**
Sale price savings	-$50.42
Mail-in rebate value	-$154.89
Store coupons	-$1.00
Manufacturers' coupons	-$57.73
Final cost before tax (92% savings)	**$23.88**

One CouponMom.com member, Dawn from Philadelphia, let us know that by using CouponMom.com strategies she was able to buy $42 worth of merchandise at Rite Aid for just $1.81. She was so excited about her success that she took a picture!

A Final Word

Who knew drugstores, which some shoppers consider a more costly option than supermarkets or discounters, could house so many fabulously frugal finds? If you'll take the time to educate yourself, sign up for store savings programs, such as loyalty cards, and combine coupons with other offers, the drugstore truly becomes a discount store.

Seventeen

- - - -

Incredible, Inedible Deals:
Savings on Non-Grocery Items

I'm willing to bet you buy more than groceries at the grocery store. Your household also needs cleaning supplies, paper products, and pet food—not to mention shampoo, cosmetics, or even greeting cards. Don't let non-food items take a big bite out of your food budget! Just as Strategic Shopping principles can help you stretch your dining dollar, they can help you find deals on the items you need to keep to your pets fed, your baby diapered, and your house, your clothes, and yourself looking great.

In this chapter we're going to discuss:

- how to pay the least on items you use most, from mascara to detergent to paper plates
- the importance of brand flexibility—and when to stay loyal to a brand
- ways to save even more by creating your own cleaning supplies

Beautiful Bargains: Saving on Cosmetics

You can buy mascara for $30 at a department store or for $1 at the grocery store or drugstore. If you're devoted to high-end cosmetic-counter brands, ask yourself a question: *Do my lashes look thirty times better when I buy luxury-label mascara from the department store?* It's easy to pay much lower prices for cosmetics at the grocery store, drugstore, or discount store by following the same sorts of strategies you use to trim your food budget with sales, coupons, and promotions.

Use coupons: Tough economic times mean that many consumers are looking for cheaper ways to glam up. To encourage women to buy their makeup at the grocery stores, cosmetics companies have been flooding Sunday coupon circular and in-store ad fliers with valuable coupons. This is great news for you! Many coupons—especially those for new lines or new products—have relatively high face values. For products such as hair color or premium moisturizer, it's common to find coupons for $5 off or more. If you use grocery store loyalty cards as discussed in chapter 6, you'll start to receive cosmetics coupons in the mail or generated at the cash register when you check out. Or check manufacturers' websites for coupons and even free samples. Then, as we discussed in chapter 7, you can stack your store and manufacturer coupons and pay next to nothing to look your best.

Wait for deals—no, steals: Most grocery stores feature a wide range of labels, including L'Oréal, Neutrogena, Max Factor, Revlon, Cover Girl, Maybelline, and Almay. You can almost always find at least one of the brands on deep discount. Watch for frequent 50 percent off sales and "buy one, get one free" offers, then put the coupons you've collected from various sources to work! My favorite Revlon eye shadow costs $6.50 at full price, but when my store sells it for 50 percent off, I use my $2 coupon to get it for only $1.25.

Become a drugstore diva: A June 2009 article in the *Los Angeles Times*[19] explained that some drugstores are swooping in to capture consumers who are turned off by high department-store prices by rolling out gussied-up beauty aisles. Even if your drugstore isn't among those adding posh new lipstick lanes, it's still a great destination for deals. Watch for sales, use a combination of store and manufacturer's coupons, and take advantage of rebate offers. The CVS/Pharmacy in my area ran a promotion offering a $10 Extra Bucks reward as an automatic rebate with the purchase of $20 in

---

19. Jones, Sandra M. "High-end Beauty on a Budget." *Los Angeles Times* (June 13, 2009).

Cover Girl products. I bought three items I use to qualify for the rebate but used three $1-off coupons as well. My final cost for $20 in cosmetics was $7—a savings of 65 percent.

Don't keep what you don't like: If cosmetics items you purchase at the drugstore or grocery store don't meet your quality standards, return them for a refund. (The cosmetics department clerk at a Walgreens in my area told me her store would accept returned items if I just didn't like the color.) Keeping products you will not use is very expensive.

Brush, Wash, and Moisturize for Free (or Close to It!)

Q: When is the one time you do not want to buy shampoo, lotion, deodorant, facial cleaners, razors, and over-the-counter medicines?
A: *When you actually need them!*

Teach yourself to seek the lowest possible price for the staples that fill your medicine cabinet or bathroom closet. When you're able to use multiple coupons, rebate offers, and in-store promotions, it's easy to stock your family up on all the health and beauty products you need for almost nothing. And because items like dental floss or emery boards don't go bad, it makes sense to stock up for your own household and to donate to charities or shelters whose clients need personal-hygiene items.

Over-the-counter remedies, such as aspirin, vitamins, or cold tablets, do have expiration dates, which generally indicate how long the product is most effective. Check labels and talk to your pharmacist to be sure you're safe.

Another cost-cutting option is buying in bulk at a wholesale club. By purchasing in large quantity, you secure a low unit cost, and wholesale clubs have attractive pricing on personal-care items that don't usually go on sale or for which you don't have coupons. If you regularly purchase specific brands of over-the-counter medications, for example, it is worth checking their prices at a wholesale club.

But if you're able to benefit from coupons and discounts, the drugstore might be the least expensive way to stock your bathroom cabinets with toothpaste, deodorant, cosmetics, cold remedies, hand lotion, and similar products. Even the best bulk bargain still pales in comparison to getting items for free by layering one Strategic Shopping tip on top of another. Cheap is good. Free is great!

I enjoy celebrating savings success with members of the CouponMom .com community, and Kimberly Shaw of Manchester, New Hampshire, shared a wonderful story of her drugstore bargain hunting. Kimberly, who learned about CouponMom.com from my appearance on *The Oprah Winfrey Show*, says she does most of her non-food shopping at CVS/Pharmacy. This careful shopper boasts that she never pays more than 70 cents for toothpaste or 49 cents for dishwashing liquid. I really loved hearing about the day she took one of her children shopping with her. Kimberly bought $40 worth of product, but by using Strategic Shopping she paid less than $10.

"My youngest daughter was with me," says Kimberly. "She was like, 'Go, Mom and her coupons!'"

What better validation could a coupon-using mom ask for?

Spend Less on Your Four-Legged Family Members

The cost of pet food can really add up, especially if you have a large pet or several furry friends living with you. Unlike bargain-seeking humans, your dog or cat is probably fairly brand-loyal. Your pet may like only one specific brand, and if he or she has health issues, your vet may recommend a particular kind of food. But even if you're limited to one brand of pet food, you can still bargain-hunt. I was able to cut the cost of our dog food by $10 per bag by buying it at the pet store with a store coupon rather than paying supermarket prices. Because the pet store is next door to the supermarket, it's worth my time to save an extra $10.

Regardless of which brand of pet food you buy, you'll generally pay the least by buying the most. In other words, the largest bag typically gives you the lowest unit price. And, you can usually find the best deals at discount stores, wholesale clubs, or large pet stores. You can also use coupons at most of the stores.

To collect coupons for your dog or cat's food, visit the manufacturer's website and sign up for their e-mail newsletters. Some pet food manufacturers issue high-value coupons in the Sunday newspaper circulars, including coupons for free items, to encourage pet owners to try new brands.

Pet stores generally accept other stores' coupons, but it's up to you to ask. I fed our dog for the least amount of money by using a $5-off competitor's coupon at our local pet store. I paid 23 percent less than what I would have spent at the supermarket, even with a sale on. If you use a brand that issues high-value manufacturers' coupons, you can combine those with store coupons to increase your savings.

By the way, even if you don't have a pet, there are animals in your community who could benefit if you're willing to put coupons and discounts to work. Animal shelter volunteers would love to accept your donation of pet food, and many shelters that aid clients with a variety of household expenses also accept pet food. It's common for the Sunday newspaper circulars to have coupons for a free can of dog or cat food to encourage trial of their new products. You can use the coupon to make a donation at no cost!

Clean Up in the Laundry Aisle: Deals on Detergent

It can be tricky to compare the costs of different laundry detergent brands, since the concentrations often vary. When I did my price comparison for laundry detergents, I found it's important to compare prices on a per-load basis rather than per ounce. You also need to consider quality, as ineffective detergents won't keep your clothes looking new for as long as higher-quality detergents will. It's cheaper in the long run to spend a little more to keep clothes looking better, longer, than to skimp on detergent and end up with drab-looking duds.

With Strategic Shopping, you'll be able to keep your clothing its cleanest. Without even changing my premium-brand preference, the following strategies helped me save about $150 a year on laundry detergent alone.

Hit the sales with coupons: Name-brand laundry detergents go on sale frequently at supermarkets, drugstores, and discount stores. And it's easy to find coupons for even the most expensive name brands. At full price I'd pay 25 cents per load on Tide liquid at my supermarket, but I'd pay only 17 cents per load if I waited until Tide went on sale and I used a coupon, a 27 percent savings. If I had more than one coupon, I could stock up on regular-size bottles. This strategy is even cheaper than buying the largest container of Tide at the wholesale club; my comparison found that the giant jug worked out to 19 cents per load, or 12 percent more than the multiple smaller bottles that I bought on sale with coupons.

Consider brand flexibility: If you're willing to switch brands, you'll pay less at large supermarkets and supercenters because they have many brands to choose from. By switching brands to take advantage of sales and coupons, I'm able to pay 10 cents per load at my supermarket. If I liked Costco's store brand, I'd also pay 10 cents per load, a 16 percent savings off my rock-bottom price on Tide.

Choose the basic version: The powdered version of your favorite brand is generally less costly than the liquid version. My sale-priced basic version of Tide, using a coupon, would cost only 11 cents per load in the powdered version, a 33 percent savings over the liquid option. Similarly, the basic version is usually less expensive than premium varieties featuring extra ingredients or new fragrances. You can add your own bleach or fabric softener when you need to rather than pay extra for detergents with add-on ingredients for every load.

Use the correct amount: Most people use more detergent than necessary. Be sure to read the package to see exactly how much you need to wash your clothes. By checking the packaging I learned that I need just one-third of a capful of my laundry detergent for a medium load and half of a capful for a large load. It's easy to assume you need an entire capful, but that's just pouring money down the drain. Especially with super-concentrated liquid detergents, it is easy to use more than you need.

Combining all of these strategies on Tide detergent drives my cost per load down from 40 cents (for the whole capful of liquid) down to 11 cents for the proper amount of sale-priced powder, a savings of $151 per year for my family of four. With some effort, I'm able to use a premium detergent at a price that compares favorably with a wholesale club's generic-brand price of 10 cents per load by shopping strategically at the grocery store, drugstore, or discount store for my favorite brand of laundry detergent.

Pay Bottom Dollar for Diapers

If you are the parent of a baby, you can save an average of $800 per child (assuming potty training kicks in by age 2½) by comparing prices and buying your diapers at the lowest unit price possible. The two-plus years your child wears diapers will cost less with the following strategies.

Compare unit cost per diaper: The key to comparing prices between various brands and varieties of diapers is to use the unit cost, or cost per diaper. Different varieties of the same brand can have different numbers of diapers in the package. For example, I compared the prices of five jumbo packages of size 3 diapers each selling for the same price, in the same store on the same day. Although each package looked the same, the five different name-brand varieties ranged from thirty-one to forty diapers per package. Obviously, I'd pay the lowest price for the variety with forty diapers.

Experiment with different brands: Generic diapers are less expensive per diaper but do not work for all babies. Having to change diapers more often drives up your cost, and you're probably going to be willing to pay more for a diaper that won't leak. Try a few brands, and once you've found the least expensive brands that work for you, compare costs between supermarket sales, discount stores, and wholesale clubs to score the best price.

Focus on sales, coupons, and rewards, and ask for help: When your baby's diapers go on sale, you want to swoop in and stock up. To make sure you get the best possible bargain, you'll want to take a stack of coupons with you. Find them in newspaper circulars and ask friends and relatives to trade (or they will probably be willing to hand them over, if their kids are out of diapers). Also check online coupon sites that frequently have diaper coupons (like Amazon.com or Diapers.com), and sign up for diaper companies' e-mail newsletters or rewards programs. Both can be sources of free coupons or even free merchandise. If you still need more, send e-mails to all of the diaper companies politely requesting coupons. They want you as a customer and will likely be happy to send you some.

Shop wholesale clubs: My price comparisons found that the wholesale clubs had the lowest cost per diaper, with the exception of the occasional rock-bottom diaper sale with coupons at traditional retailers. If you are a

Busy Shopper, you can save with no effort by buying large packages of name-brand diapers at the clubs at their everyday prices, and if you are a Rookie or Varsity Shopper, you can save even more with coupons at the clubs. Costco's store coupon booklet occasionally has diaper coupons. BJ's Wholesale Clubs also accept manufacturers' diaper coupons. Sam's Club does not take coupons, but offers a Click 'n' Pull system, where shoppers can order diapers online and pick up their orders. You can load up diapers without having to tote your baby around the store. That's a bargain right there!

Shop online retailers: At full price, online retailers, such as Amazon.com, generally have higher diaper prices than wholesale clubs, but Amazon's diaper prices are very competitive when you're able to use special coupon codes and take advantage of free shipping. Sign up for Amazon's Subscribe and Save program to save an additional 15 percent. Amazon's diaper deals have had lower per-diaper costs than the wholesale clubs in the past, and customers get the convenience of having them delivered at no cost, and with no membership fees.

These savings approaches work with other baby supplies as well, such as baby wipes, formula, and bath products.

Sparkling Savings: The Best Deals on Cleaning Products

It's easy to stock up on glass cleaner, all-purpose spray cleaners, dishwashing liquid, and dishwasher detergents at significant savings. If you are a Busy Shopper, you can pay less for cleaning products at discount stores or wholesale clubs by purchasing them in very large quantities. But Rookie and Varsity Shoppers will be able to get many name-brand items by combining store sales with coupons.

The true bargain hunter can wash windows using a little extra elbow grease with newspaper instead of paper towels, clean with washable cloth rags, and turn vinegar, baking soda, and ammonia into glass and surface cleaners. As a bonus, vinegar—which contains acetic acid and kills viruses, germs, and mold—and baking soda are nontoxic and eco-friendly. If you decide to make your own cleaners, use a new spray bottle rather than one that's contained commercial cleaning chemicals. You can find inexpensive spray bottles at the dollar store or a discount store.

These natural, nontoxic cleaning product alternatives cost up to 80 percent less than commercial products. I tested them, and they work for me. They include the following.[20]

Cleaner	Substitute	How-to
all-purpose cleaner	vinegar	equal parts white vinegar and water in spray bottle (do not use on marble)
cleanser	baking soda	sprinkle on surface and scrub (safe to use on marble)
dishwasher detergent	borax, baking soda	mix one Tbsp. borax and one Tbsp. baking soda per load (borax is sold as 20 Mule Team Borax) for sparkling clean dishes!
dishwasher rinse agent	vinegar	fill the rinse agent well in dishwasher with white vinegar
glass cleaner	vinegar	equal parts white vinegar and water in spray bottle
oven cleaner	baking soda	sprinkle on cool oven; spray and soak with water every few hours; scrape off and wipe down
stainless-steel cleaner	rubbing alcohol	undiluted in spray bottle or use on soft cloth and wipe—no streaks!
toilet bowl cleaner	vinegar	pour 2 cups white vinegar in and leave overnight; scrub in morning

Price-Conscious Partying

Buying gift wrap, greeting cards, plastic utensils, cupcake foils, and other party supplies at the grocery store is awfully convenient. It can also be your most expensive option.

Before you turn your child's end-of-year celebration or the neighborhood pool party into a budget-busting ordeal, check out the dollar store or discount store. You'll save 50 to 75 percent on gift bags, cake decorations,

---

20. Huffstetler, Erin. "Frugal Living Guide." Frugalliving.about.com.

party favors, invitations, gift bags, streamers, balloons, colored paper plates, plastic cutlery, and more. It's easy to find greeting cards for 50 cents each, too. Dollar stores stock disposable foil pans—perfect for sending treats to school—for less than half of what you'll pay at the grocery store. Drugstore spice sections are good sources for large $1 bottles of colored sugars and sprinkles. I've found 4.6-ounce bottles there for $1 or less, a nice alternative to the $2.69 2-ounce bottle I found at my supermarket. That's a 75 percent sprinkles savings!

A Final Word

Strategic Shopping isn't just about eating for less. It's about spending less, period. Once you've found ways to stock your pantry for pennies, it should pain you to pay full price for non-grocery items. Luckily, you never have to!

Eighteen

— — — — —

Go Green, Save Green: Saving on Organic Products

G reen may be the new black, but it doesn't have to leave you in the red. I can't promise that you'll be able to get cartloads of organic food free every week, but it's still possible to trim your costs.

If buying organic food is a priority for your household, using Strategic Shopping principles can help you stock up on items that are both eco-friendly and budget-friendly.

In this chapter we're going to discuss:

- exactly what terms like "organic" and "natural" mean, to help you make the best buying decisions
- how to compare prices at multiple sources to get the best deals
- advice on the ultimate organic experience: gardening

Who's Buying Organic?

Many shoppers value organic products. A 2008 Hartman Group report[21] found that 69 percent of U.S. adult consumers said they buy organic

---

21. Published by The Hartman Group in 2008.

products at least occasionally. About 19 percent of adults said they are weekly organic users. The most popular organic categories are produce, dairy, prepared foods, meats, breads, and juices, according to the study.

Organic food can cost 20 to 100 percent more than conventionally grown items, but even so, since 2001, organic food sales have soared to $19 billion per year, and organic foods are now available at neighborhood specialty markets; large natural markets, such as Whole Foods; traditional supermarkets; wholesale clubs; Trader Joe's; and even Wal-Mart and Target.[22]

But the growth of organic food sales is beginning to slow. In a 2008 survey of one thousand organic shoppers conducted by Information Resources, a market-research firm, nearly half said they were buying fewer organic foods because they were too expensive.[23] However, even in these tough economic times, there are ways to save real money on organic products. I'll show you how.

First, Understand What You're Buying

The USDA defines organic foods as those free of antibiotics, hormones, pesticides, irradiation, and bioengineering. "Conventionally grown" refers to fruits and vegetables grown with pesticides and fertilizers. This allows farmers to extend the growing season and increase their harvest and translates into lower prices.

A good first step to buying organic is to make sure you know exactly what you're paying for. The USDA Certified Organic seal, for example, can be affixed only to items that meet specific criteria. Before deciding whether it's worth it to pay for the seal—or for items labeled "natural" or "antibiotic-free"—it's important to learn the lingo. Here's a primer to help you understand the terms.

Organic: The makers of the foods with the highest concentration—95 percent or more—of organic ingredients are allowed to use the USDA seal. The four organic standards are explained in the following table.

22. http://www.newsweek.com/id/135377.
23. "Budgets Squeezed, Some Families Bypass Organics." *New York Times* (Oct. 31, 2008).

USDA ORGANIC LABELING STANDARDS

100 percent organic (can use USDA seal)	Foods containing all organically produced ingredients and processing aids, excluding water and salt. Processing aids used in the production of the food may include lime or calcium.
organic (can use USDA seal)	The product must contain at least 95 percent organically produced ingredients.
made with organic ingredients (cannot use USDA seal)	Processed foods that must contain at least 70 percent organic ingredients. The packaging can list up to three of the organic ingredients on the "principal display panel," a surface on the packaging that the consumer is most likely to notice.
less than 70 percent of content is organic (cannot use USDA seal)	Foods that cannot use the term "organic" anywhere on the principal display panel, but the organic ingredients can be listed on the information panel.

If the organic "seal of approval" is important to you, spend your money wisely by ensuring you're getting the real thing. Look for the USDA seal and read ingredient labels, and don't rely on marketing claims on the packaging. Don't assume items sold in the health-food section are all organic or natural—look for the USDA seal to be sure. And beware of marketing that gets ahead of science. "Organic fish," for example, is a marketing label, not an official designation.

Natural: The USDA defines natural products as those containing no artificial ingredients or added color. Also, such items minimally processed in a manner that does not fundamentally alter the raw product. The label must explain the use of the term "natural," such as noting "no added colorings or artificial ingredients." The FDA does not officially define "natural."[24]

For the USDA Agricultural Marketing Service to define meat as "natural," the product must come from "animals that have been raised without growth promotants and antibiotics and have never been fed mammalian or avian by-products."[25]

If you're looking for officially sanctioned "natural" products, rely on

24. IFT.org. "Is There a Definition of Natural Foods?" June 2008 http://www.am-fe.ift.org/cms/?pid=1000744.
25. USDA Agricultural Marketing Service. http://www.ams.usda.gov/AMSv1.0/.

USDA labels rather than promotional packaging. The ingredient list is also a helpful guide. Nuts are natural; sixteen-syllable ingredients you can't pronounce might not be.

Certified Naturally Grown: The USDA requires certification of organic farms that earn more than $5,000 a year. Companies such as Kraft and Dole that own the largest organic companies have the resources to pay for the certification process. Smaller farms generally cannot afford to complete the certification process, even if their products are naturally grown.

To provide an affordable alternative to the USDA certification prices, a group of farmers assembled and created Certified Naturally Grown (www .naturallygrown.org), a nonprofit certification program. Member farmers use the Certified Naturally Grown label. CNG farmers, like organic farmers, produce organic foods with an emphasis on natural, sustainable agriculture. The Certified Naturally Grown effort uses the standards of the USDA's National Organic Program.

Locally Grown: The farm-to-table movement is popular with shoppers who prefer to eat food grown across town rather than across the country. Putting locally grown food on the menu is environmentally friendly, since transporting veggies up the road uses far less fuel and creates much lower emissions than shipping them across the country.

Your grocery store may sell locally grown produce in season, but local farms and farmers' markets are sure bets. Search at farmersmarket.com or localharvest.org for ones near you.

Keep It Clean

The Environmental Working Group, a nonprofit public health advocacy group, created lists of items it says absorb the most and the least amounts of pesticides. Their guide, meant to help consumers reduce their pesticide exposure, is available at foodnews.org/walletguide.php, and there's even an application for your iPhone, if you want to download it for easy reference when shopping. The EWG's Dirty Dozen list of produce it says absorb the most pesticide residue includes peaches, apples, bell peppers, celery, nectarines, strawberries, cherries, kale, lettuce, imported grapes, carrots, and pears. The EWG's Clean 15 list of items it says absorb the least amount of pesticide residue includes onions, avocados, sweet corn, pineapples, mangos, asparagus, sweet peas, kiwifruit, cabbage, eggplant, papaya, watermelons, broccoli, tomatoes, and sweet potatoes.

If your budget allows you to shop only sparingly for organic produce, it makes sense to choose the items the EWG deems most likely to contain pesticide residue.

The Green Scene: Where to Find Organic Produce

Supermarkets: Most supermarkets' produce departments have organic sections. My large supermarket carries organic produce but has a limited selection of each item. For example, it has a dozen varieties of conventionally grown apples but only one variety of organic apples. Because apples are at the top of the EWG's Dirty Dozen list and their price is the same as conventional apples at my stores, I'd rather buy organic apples. If I wanted a broader selection, I'd go to a natural produce market.

Large natural markets: Large natural foods markets, such as Whole Foods, which operates 270 locations across the country, offer larger selections. These stores carry a wide variety of conventional produce as well. In most cases, the organic options cost more. A price comparison of twenty common produce items at the Whole Foods in my area found the organic price tags were about 30 percent higher. To stretch my dollars, I'd selectively purchase the organic versions of the EWG's Dirty Dozen items and purchase the conventional versions of the group's Clean 15 list.

Farmers' markets: Take advantage of organically grown local produce during the growing season in your area. Unlike supermarket cashiers, farmers and the employees who staff farmers' markets will often work with you on price. They'd rather sell at a discount than haul produce back to the farm, so shopping toward the end of a farmers' market hours might yield bargains. The Produce chapter gives specific details on how to find farms and farmers' market in your area.

Wholesale clubs: You can find a few high-quality produce items selling at bargain prices at wholesale clubs. Both my local Sam's Club and Costco sell large 1-pound containers of organic spring mix salad for about $4. The supermarket and natural market prices in my area are typically $6 to $7 for the same item. My local Sam's Club and Costco also sell fresh organic spinach, berries, lettuce, and carrots at much lower prices than traditional supermarkets.

Organic shoppers buy a wide range of products, although organic preference varies by category. For example, 73% of organic shoppers routinely buy organic fresh produce, while only 22 percent of organic shoppers routinely buy organic snack foods.

ORGANIC SHOPPERS' PURCHASES BY CATEGORY

fresh produce	73%
nondairy beverages	32%
bread and baked goods	32%
dairy products	25%
packaged goods	22%
meat	22%
snack foods	22%
frozen foods	17%
prepared meals	12%
baby food	3%

The organic versions of these items sell at a premium, but you can cut the cost of organic products by taking the Strategic Shopper's approach of tracking prices, mastering store savings programs, and using coupons.

Here are some tips to drive down the cost of organic items:

Compare prices at different stores: Include your supermarket's health food section; mom-and-pop health-food stores and natural markets; larger chains, such as Whole Foods and Trader Joe's; Amazon.com; wholesale clubs; and discount supercenters such as Wal-Mart and Target. You can also check prices at Sam's Club at www.samsclub.com. The time you'd spend researching prices can translate into significant annual savings.

If you are one of the 32 percent of organic shoppers who buy non-dairy products like soy milk, wholesale clubs may be your best bet for savings. CouponMom.com members report finding the lowest prices on soy milk at clubs such as Sam's and Costco. In my comparisons, I found that the price of Costco's Kirkland brand of soy milk at $1.08 per quart was less than half the cost of my supermarket's name-brand price of $2.69.

Shop store-brand organics. Traditional supermarkets are competing for your organic dollar with store-brand organics, and the price difference between name-brand and store-brand organics can be significant. For example, a name-brand 26-ounce jar of organic pasta sauce at a supermarket in my area costs $7.99, while its store-brand counterpart costs $3.39. Name-brand organic raisin bran cereal costs $4.89, while the store-brand option cost $2.50. The most dramatic example I found was name-brand organic wheat pasta at $5.98 per pound. The store-brand was $1.79 per pound. You can find the store brand's organic items in the health-food section of your supermarket, but keep an eye out for organic options throughout the store. Large natural markets, such as Whole Foods, stock an extensive line of store-brand alternatives. Because larger selections mean better deals, shopping at a supermarket with a large line of organic store brands is a good idea.

Trader Joe's: Trader Joe's prices are reasonable, and with its colorful displays and friendly employees all wearing Hawaiian shirts, it's just fun to shop there!

This privately held chain operated three hundred stores in twenty-five states as of June 2009. Trader Joe's primarily carries its own brand of reasonably priced organic and natural products. Stores do not accept coupons or have sales but focus on everyday low prices for their private-label items. Trader Joe's shoppers like the stores' quirky ambience and specialty products, such as Joe Joe cookies or its famous Two Buck Chuck wine. Some of Trader Joe's best values are prices on conventional frozen fish, frozen prepared foods, produce, nuts, gourmet cheeses, eggs, and milk. Organic packaged food prices are competitively priced as well. For example, Trader Joe's organic pasta and pasta sauce prices were the lowest option in my area. The sauce was $2.29 per 26-ounce jar, while my supermarket's store brand price was $3.39 for a 26-ounce jar.

- **Shop the bulk department:** When I use the term "bulk" here, I am not referring to super-size packages. Bulk departments sell basic dry goods out of large bins, and you can use plastic bags provided by the store to scoop out the amount you desire. Some markets also sell products such as honey and nut butters out of bulk containers. You can buy organic beans, teas, grains, flour, oatmeal, or spices this way, and you are less likely to waste food you can't use. Don't assume every item sold in bulk is cheaper; bring your calculator when you shop and compare prices by the ounce or pound to prepackaged items.

Coupons for Organic Products

Look for both store coupons and manufacturers' coupons and remember that in most cases, you can combine a store coupon with a manufacturers' coupon. Ask if your store accepts competitors' coupons or doubles coupons, to further your savings. I was able to get $25 worth of organic and natural groceries practically free at my supermarket by using these coupon strategies. Here are some ideas for where to find coupons for organic items.

The newspaper: Organic food coupons are often featured in Sunday newspaper circulars, and you can use the Grocery Coupon Database at CouponMom.com as a guide by searching for the term "organic."

In-store coupon booklets: Neighborhood health-food stores and chains, such as Whole Foods, feature booklets with store coupons for name-brand items. Whole Foods's in-house magazine, *The Whole Deal*, features recipes, money-saving tips, product information, and about $30 worth of store coupons. You can pick up the magazine in stores or download it from www .wholefoods.com. The online version doesn't always feature all of the coupons found in the hard copy, so be sure to seek out the version in the store.

Online: Manufacturers' websites often feature coupons you can print. Be sure to sign up for e-mail newsletters, which also may include coupons. We found printable coupons at more than fifty organic manufacturers' websites, and you can find the complete list in the appendix at the back of the book.

E-mail requests: Tough economic times put consumers in powerful positions. Ask for coupons, and often you'll receive some. We sent polite e-mail requests to 57 companies and received coupons back from 26 of them, totaling a face value of $83. A few were for free items. I received two coupons for free one-pound containers of my favorite organic spring salad mix, priced at $5.99, and one for a free box of tea that costs $5. Response time averaged six days, ranging from two to 21. The list of companies that sent coupons can be found in Appendix 2.

Earth Day coupon booklets: Look for grocery coupon booklets distributed in many supermarkets beginning April 1 to promote Earth Day. The 2009 Go Organic for Earth Day coupon booklet featured $12.50 worth of coupons for a wide range of products. These booklets are usually distributed via in-store displays. Find one near you at www.organicearthday.org.

Store mailing lists: Visit the websites of your natural-food stores and sign up for their e-mail newsletter and mailing list to receive coupons and information about sales and special offers.

It may take a little more effort to find coupons and combine them to cut your costs on organic groceries, but it can pay off. I tested the Strategic Shopping concept at my supermarket, using coupons from manufacturers' websites, coupon booklets, newspaper circulars, and my e-mailed requests.

I bought $35.37 worth of items and after applying all my coupons I paid $9.61. I saved $25.76, or 73 percent, on a box of Cascadian Farms organic cereal, two boxes of Kashi Organic Promise cereal, two 5-ounce containers of Earthbound Farms organic spring salad mix, one 10-ounce Stonyfield Farms organic yogurt smoothie, one 5-ounce container of Oikos organic yogurt, one 32-ounce tub of Stonyfield organic yogurt, two boxes of Morningstar Farms veggie burgers, and one box of Traditional Medicinals tea.

Who said buying organic has to be pricey?

Create Your Own Savings: Skip the High Price of Convenience

I bet your grandmother lived the organic lifestyle generations before it was hip and trendy. Try these retro ideas to save on your modern family's organic choices.

Instead of buying boxed organic chicken stock for $3.99 a quart, use the leftover bones from your organic chicken with organic vegetable scraps and simmer your own stock. Then, freeze concentrated stock in ice-cube trays and keep the cubes in a bag in the freezer to have convenient portions ready when you need them.

Soak dried organic beans rather than buying canned beans. Add your own seasonings to organic rice you purchase in bulk rather than buying more expensive rice mixes. Make your own soups, cookies, muffins, pizza crusts, and casseroles rather than paying a premium for preparation. If you make several batches at once and keep the extras in the freezer, you create your own "convenience foods" without paying the preparation premium.

Organic Adventures: The Hard-Core How-To List

If you're up for experimenting, you can save by making your own soy milk. The least expensive prepared soy milk option I found was $1.08 per quart for the Costco Kirkland brand purchased in a twelve-count case. My supermarket's name-brand option was $2.69 per quart. I could make my own by purchasing packaged organic soy flour for $2.68 per pound at the supermarket or $1.69 per pound by buying from the bulk bin at the health-food store. By mixing 1 cup of soy flour with 3 cups of water as directed, I would have homemade soy milk for as little as 42 cents per quart, a savings of 61 percent off the lowest price I found for prepared soy milk. Recipes recommend adding flavorings such as honey, vanilla, or almond extract to the homemade soy milk.

Soy flour is also an inexpensive substitute for eggs in baking. One tablespoon of organic soy flour added to 1 tablespoon of water can replace one egg and costs 2.6 cents at the lower bulk price. Organic eggs can cost 20 cents or more each. Conventionally produced eggs cost about 10 cents each.

Other eco-friendly projects include making your own organic baby food. It's much less expensive to cook organic carrots and puree them than it is to buy jarred baby food. Take the same approach with other organic fruits and vegetables and you'll be reducing unnecessary packaging as well.

Finally, consider joining a co-op or community-supported agriculture program. Search localharvest.org for one near you.

Grow Your Own Savings

Nothing beats the price—and the taste—of a tomato you harvest from your own backyard or even your deck, if you have limited time and space. If you're willing to get your hands a little dirty, you can put fresh veggies on the table for next to nothing. Here are some tips from two gardening experts.

The $25 Victory Garden

Gardening expert Joe Lamp'l hosts *Fresh from the Garden* on DIY Network and appears on *Today*, *Good Morning America*, and *The Victory Garden*. The author of *The Green Gardener's Guide*, he writes a nationally syndicated column and posts all sorts of helpful advice on his website, joegardener.com.

Joe serves on the Garden Writers Association's trends committee, which found that forty-three million households were growing at least some of their own food in 2009. That's an additional seven million, or a 19 percent increase from the year before. A sluggish economy, it seems, means many folks are turning the earth for the first time.

"The only thing many people have to spend these days is time," says Joe. To help these new gardeners, he decided to tackle a timely challenge: feed his family of four fresh veggies for the entire summer at a cost of no more than $25, and chart his progress on his blog, joegardener.typepad.com/dailycompost.

He was even more successful than he'd imagined.

"My first investment was $7 for seed-starting mix," said Joe. Instead of buying seeds, he put the word out through the Twitter and Facebook social networking websites, and his mailbox was soon full of seeds sent by virtual friends. Next he snatched items bound for the recycling bin and turned them into a seed-starting apparatus. The bottom of a pizza box, he realized, was just deep enough for seeds to sprout. The plastic cover that came with a store-bought birthday cake served as a cover, creating a mini greenhouse.

Instead of buying soil, Joe drove to his city's free compost site and filled the bed of his pickup. And after posting a query on Freecycle.com, a site where members can ask for or offer items at no cost, Joe heard from a neighbor who was tearing down an old barn. The neighbor was happy for Joe to come claim some of the lumber to build a retaining wall around his raised-bed garden. Similarly, a neighbor whose yard was overrun with bamboo—a very invasive species—was overjoyed when he asked to cut some for critter fences and stakes for pole beans.

Early in the summer, Joe had spent just $14 of his $25 victory garden budget. Other than the $7 seed mix, he had made two other cash purchases, spending $5 for two tomato plants at a roadside stand and a couple of dollars for twine to stake plants. He used garden tools he already had, and he notes that new gardeners can find shovels, trowels, and such for a few dollars each at yard sales.

If insects threaten his bounty, he'll ward them off by spraying a home-made repellent: a quart of water mixed with a teaspoon of Ivory soap and a teaspoon of cooking oil. He'll water using his rain barrel, which fills with gray water or "warm-up water" captured while waiting for the bath water to heat up. And if he does decide to use fertilizer, he'll turn to the bag he found for 25 cents at a yard sale.

"I wanted to approach this as though I was a true first-time gardener," says Joe.

A few months after his shovel hit the earth, his family was feasting on homegrown tomatoes, cucumbers, squash, lettuce, Chinese cabbage, peppers, basil, chard, beets, summer spinach, and pole beans. He plans to donate surplus vegetables to a local food bank.

If Space Is Tight, Consider Container Gardening

Not everyone has the 8x30-foot patch of dirt Joe uses for his victory garden. But limited space need not keep you from gardening.

Gwendolyn Bounds writes the "About the House" column for the *Wall Street Journal*, authors the PureShelter.com blog, and serves as an on-air home-improvement contributor to *Good Morning America*. Those with limited time and space can become a "lawn-chair" gardener, she says.

"If you have a deck, balcony, sunny porch, or even sunny windowsill, you can grow food in a pot," Gwendolyn says. "Containers are a low-cost way to begin greening your thumb no matter how little space you have or what the quality of your soil."

Like Joe, she recommends scouring secondhand sources for supplies.

"Buying your own pots and good potting mix is the cheapest solution in terms of upfront costs," she says. "You can do it for under $10 by purchasing cheap plant containers at garage sales and flea markets, or making your own out of old buckets, jars, plastic trash containers, ceramic pots, or other well-cleaned containers you have around the home."

Good drainage is key. Make sure your containers have holes in the bottom or along the sides, about ¼ inch to ½ inch from the bottom. And don't simply dig up soil from the yard, Gwendolyn cautions. It's likely too dense for container gardening. Store-bought potting mix, on the other hand, is designed to give proper nutrients and breathing room for your plants. A less expensive alternative is to buy a bag of peat (or coir, coconut fibers) and a bag of compost and blend them two parts peat to one part compost and use that in your containers, she says.

To help get started, consult websites for creative ideas on do-it-yourself container gardening. Gwendolyn recommends the National Gardening Association's website (www.garden.org) and *Organic Gardening* magazine's website (www.organicgardening.com). Also, she says that while most vegetables and herbs grow well in pots, it's a good idea to check with a local nursery or a state's agricultural cooperative extension program to determine the best varieties and planting times for your region.

Finally, Gwendolyn says new container gardeners should focus on a few favorites and start with those.

"If you don't really love eggplant, why fuss with it? Staples like lettuce, tomatoes, peppers, and herbs can provide the most bang for your buck the first time out of the gardening gate," she says. "My first year as a container gardener, I munched on homegrown Swiss chard, three varieties of lettuce, arugula, mint, chives, oregano, sage, basil, potatoes, tomatoes, and broccoli. I grew it all on my back deck near the kitchen, and the garden needed very little maintenance other than watering and some occasional insecticidal soap to keep pests away."

A Final Word

Organic food that comes from small farms that don't use pesticide typically will cost more than food produced on giant corporate farms. But if buying organic is important to you for health or environmental reasons, taking the time to research savings possibilities will pay off.

Nineteen

— — — — —

Cheap Eats:
Deals in Your Dining Room

You've collected every coupon you could get your hands on and have a month's worth of grocery-store circulars stacked neatly and ready for action. You're on a first-name basis with the entire staff of every supermarket in your area, since you never hesitate to ask about markdowns or rain checks. And along with the photos of your kids, your wallet is stuffed with rebate offers you've printed from various websites.

Don't let all this effort go up in flames when you start preparing dinner. Strategic Shopping needs to have a seat at your dining-room table! Even if you're able to score the most incredible bargain on every single grocery item you purchase, that triumph is wasted unless you whip those budget buys into meals and snacks your family will actually eat and serve them for the lowest cost per person.

In this chapter we're going to discuss:

- matching meals and deals by planning menus around what's on sale, and learning to calculate the cost of what you feed your family
- learning to work Cheap Superfoods into your diet and adopting recipe flexibility so you're able to cook with items you have on hand, saving time and money

- creating your family's personalized Greatest Hits list of recipes that you and your wallet will love, and ideas of low-cost dishes for every meal

BARGAINS FOR THE BUSY

I like to cook, but I don't have time to prepare every part of every meal from scratch. Who does? If you're like me, you need to pull meals together in a hurry before everyone heads in different directions to school, work, sports, or community functions. But even while maintaining busy schedules, I'm committed to feeding my family healthy meals at home. Strategic meal planning, like Strategic Shopping, helps me stretch our food budget while making sure we carve out some precious family time around the table.

Here's a checklist for making sure every meal is a good deal both in terms of cost and nutrition.

1. **Plan, plan, plan:** On your last family vacation, did you bundle everyone in the car, gun the engine, and then decide where you were going? Of course not! Mealtime isn't exactly as exciting as your family's big summertime trip, but it needs to involve a similar level of forethought. Effort on the front end takes the stress out of searching for healthy, inexpensive options when it's time to eat. You want to be sure to do the following.

    Shop the sales: Start your weekly shopping with a spin through the grocery-store circulars, and you'll be amazed at how much you'll save. Every week I scan the front page of my stores' ads to see which main-dish ingredient is selling for 50 percent off or more that week. If it's chicken, we're eating dishes that use chicken that week. If it's pork, then pork is about to have a starring role on our dinner plates. Determine the deal of the week, and then start building meal plans for that week—and beyond, if you have room to freeze some of the weekly bargain for future use. Over time, you can build up a variety of items. You'll be able to "shop your freezer" and offer your family variety at mealtime while keeping your costs consistently low. At my house, we may not eat the same thing night after night but you can be certain that we dine on main-dish ingredients I've purchased at a discount of 50 percent or more.

Cook once, serve twice: Once you've come up with a meal plan, double any recipes you can to make it easy on yourself later in the week. Double a batch one night and you're able to essentially give yourself the night off down the line. This is an especially handy strategy if you know your calendar's going to be cramped—if your kids all have a game on the same night your spouse is going to be out of town on business, for example. And it just makes sense to get a lot of work out of the way at once. If we're firing up the grill to make my favorite marinated grilled chicken, for example, I marinate two packages of chicken and my husband grills them all at the same time. I'll serve half the chicken that night and serve the rest of the chicken the second or third night with different side dishes. It saves me preparation time and also saves the expense of charcoal (or propane) by doing it all at once. I take the same approach with soups, casseroles, and many side dishes.

Look forward to leftovers: Two extra pieces of chicken can go a long way for your family of four. Toss it in jarred marinara sauce and serve over spaghetti for dinner on leftover night. Slice up the chicken and mix with cheese and veggies, and you have sandwich wraps or entrée salads. Or perhaps you'd prefer chicken fried rice or homemade chicken soup. However you use it, the unused portion from tonight's dinner can easily become the foundation of fast, easy meals later in the week. Chances are, the repurposed menu items won't even seem like leftovers. It's also a good idea to make plans to use leftover ingredients, knowing how much you'll have to use throughout the week. This saves time and money. For example, if you are having chicken, rice, and broccoli for dinner one night, you can make a little extra rice and broccoli and serve a yummy frittata with eggs and cheese the following night. If you're making roasted vegetables to serve with pork loin tonight, you can double the batch of vegetables and use them to make a roasted-vegetable pizza tomorrow. Or you can double the amount of rice you're making as a side dish and make fried rice to accompany leftover pork or chicken.

2. **Cost out each meal:** When I first started tackling my family's grocery budget, I learned to figure out what each meal cost. Cutting out unimportant ingredients or swapping them with less costly options allowed me to bring the cost down while keeping our favorite meals on the table. Once I knew what meals cost, I could plan a couple of Ultra-Budget meals during the week to be able to afford more expensive meals, too. As long as I used good recipes, my family didn't realize that some of their favorite meals were in the Ultra-Budget category!

For an easy comparison, here's a look at what you could spend on a simple spaghetti supper. The Strategic Shopping family is able to dine on this simple standby meal for about a third of the cost of the typical family, because the typical family had to pay full price on a last-minute trip to the store to pick up something for dinner.

Pasta Dinner for 4	Strategic Shopping Family	The Typical Family
pasta, 12-oz. box	name brand bought with coupon—FREE	Store brand, on sale, $1.00
pasta sauce, 26-oz. jar	name brand bought with coupon, 50 cents	Store brand, on sale, $1.29
ground beef, 1 lb.	$1.50, bought on sale and stocked in freezer, thawed	Fresh, $2.49
salad	romaine salad made from bunch of lettuce, 67 cents	Bagged salad 12 oz. romaine, $2.50
bread	flour tortillas broiled with cheese, cut in wedges, 50 cents	French bread from bakery, $1.99
total cost	**$3.17**	**$9.27**

While $9.27 does not sound expensive for a dinner for four people, it's still $6.10 higher than it could have been. If the Strategic Shopping family saved that amount on dinner every night of the year, they'd spend $2,226.50 less annually than the typical family—just on dinner. Plus, the Strategic Shopping approach saves time. Because this family planned their meals for the entire week, there was no need to run to the store for ingredients just for one meal.

It's useful to figure out how much meals and snacks cost to determine whether meals are Ultra-Budget, Moderate, or Upscale options, and which ingredients are budget-killers. It will also help you find ingredient substitutions for budget-killers and lower your grocery bill. Although ingredient prices change over time, start with the prices you've paid recently (or prices you've tracked in a price book) to estimate what your meals cost. Keep your calculations in a note-book or in a three-ring binder that you can also use to collect recipes. When you add recipes to your book, note the cost of each item and the recipe for future reference.

Include the cost of condiments or seasonings, within reason. Don't worry about figuring the cost of a pinch of salt, when the 26-ounce box cost 33 cents. On the other hand, you do want to know the price of a tablespoon of capers that costs $1 or a casserole topping using a $3 container of fried onions. It may even spark some creativity. When I can feed my family of four a complete spaghetti dinner for $3, I'm reluctant to spend that much just on a casserole topping. Spending a dime on toasted cornflakes or breadcrumbs works just fine for me, and saves calories as well as money!

As you start to cost out meals, start a page of standard ingredients and list what their unit cost is, to use as an easy reference. Say you have a recipe calling for 3 cups of flour. You may know how much a 5-pound bag of flour costs, but how many cups are in a bag of flour? A glance at your reference page will tell you there are about 20 cups in that bag.

If you paid $1.50 for the bag, then a cup of flour costs about 8 cents. Write that down as the first item on your ingredient list and you're off! A page from my ingredient list looks like the following table.

Ingredient	Item Cost	Number of Units	Cost per Unit
butter	$2.50 per pound	4 half-cup sticks	63 cents per stick
cornmeal, yellow	$1.09 per 24 oz.	4.3 cups in canister	25 cents per cup
eggs, large	$1.20 per dozen	12 eggs	10 cents per egg
flour, wheat	$1.88 per 5 lb. bag	20 cups	9 cents per cup
flour, white	$1.50 per 5 lb. bag	20 cups	8 cents per cup
lemon juice	$2.00 per 32 oz.	64 Tbsp.	3 cents per Tbsp.
lime juice	$2.19 per 15 oz.	30 Tbsp.	7 cents per Tbsp.
margarine	$1.09 per pound	4 half-cup sticks	27 cents per stick
mayonnaise, light	$2.48 per 32 oz.	64 Tbsp.	4 cents per Tbsp.
milk	$1.99 per gallon	16 cups	12 cents per cup
peanut butter	$1.39 per 18 oz.	36 Tbsp.	4 cents per Tbsp.
shortening	$2.50 per 3 lb. tub	6 cups	42 cents per cup
sugar, brown	$1.19 per 2 lb.	4.5 cups, packed	26 cents per cup
sugar, white	$2.19 per 5 lb. bag	11 cups	20 cents per cup; 1.2 cents per Tbsp.
vanilla extract, imitation	$1.00 per 8 oz.	48 teaspoons	2 cents per tsp.
vanilla extract, real	$5.99 per 16 oz.	96 teaspoons	6 cents per tsp.
vegetable oil	$2.39 per 48 oz.	6 cups	40 cents per cup; 2.5 cents per Tbsp.

3. **Swap in substitutions:** In some cases, only the real thing will do. But for everyday cooking, you can save time and money by using inexpensive substitutions in your cooking and baking. Apply the 5-minute "do it yourself" rule. Get to work when prep time is less than 5 minutes and the savings potential is significant. The following table includes some cost-saving, time-saving substitutions I use every day.

Ingredient	Cost	Inexpensive Substitution	Cost	Saves
almonds, toasted slivered (added to salads or vegetables, or baked in breads)	$5.38 per lb.	toasted sunflower seeds	$1.99 per lb.	63%
breadcrumbs, 15-oz. canister	$1.29	use blender or food processor to make breadcrumbs from ends of bread	usually thrown out	100%
buttermilk, 1 cup	$0.57	combine 1 cup milk and 1 Tbsp. lemon juice, then let sit for 5 minutes	$0.18	68%
chicken broth, 15-oz. can	$0.39	chicken bouillon cube, 2 cubes to make 16 oz.	$0.10	74%
cornflake crumbs, 21-oz. box	$3.79	crush your own cornflakes, 21 oz.	$1.75	54%
croutons, 5-oz. bag	$1.79	make your own croutons from 5 pieces of bread	$0.31	83%
graham-cracker crust, ready-made	$2.17	make your own graham cracker crust (see chapter 20)	$0.61	72%

lemon juice, one lemon	$0.42	reconstituted lemon juice, 2 Tbsp. equal to one lemon	$0.06	86%
lime juice, one lime	$0.42	reconstituted lime juice, 2 Tbsp. equal to one lime	$0.14	67%
onion, small (⅓ cup chopped)	$0.25	1 tsp. onion powder	$0.02	92%
pizza crust, two 12-inch prepared crusts, 24 oz. total	$4.29	make pizza crust dough, two 12-inch pizzas, 24 oz. total (see chapter 20)	$0.29	93%
rice mix, in box, 6 oz.	$1.19	make rice pilaf with rice and seasonings (see chapter 20)	$0.37	69%
tomato juice, 32 oz. can (called for in soup recipe)	$2.00	1 6-oz. can tomato paste mixed with 4 cans water plus 4 Tbsp. water	$0.39	81%

4. **Stretch your food dollar with Cheap Superfoods:** I work foods that offer the greatest nutrition at the lowest price into my family's regular diet. This is great for our physical and financial health! This is my own personal list of foods. I hope you'll use it as inspiration to start creating your family's list of cheap, nutritious Greatest Hits. We like green cabbage, romaine lettuce, carrots, spinach, green peppers, fresh or frozen broccoli, and fresh or canned tomatoes (depending on the season), bananas, oranges, 1% milk, beans, lentils and split peas, fresh chicken and turkey, eggs and egg whites, canned tuna, brown rice, whole-wheat pasta, and oatmeal and whole-grain hot cereals.

For an item to make my Cheap Superfoods list, it needs to be both cost-effective and healthy. Chicken breast—at 60 cents per 4-ounce serving and 2 cents per gram of protein—is at the top of my list. T-bone steaks, on the other hand, cost $2 per 4-ounce serving and cost 8 cents per gram of protein. Even a small fast-food hamburger that costs only $1 still costs 8 cents per gram of protein. Of course, we do enjoy steak on occasion, but we eat chicken or other healthy bargain options far more frequently.

Calculating the cost per gram of protein is just one way to assess how nutritionally and financially healthy certain foods are. To measure by vitamins, calorie count, or other criteria, see nutritiondata.com, or study product labels.

This chart assumes the typical prices I pay for these items before using grocery coupons, with the exception of the fresh produce items listed at their regular prices. As a Strategic Shopper, you can get some of these items free or close to it, by using coupons. Canned tomatoes, frozen vegetables, tuna, canned beans, whole-wheat pasta, and oatmeal are common coupon bargains or freebies and you can easily stockpile them for several months if you collect multiple coupons to get several deals at a time.

Cheap Superfood Item Serving Size	Nutrition Highlights Vitamins Noted with % Daily Value for Age 4 or Older*	Cost per Serving (At Lowest Prices Before Coupons)
bananas, 1 medium (118 g)	105 calories, 3 g. fiber, 17% vitamin C, high in potassium and vitamin B_6	$0.19
beans, black, ¼ cup dried	100 calories, 7 g. protein, 5 g. fiber, 10% iron, 4% calcium	$0.09 per serving 1.3 cents per g. protein
broccoli cuts, 1 cup cooked (87 g)	30 calories, 2 g. fiber, 50% vitamin C, 2% calcium	$0.20 (frozen)
cabbage, green, 1 cup shredded (70 g)	17 calories, 2 g. fiber, 43% vitamin C	$0.11, assuming cabbage costs $0.69/lb.

carrot, 1 medium	30 calories, 2 g. fiber, 110% vitamin A, 10% vitamin C	$0.09, assuming 1 lb. carrots cost $0.69
chicken, fresh, boneless breast, 4-oz. serving, cooked	130 calories, 27 g. protein; high in niacin and vitamin B$_6$	$0.60 per serving 2.2 cents per g. protein ($2/lb. sale price)
egg, one large	71 calories, 6 g. protein; good source of riboflavin, vitamin B$_{12}$, and phosphorus	$0.10 per serving 2.1 cents per g. protein
lentils, 1 oz.	99 calories, 10 g. protein, 8.5 g. fiber; good source of thiamine, folate, iron	$0.06 per serving $0.01 per g. protein
lettuce, romaine, 2 cups shredded leaves (85 g)	14 calories, 2 g. fiber, 148% vitamin A, 34% vitamin C	$0.16, assuming romaine costs $0.84/lb.
milk, 1%, 8 oz.	100 calories, 8 g. protein, 30% calcium, 10% vitamin A	$0.12, assuming $2 per gallon 1.5 cents per g. protein
oatmeal, ⅓ cup dry	102 calories, 4 g. protein, 3 g. fiber	$0.06 per serving 1.5 cents per g. protein
orange juice, 8 oz.	110 calories, 160% vitamin C, 15% folate, 10% thiamine	$0.16, frozen concentrate
oranges, 1 whole navel (140 g)	69 calories, 3 g. fiber, 138% vitamin C	$0.50
pasta, whole wheat, 2 oz. dry (56 g.)	200 calories, 6 g. fiber, 7 g. protein, 8% iron; high in phosphorus and magnesium	$0.21 per serving $0.03 per g. protein
pepper, green bell, ½ medium (60 g)	12 calories, 1 g. fiber, 80% vitamin C	$0.38, assuming 1 pepper costs $0.75
potato, 1 medium (173 g)	161 calories, 4 g. fiber, 28% vitamin C, 10% iron	$0.25, assuming 5-lb. bag costs $3
rice, brown, ¼ cup dry	160 calories, 2 g. fiber, 4 g. protein, 4% iron	$0.07 per serving 1.7 cents per g. protein

spinach, ⅓ cup cooked	30 calories, 50% vitamin A, 8% calcium	$0.22 (frozen)
tomatoes, canned, ½ cup (121 g)	25 calories, 15% vitamin C, 10% vitamin A	$0.15
tuna, canned chunk light in water, 5-oz. can, drained	99 calories, 22 g. protein; high in niacin, vitamin B$_{12}$, and selenium; 230 mg. of omega-3's (equal to adult daily recommendation)[26]	$0.62 per serving 2.8 cents per g. protein
turkey breast, fresh, 4-oz. serving, cooked	116 calories, 20 g. protein; high in selenium	$0.56 per serving 2.5 cents per g. protein ($0.99/lb. frozen bone-in turkey breast)

*Note: Conversions used assume 453 grams in a pound, 28 grams per ounce.

5. **Eat at home:** My family treats eating out—even drive-through meals—as special occasions. Most of the time, we eat at home. When family activities pack our schedules, we pack our meals to go. When your kitchen is your family's primary source of meals, everyone's diet becomes healthier and less expensive. Here are some ideas for planning breakfast, lunch, and dinner menus that will help you avoid unplanned restaurant meals.

Breakfast: Even though you're in a rush, eating at home costs less and takes less time than picking up coffee and a bagel later. And it demonstrates to your children that eating a good breakfast before school is a priority. Kids don't always feel like eating first thing in the morning, so I offer light meals like eggs, fruit smoothies, yogurt and fruit, and toast or a slice of pumpkin or banana bread. We also have a wide variety of cold cereals that everyone likes, since it's easy to buy cereal

26. Although there is no official FDA recommendation of omega-3 daily intake, it is commonly believed to be a "good fat" and helpful in promoting good health. A National Institutes of Health workshop recommendation for omega-3 intake was 160–220 mg. per day for healthy adults and children.

on sale with a coupon or store-brand cereal for $1.50 per box or less. Put these simple ideas to use and everyone in your family eats the most important meal of the day for less than 75 cents each—a far cry from the $5 or more you could spend by grabbing breakfast at the coffee shop.

Bargain Breakfast Ideas	Total Cost per Person
6-oz. container yogurt ($0.40), banana ($0.19), 8 oz. orange juice ($0.16)	$0.75
2 scrambled eggs with cheese or omelet ($0.36), 2 pieces wheat toast ($0.20), 8 oz. orange juice ($0.16)	$0.72
breakfast burrito: scrambled eggs with cheese in wheat tortilla ($0.59), salsa optional, 8 oz. orange juice ($0.16)	$0.75
frozen-fruit smoothie with ½ cup milk ($0.06), ½ frozen banana ($0.10), 5 frozen strawberries ($0.29), ½ cup vanilla yogurt ($0.20)	$0.65
1 egg muffin with cheese (see chapter 20 for recipe) ($0.45), 8 oz. orange juice ($0.16)	$0.61
2 fried eggs ($0.20), 2 pieces white toast ($0.20), 8 oz. orange juice ($0.16)	$0.56
1 cup cold cereal with 8 oz. milk ($0.20), 2 pieces wheat toast ($0.20), 8 oz. orange juice ($0.16)	$0.56
1 cup oatmeal with 8 oz. milk ($0.18), banana ($0.19), 8 oz. orange juice ($0.16)	$0.53
thick slice homemade banana bread ($0.17), 8 oz. milk ($0.12), ⅛ melon in season ($0.20)	$0.49
2 slices French toast with light syrup ($0.32), 8 oz. milk ($0.12)	$0.44
homemade bagel, peanut butter, and jam ($0.09); banana ($0.19); 8 oz. milk ($0.12)	$0.40

Planning ahead saves time, which helps you save money. I make batches of banana, pumpkin, and poppy-seed quick breads to have on hand for busy mornings. One loaf will make nine to twelve thick slices that are perfect breakfast portions, and extra loaves can go into the freezer. Other make-ahead ideas include homemade bagels, pancakes, waffles, or French toast. Freeze them in individual portions and then pop them in the toaster or microwave when you're ready to eat. Most of these meals do not require a recipe, but we have included some easy recipes in the following chapter.

Lunch: Whether you eat lunch at home, school, or the office, you'll pay a lot less if you make it yourself. Plus, you tend to eat better when you dine on a prepared meal, with no tempting menu staring you in the face. When we first began trimming our family's spending almost eighteen years ago, one of the most helpful cuts was the daily restaurant lunch. Even eating in the company cafeteria added up over time! Just by packing our lunches, my husband and I saved $100 per month. Pack a $2 lunch instead of paying $10 or more per person at a restaurant, and you'll easily save $2,000 per year—just on lunch!

Brown-bagging is even easier when you work at home. Last night's leftovers are the beginnings of today's lunch. Use leftover meat, chicken, or turkey for a salad or a sandwich. Plan ahead by making a big pot of your favorite soup one morning and have it a few days during week. You could freeze some for future meals as well. Bake extra chicken breasts to slice for sandwiches or to make chicken salad. Roast a turkey breast for gourmet turkey sandwiches. With a little creativity, you can eat well and inexpensively. Making your lunch does not mean peanut-butter sandwiches day after day!

Here are some low-cost lunch ideas. You can customize by subbing tortilla chips for pretzels, drink water for free or, add a low-cost beverage such as iced tea, lemonade, milk, or seltzer with a splash of juice for 20 cents or less.

Bargain Lunch Ideas	Cost
tarragon chicken salad on pita bread (see chapter 20 for recipe) ($0.68), ⅛ melon ($0.20), 1 oz. pretzels ($0.08)	$0.96
chicken sandwich on a bun (2 oz. chicken, 1 slice cheese) ($0.55), carrot sticks ($0.09), 1 oz. pretzels ($0.08)	$0.72
turkey sandwich on wheat bread (2 oz. turkey) ($0.44), celery sticks ($0.10), 1 oz. pretzels ($0.08)	$0.62
tuna salad on wheat bread ($0.40), carrot sticks ($0.09), 1 oz. pretzels ($0.08)	$0.57
chicken tortilla wrap with 2 oz. chicken, lettuce, 2 Tbsp. salsa ($0.41), 1 cup low-fat tangy creamy coleslaw (recipe follows) ($0.16)	$0.57
pasta salad with vegetables, 2 oz. chicken and 1 oz. cheese ($0.56)	$0.56
2-egg cheese omelet ($0.30), toasted bagel ($0.05), banana ($0.19)	$0.54
egg-salad sandwich on wheat bread ($0.29), celery sticks ($0.10), 1 oz. pretzels ($0.08)	$0.47
grilled cheese sandwich ($0.25), 1 oz. pretzels ($0.08), carrot sticks ($0.09)	$0.42
homemade lentil-vegetable soup, 2 cups (see chapter 20 for recipe), ($0.26), 10 wheat saltines ($0.08)	$0.38

Dinner: I've found that dinnertime is easiest when I rotate a few standard favorites that I can get on the table quickly. I reserve real "cooking" that takes multiple steps and a couple of hours in the kitchen for leisurely afternoons or weekends. During the week I usually need to prepare dinner in an hour or less.

I've included some of my favorite recipes in this book, but staying flexible helps you stay on budget. Once you've memorized some basics, you can improvise recipes based on what you have on hand.

To the Strategic Shopper, the best recipes are healthy bargains. Learn ways of preparing foods that allow your savings to follow you home from the grocery store. For example, you may know how to roast a whole chicken, but maybe you haven't made chicken thighs before. Because at least one type of chicken is always on sale, learning easy ways to prepare various types of chicken will expand your savings options.

Approach each type of bargain meal creatively. Once you know what the basic building blocks are for each meal, you can jazz the meals up with different variations. If your family likes homemade pizza (and who doesn't?), you can use different toppings to keep that bargain meal interesting. The same is true for other cheap eats, such as soups, pasta casseroles, chili, or skillet meals.

As you get more familiar with the cost of various meals and collect more recipes using affordable ingredients, you'll start recognizing true ingredient bargains at the store. After time, you'll spot a bargain and start planning a menu around it. For example, sweet red peppers are $2.50 each at my supermarket, so I usually buy green bell peppers. But when I see red peppers on sale for $1 or less each, I start planning to serve kebabs, roasted-vegetable pizza, or a vegetable stir-fry for dinner that week to take advantage of the bargain.

Try to group together recipes that use a common ingredient if you need to use only part of the ingredient in one meal. For example, I have a few recipes that call for cilantro. It costs $1 per bunch at my store, and no single recipe uses the entire bunch. I'll make a few recipes during the week that call for cilantro so it becomes a less expensive ingredient and doesn't go to waste. If I'm having arroz con pollo one night, I'll plan to have marinated chicken fajitas another night and black-bean salad on a third, making good use of my $1 bunch of cilantro.

Enjoy Restaurant-Quality Meals at Home

You don't have to give up your pricier favorites just because you are trying to save money on groceries. In fact, you may be able to enjoy them more often if you manage your budget well. When you classify meals as Ultra-Budget, Moderate, or Upscale, it forces you to pay close attention to cost. By holding the line on ingredients, serving plenty of the lowest-cost meals, and eating out less often, you'll create some room in your budget for more regular at-home splurges.

My favorite meal is grilled salmon with broccoli and rice, which I can serve my family of four for about $16. Although that's on the expensive end for my home meals, it is far less than the cost of eating the same meal in a restaurant. We would rather eat frequent Upscale meals at home than spend money on frequent fast-food meals away from home, which may be the same cost. When I consider the total cost of a meal, I include side dishes, such as salad, vegetables, rice, potatoes, or beans, but not beverages or dessert.

Here's a rundown of some of our family's favorite dishes, separated by price point.

Ultra-Budget dinners, costing $1 or less per person for our family of four, include:

Homemade pizza: Making pizza from scratch is much easier than you might think. Use a pizza-crust mix or make your own dough in a bowl in 10 minutes or less. Or use a bread machine. After the dough rises, roll it out, add toppings, and bake. It costs between $1 and $2 for a medium pizza, depending on toppings. One batch of pizza dough makes two medium pizzas, enough to feed my family of four. Add a tossed romaine salad, and we all eat for about $1 each—or about what it would cost just to tip a pizza delivery guy. (See chapter 20.)

Homemade soups: Soup is my favorite dish to make. It seems like magic to me that you can take 10 minutes to fill a pan with water; add some vegetables, legumes, seasonings, a can of tomatoes, and meat; and in a couple of hours you have a great meal. I make a pot of soup every week. A basic 13-cup pot makes the equivalent of six cans of soup, in many cases for less than the cost of one can of soup at the store. I think homemade soup tastes better than canned, and by making it yourself you reduce the packaging your family uses. (Imagine if every family in the country made one pot of soup and used six fewer cans every week!) My favorite vegetable-lentil soup makes six healthy meals at a total cost of $2, while heartier dinner soups and chili still cost only $3 or $4 to make. If you've never made homemade soup before, I encourage you to give it a try. It's good for your budget and your waistline, and it can save you a lot of time in the kitchen when you can cook a dish that will last for more than one meal. You can decide which seasonings and recipes your family likes the best. I've included my favorites in chapter 20.

Egg dishes: When I'm out of both ingredients and time, I throw together simple frittatas, omelets, quiches, or stratas. For a very fast dinner, I'll make a frittata on the stove using leftover rice, pasta, or potatoes or green vegetables. With a half-dozen eggs and a cup of cheese, I'll have a good main dish in about 15 minutes. If I have more time, I'll put a strata casserole or quiche in the oven using a little ham or turkey sausage, eggs, and cheese to be ready in an hour. Add a green vegetable, salad, and muffins or tortillas, and we're all eating for about $1 per person. (See chapter 20.)

Vegetable stir-fry: The basic stir-fry recipe goes like this: Take whatever you have on hand, sauté it with a simple marinade, and serve over rice. Dinner is served! Even better, you need only one pan or wok, so cleanup is easy, too.

Pasta: Dry pasta, canned tomatoes, and pasta sauce should be among the pantry staples a Strategic Shopper always has on hand, since sales and coupons make it easy stock up for little or even nothing. Top the pasta and sauce with vegetables, leftover chicken, or meat, and sprinkle cheese on top. Broil flour tortillas with cheese and slice into wedges and add a green salad, and again, your family is dining for $1 or less per person.

Sandwich wraps: Cut the cost of dinner by cutting the amount of the main-dish ingredient served per person. Warm burrito-size large tortillas in the oven or microwave to soften, and then fill the wraps with two ounces of chicken or meat with cheese, canned beans, lettuce, salsa, or other condiments. This is a great meal idea when you want to stretch one or two leftover servings of chicken or steak, or you can skip the meat entirely. Add fruit, salad, coleslaw, or Mexican rice (see chapter 20) on the side for a light dinner at a total cost of about $1 per person.

Moderately Priced Meals

My husband likes to grill, so I can marinate the main-dish ingredients and he cooks them. We add fresh or frozen vegetables, depending on what's on sale that week, and usually have some type of rice, potato, or bean side dish. A green salad, our standard with every dinner, is very inexpensive when you wash your own lettuce—and as a dedicated Strategic Shopper, you're of course washing your own lettuce! Every one of these full meals costs about what a small hamburger at a fast-food restaurant would cost, not including the fries, but offers far greater nutritional value.

Some of our favorite Moderate-Cost Meals, costing between $1.25 and $1.75 or less per person or $5–$7 for a family of four, include:

- Roasted chicken (using a 3-pound fryer); brown rice; a green vegetable, such as broccoli or green beans; and romaine salad. Cost: $5 for four, $1.25 each.
- Grilled cheeseburgers (using 1.25 pounds ground chuck to make four burgers), a slice of cheese for each burger, homemade coleslaw, and baked beans. Cost: $5 for four, $1.25 each.
- Grilled, marinated boneless chicken breasts (using 1.5 pounds of chicken), a green vegetable, pasta salad, and romaine salad. Cost: $5 for four, $1.25 each.
- Roasted pork loin (two-pound roast), carrot-rice pilaf, a green vegetable, and romaine salad. Cost: $6 for four, $1.50 each.
- Oven-fried chicken tenders (using 1.5 pounds of chicken breasts), coleslaw, a green vegetable, and cornbread. Cost: $6 for four, $1.50 each.
- Oven-baked boneless pork loin chops (using 1.5 pounds of pork chops), a green vegetable, scalloped potatoes, and romaine salad. Cost: $5 for four, $1.25 each.
- Arroz con pollo (Spanish chicken with rice, using 1.5 pounds of chicken breasts), broccoli, and romaine salad. Cost: $5 for four, $1.25 each.
- Pasta casseroles with meat and cheese, such as lasagna or rotini with sausage and cheese. Cost: about $5 for four, $1.25 each.

You can use chicken, beef, or pork you buy for $2 or less per pound in many recipes with simple ingredients and serve everyone for a dollar or two apiece. Search the Web, cookbooks from the library, magazines—or the recipe chapter that follows.

Upscale Meals

This is sort of a funny term, considering most meals at fast-food restaurants cost more, but to the Strategic Shopper and meal planner, these dishes at $3–$4 per person are the epitome of high-rent dining!

Some of our favorite Upscale meals include:

- Chicken or steak kebabs with green and red peppers, mushrooms, and red onion; rice pilaf; and romaine salad. Cost $14 – $16 for four, about $3.50 each.
- Grilled marinated top sirloin steak, baked potatoes, a green vegetable, and romaine salad. Cost: $12 for four, $3 each.
- Grilled marinated salmon (or other fish), rice pilaf, steamed fresh broccoli, and romaine salad. Cost: $16 for four, $4 each.
- Pork tenderloin with spicy rub, roasted potatoes and vegetables, and romaine salad. Cost: $12 for four, $3 each.

A Final Word

Strategic meal planning and shopping go hand in hand. Once you've trained yourself to wait for sales, combine coupons and promotions, and stock up when prices are at their lowest, it should be second nature to learn the best ways of putting all those bargains on the table for the least amount of money.

Twenty

Recipes

Salads

Barbara's Asian Coleslaw
SERVES 6–8, ABOUT $1.75 PER BATCH

I've tried many recipes for Asian coleslaw, and my aunt Barbara's is my favorite. You can use low-fat ramen noodles if you'd like to make it even healthier.

2 Tbsp. toasted sesame seeds
2 Tbsp. sliced or slivered toasted almonds
½ medium head cabbage (1¼ lb.), shredded
½ package uncooked ramen noodles, crumbled
    (do not use the seasoning packet)
2 green onions, chopped (optional)

DRESSING:
2 Tbsp. sugar
⅓ cup vegetable oil
1 tsp. salt
⅛ tsp. pepper
3 Tbsp. distilled white vinegar
dash soy sauce
dash ground ginger

Combine all the salad ingredients in a bowl. Shake all the dressing ingredients in a jar or whisk them together in a separate bowl. Pour the dress-

ing over the salad and toss together. Keep salad in refrigerator until ready
to serve.

Low-fat Tangy Creamy Coleslaw
SERVES 6–8, ABOUT $1.35 PER BATCH. MAKES 1¾ LB. PREPARED
COLESLAW.

DRESSING:
¾ cup light mayonnaise
1 Tbsp. distilled white vinegar
1 Tbsp. sugar
¼ tsp. salt, to taste

½ medium head cabbage, shredded (1¼ lb.)
1 carrot, shredded

Mix dressing ingredients together and toss with the cabbage and
carrot.

Laura's Easy Fruit Salad
SERVES 6–8 HALF-CUP SERVINGS, ABOUT $3.00 PER BATCH

I like this recipe because it's easy to remember and it uses inexpensive fruit,
so I always have a fruit-salad option, even if summer fruits are out of
season. My friend Laura told me this recipe years ago and said, "Just remember two of each ingredient," and that worked. It goes nicely in custard cups
as a fruit compote alongside sandwiches.

2 apples, peeled and diced
2 navel oranges, peeled and diced
2 bananas, sliced
2 Tbsp. sugar

1 Tbsp. lemon juice, to prevent browning of bananas
(optional if serving immediately)

Mix fruit and stir in sugar and lemon juice. Cover and refrigerate until ready to serve.

Our Favorite Mandarin Orange Salad
SERVES 6–8, ABOUT $2.25 PER SALAD, 28 CENTS PER SERVING

½ cup chopped or sliced almonds, pecans, or walnuts
3 Tbsp. sugar
½ large bunch romaine lettuce, torn for salad
1 stalk chopped celery
2 green onions, white part, chopped (optional)
1 11-oz. can mandarin oranges in juice, drained

DRESSING:
¼ cup vegetable oil
½ tsp. salt
2 Tbsp. sugar
2 Tbsp. distilled white vinegar

In small nonstick pan over medium heat, cook the nuts and 3 Tbsp. sugar until nuts are coated and sugar is dissolved, stirring constantly to prevent scorching. Cool on a plate or in a bowl, then store in an airtight container once cooled.

Whisk together all dressing ingredients and chill, if desired. Toss lettuce, celery, and onions. Just before serving, add the candied nuts and oranges. Toss with dressing. *Note:* To reduce calories, you can toast the nuts instead of sugaring them. We also make this dressing for our everyday dinner salads.

Side Dishes

Homemade Tortilla Chips

MAKES 30 CHIPS FROM 5 CORN TORTILLAS, 25 CENTS, OR 30 CHIPS FROM
3 LARGE BURRITO TORTILLAS, 45 CENTS

    5 corn tortillas *or* 3 large flour tortillas (burrito-sized)
    Cooking spray or vegetable oil
    Salt or other seasonings

Spray corn or flour tortillas on both sides with cooking spray or brush
on both sides with vegetable oil, then sprinkle with salt or other seasonings.
Cut each tortilla into 6–8 wedges, and place on an ungreased cookie sheet,
without overlapping to allow even baking. Bake at 350 degrees for 15
minutes or until golden brown. Cool and dip in salsa or eat the chips on
their own.

Black Bean Salsa

MAKES 3½–4 CUPS, ABOUT $2.50 PER BATCH

    2 cloves garlic, minced
    1 15-oz. can black beans, rinsed and drained
    1 7-oz. can shoepeg corn, drained
    ½ cup Italian salad dressing
    3 Tbsp. chopped fresh cilantro leaves
    ½ tsp. hot pepper sauce
    ¾ tsp. chili powder
    1 medium tomato, chopped
    ½ green pepper, chopped
    ½ onion, chopped

Combine all ingredients and marinate for 4–5 hours or overnight. Serve with tortilla chips or use as a filling for tortillas.

Cindy's Sweet Potato Casserole
SERVES 10, ABOUT $2.40–$3.50 PER BATCH OR 24–35 CENTS PER SERVING, DEPENDING ON THE TOPPINGS YOU USE

Sweet potato casserole must be healthy because it has sweet potatoes, although my friend Cindy's recipe is as good as a dessert. It's a standard holiday dinner side dish for our family now. It costs about $3.50 to make with the pecan topping or $2.40 to make with the crumb topping.

SWEET POTATOES:
½ cup butter, melted
3 cups cooked sweet potatoes (about 5 small or 3 large potatoes, boiled)
¾ cup sugar
½ tsp. salt
½ cup whole or low-fat milk
2 eggs
½ tsp. vanilla

Mix all ingredients well. Place in a 9x13-inch greased baking dish.

PECAN TOPPING:
3 Tbsp. butter
1 cup brown sugar
½ cup flour
1 cup chopped pecans

INEXPENSIVE CRUMB TOPPING:
½ cup quick-cooking rolled oats
½ cup packed brown sugar
¼ cup cold butter or margarine, cut into pieces

¼ cup all-purpose flour

½ tsp. ground cinnamon

dash salt

Combine all ingredients for the topping you are using. Mix well, using a pastry cutter or two knives to cut ingredients and butter into a crumble. Sprinkle on top of potatoes. Bake at 350 degrees for 30 minutes.

Carrot Rice Pilaf

Makes 4 servings, $1 per batch with sunflower seeds, 75 cents without

2 cups water

2 chicken bouillon cubes

1 cup long-grain rice

2 large carrots, grated

dash black pepper

2 tsp. cumin

2 Tbsp. toasted almonds or sunflower seeds (optional)

Bring water, bouillon cubes, rice, carrots, pepper, and cumin to boil. Reduce heat to low, and cover and cook over low heat for 17 minutes until rice is tender but firm and the water has been completely absorbed. When rice is cooked, stir in nuts or sunflower seeds (if using) and serve.

Breads

Our Favorite Banana Bread

This recipe makes one large loaf using a 9x5x3-inch loaf pan, about $1.70 per loaf

½ cup whole-wheat flour

2 cups all-purpose flour

2 tsp. baking powder

1 tsp. baking soda

1 tsp. ground cinnamon

4 ripe bananas, mashed (2 cups)

½ cup natural applesauce

1 cup white sugar

2 large eggs

1 tsp. vanilla

½ cup chopped walnuts (optional)

Preheat oven to 350 degrees and spray a 9x5x3-inch loaf pan with cooking spray. Mix the first five ingredients together in a bowl. In a separate bowl, mix the bananas, applesauce, sugar, eggs, and vanilla until well blended. Add the flour mixture to the wet mixture and stir to blend. Add walnuts last (if using). Pour the batter into the loaf pan and bake 50–60 minutes, or until a knife inserted in the middle comes out clean. Allow bread to cool before slicing.

Spiced Pumpkin Bread

THIS RECIPE MAKES 2 LOAVES AT ABOUT $1.25 EACH WITHOUT NUTS, OR $1.75 EACH WITH NUTS

I like to make pumpkin bread because it's easy, nutritious, and is a great way to use sale-priced canned pumpkin that I stock up on during the November and December holiday season. It freezes well and also makes a nice gift. This recipe makes two loaves, so you can serve one to your family and share another as a gift. Write the recipe on an index card with colorful markers and tie it on the loaf with curling ribbon to dress up the wrapping and you have a thoughtful, inexpensive gift.

3 cups sugar

1 cup vegetable oil

3 large eggs

1 16-ounce can solid-pack pumpkin

3 cups all-purpose flour

1 tsp. ground cloves

1 tsp. ground cinnamon

1 tsp. ground nutmeg

1 tsp. baking soda

½ tsp. salt

½ tsp. baking powder

1 cup chopped walnuts (optional)

Preheat oven to 350 degrees. Mix the first 4 wet ingredients (including the sugar) together in a large bowl, and mix the next 7 ingredients (flour through baking powder) together in a separate bowl. Mix the dry ingredients into the wet ingredients, then fold the walnuts into the batter if you are using them. Divide batter equally between two 8x4-inch greased loaf pans. Bake for about 1 hour and 10 minutes until toothpick inserted in center comes out clean. (Start checking at about an hour.)

Homemade Pizza Crust

MAKES 2 MEDIUM CRUSTS OR 1 EXTRA-LARGE CRUST, 35 CENTS
PER BATCH WITH YEAST PURCHASED IN BULK; 65 CENTS PER
BATCH WITH YEAST PACKET. MAKES 4-6 SERVINGS.

I've tried many pizza crust recipes, and the best one I've found is right on the back of the Fleischmann's yeast packet. It takes much less time than I expected and is worth it. This recipe makes two medium crusts or one extra-large crust at a cost of 35 cents if you buy yeast in bulk, or about 65 cents if you buy it by the packet on sale.

2¼ teaspoons yeast in bulk, or 1 envelope active dry yeast

1 cup warm water (100–110 degrees)

2½–3 cups all-purpose flour, divided

¾ tsp. salt

2 Tbsp. olive oil or vegetable oil

Soften the yeast in the warm water, in a mixing bowl. Add 2 cups of the flour, and the salt and oil. Stir in enough of the remaining flour to make a soft dough. Knead on a lightly floured surface until smooth, about 4–6 minutes. Place dough in a bowl sprayed with cooking spray or greased with a little cooking oil; cover with a towel or plastic wrap and let rise in a warm place until doubled in size, about 30–45 minutes. Preheat the oven to 400 degrees. Punch the dough down. Pat the dough into a large pizza pan for one extra-large pizza, or divide it into 2 pieces and roll out 2 medium-size pizzas. Top the dough with desired toppings. Bake for 20–30 minutes or until slightly browned.

Egg Dishes

Egg Muffin
MAKES ONE SERVING, 35–58 CENTS

It takes less time to make this breakfast than it does to zip through the drive-through on the way to work. At only 35–58 cents each, depending on your preferred ingredients, it's an easy, delicious bargain you can make at home in less than 5 minutes.

    1 English muffin, split (25 cents), or two pieces of bread (15 cents)
    1 large egg (10 cents)
    1 slice American cheese (10 cents)
    1 1-ounce piece of ham (13 cents), optional

Toast the bread or English muffin while you are cooking the egg. Spray a custard cup with cooking spray. If using ham, put it in the bottom of the custard cup. Beat the egg in a separate dish, then pour it into the custard cup. Cook the egg in the microwave for 75 seconds on high. Place the slice of cheese on top of the cooked egg and microwave for an additional 15 seconds on high. Turn the custard cup upside down on top of one piece of toast or muffin, releasing the egg, top with the second piece of toast or muffin, and enjoy!

Easy Quiche
SERVES 6, ABOUT $2 BEFORE OPTIONAL ADD-INS, 33 CENTS PER SERVING

I like this because it's a cinch to make and my kids love it.

  2 cups or 8 ounces shredded cheese (any type you prefer)
  ½ cup add-ins, such as chopped ham, diced peppers, diced onions,
      chopped broccoli, etc. (optional)
  3 eggs, beaten
  1½ cups milk
  ¾ cup baking mix, such as Bisquick

Preheat oven to 400 degrees. Grease an 8x8-inch square glass dish or a 9-inch round pie pan. Spread cheese on bottom of the pan. Spread any optional add-ins over the cheese. Mix the eggs, milk, and baking mix together, and pour over the cheese. Bake for 30–35 minutes or until a knife inserted in the middle comes out clean. Allow to cool slightly and serve whole or cut in half.

Marinades and Rubs

Using marinades and rubs adds variety and flavor to inexpensive chicken, pork, beef, or fish. These are some of our favorites.

The Best Chicken Marinade
MAKES 20 OZ. (2½ CUPS), ABOUT $1 PER BATCH

I had this delicious marinade on grilled chicken at a friend's house fourteen years ago, and it is still my favorite for entertaining guests, as well as for everyday family meals. I also like it because it uses brown mustard, which is often a good coupon freebie. I make this large batch in the blender and then keep it in a glass jar in the refrigerator.

2 tsp. minced garlic

1 Tbsp. salt

1 cup packed brown sugar

⅓ cup grainy brown mustard

½ cup apple-cider vinegar

4 Tbsp. bottled lime juice (or juice of 2 limes)

2 Tbsp. bottled lemon juice (or juice of 1 lemon)

¾ cup vegetable oil

Puree all ingredients in a blender. Makes enough to marinate about 4 batches of grilled chicken, assuming 1½ to 2 lbs. of chicken per batch. Marinate 1½ to 2 lbs. of boneless, skinless chicken breasts with ¾ cup marinade in a resealable bag for at least 1 hour and up to 24 hours in the refrigerator before grilling, which is preferable to baking because grilling carmelizes the marinate nicely You can grill the chicken on a grill, under a broiler, or in a grilling pan on the stove.

Our Favorite Stir-Fry Marinade
MAKES ¾ CUP, ABOUT 75 CENTS PER BATCH

When I met my husband twenty years ago, his stir-fry dinner was the one his friends raved about. We still rave! You can use this marinade for beef, pork, or chicken, and stir-fry it with whatever fresh, crunchy vegetables you have on hand. Serve over rice.

½ cup dry white wine, sherry, vermouth, or cooking sherry (I use cheap white
  wine at $3 per bottle, which is much cheaper than cooking sherry
  purchased at the grocery store.)

1 tsp. sesame oil

½ tsp. minced fresh ginger

½ tsp. minced fresh garlic (I use jarred minced garlic for convenience)

1 tsp. sugar

¼ cup soy sauce

Mix ingredients in a bowl with a fork or whisk, and marinate the meat for at least 15 minutes. This is the right amount for about 1½ pounds of meat.

Steak Marinade

MAKES 1¼ CUPS, ABOUT 90 CENTS PER BATCH

2 Tbsp. bottled lemon juice (or juice of 1 lemon)
½ cup soy sauce
¼ cup dry red wine
3 Tbsp. vegetable oil
2 Tbsp. Worcestershire sauce
½ tsp. minced garlic

Mix ingredients together. This is enough to marinate 1½–2 pounds of meat in a glass dish, turning occasionally, for 2–12 hours in the refrigerator.

Rubs are great, but they call for a large number of dried herbs and spices. If you buy the name-brand spices at your supermarket, these rubs will be fairly expensive to make. Instead, check the spice aisle at your drugstore or Wal-Mart to buy these basic spices for 50 cents to $1 for a large jar. You can also buy them in the bulk section of your local health-food store rather than paying $2–$3 for a small jar of just one of the spices at a supermarket.

Spicy Southwest Rub

MAKES ¼ CUP, ENOUGH FOR A LARGE STEAK. ABOUT 36 CENTS PER BATCH.

This has a kick to it and is great on pork tenderloin or a steak.

2 Tbsp. chili powder
2 Tbsp. packed brown sugar
1 Tbsp. ground cumin
2 tsp. minced garlic

2 tsp. cider vinegar

1 tsp. Worcestershire sauce

¼ tsp. ground red pepper

Mix ingredients together and use immediately. You can also store left-over rub in the refrigerator.

Jane's Oregon Herb Rub

MAKES ABOUT ½ CUP OF DRY RUB, ENOUGH FOR 7 STEAKS OR ROASTS AT
1 TABLESPOON EACH. ABOUT 42 CENTS PER BATCH.

Everything my aunt Jane makes is wonderful, including this seasoning mix she uses when grilling meat. We use this dry rub when grilling pork loins or beef roasts. Moisten the meat and cover it with 1 tablespoon of the rub before grilling.

¼ cup salt

2 tsp. garlic salt

2 tsp. celery salt

1 tsp. black pepper

1 tsp. onion powder

1 tsp. paprika

½ tsp. dill

½ tsp. sage

½ tsp. rosemary

Mix ingredients together and store in a jar.

Carole's Sweet Soy Salmon Marinade

MAKES ABOUT 1 CUP, 82 CENTS PER BATCH

½ cup pancake syrup (for fewer calories, you can use light syrup)

½ cup soy sauce

1–2 lbs. salmon (estimate 1 lb. for 2 to 3 people)

Mix pancake syrup and soy sauce. Pour over salmon, and let it marinate in the refrigerator for at least 4 hours. Line a cookie sheet with foil and place the salmon pieces on it, baking at 350 degrees for 15–20 minutes.

Citrus Teriyaki Salmon Marinade

MAKES 1 CUP, ENOUGH TO MARINATE 1 POUND OF SALMON, ABOUT 54 CENTS PER BATCH

    4 Tbsp. soy sauce
    ⅓ cup orange juice
    ½ cup packed brown sugar
    1 tsp. minced fresh ginger
    1 lb. salmon

Mix the first four ingredients in a shallow dish. Add the salmon and turn several times to coat. Cover and refrigerate at least 1 hour, turning once. Bake at 350 degrees for 15–20 minutes.

Main-Dish Entrées and Soups

Lentil-Vegetable Soup

MAKES 6 LARGE 2-CUP BOWLS, ABOUT 30 CENTS PER SERVING

I'll make this on Monday morning and have it all week for lunch with wheat saltines. At only 30 cents a bowl and 2 minutes in the microwave, it's my idea of good fast food.

    4 large carrots, chopped
    ⅛ head green cabbage, chopped finely (or 2 stalks celery, chopped)
    1 14.5-oz. can diced tomatoes or diced tomatoes with onion, with juice

¼ cup chopped onion (optional if using canned tomatoes with onion)

½ tsp. minced fresh garlic

1⅓ cups lentils, rinsed

⅓ cup barley

3 chicken bouillon cubes

1 or 2 bay leaves

Fill a large (13-cup) saucepan with 8 cups of water, about 2/3 of the way up the pot, and bring to a boil. While you wait for the water to boil, prepare the rest of the ingredients and add them to the pot, adding enough water to fill the pot as necessary. Once everything is boiling, turn the heat down and simmer for at least 1 hour, or up to 2 hours for the best flavor. Remove the bay leaves before serving.

Healthy Minestrone
MAKES 6 LARGE SERVINGS, ABOUT 63 CENTS PER SERVING

I use either ground turkey or ground beef in this recipe. I buy the 91 percent lean frozen ground beef in 1-lb. rolls from Costco at about $2.40 per pound or will buy less expensive ground beef on sale and rinse it under hot water in a colander to remove the extra fat after cooking. This recipe could cost less for coupon users, because they may get canned tomatoes, beans, and pasta for pennies or free with coupons.

1 lb. lean ground beef or ground turkey

1 Tbsp. vegetable or olive oil

1½ cups chopped yellow onion

2 celery stalks, chopped

2 large carrots, chopped

1 28-oz. can diced tomatoes with juice

2 cups pinto beans or white beans, soaked and cooked (or substitute 1 15-oz. can of beans)

6 cups water

6 cubes beef bouillon

1½ tsp. dried marjoram

1 tsp. salt

pepper to taste

1 cup uncooked small pasta (such as elbow macaroni, or whatever you have
    on hand)

hot-pepper sauce, to taste (optional)

grated Parmesan cheese, to taste (optional)

Brown the ground beef and drain off the fat; set the beef aside on a plate. Use the same pan to heat the oil. Add the onion, celery, and carrots, and sauté until the onion softens. Add the diced tomatoes with their juice, bring to a boil, reduce the heat to medium-low, and simmer the vegetables for 10 minutes. Add the beans, water, bouillon, reserved beef, marjoram, salt, and pepper. Bring the soup to a boil and add the pasta. Cook for 10–15 minutes or until the pasta is done. Add hot-pepper sauce to taste (if using). Sprinkle the soup with Parmesan cheese if you have it on hand and serve.

Cathy's Southwest Turkey Chili
Makes 6 servings, about 70 cents per serving

I tried this at my sister's, and it gets rave reviews at my house now.

1 lb. ground turkey, browned and drained

1 tsp. chili powder

1 tsp. ground cumin

¼ tsp. salt

1 green pepper, chopped

½ small onion, chopped

1½ tsp. minced fresh garlic, or 3 cloves, minced

1 15.5-oz. can chili beans in spicy sauce, undrained

1 14.5-oz. can diced tomatoes with juice

¾ cup salsa or picante sauce

Fresh cilantro leaves (optional)
Shredded cheese (optional)

This can be made in a slow cooker or on the stovetop, combining all ingredients and simmering until vegetables are cooked (at least 30 minutes). To cook in the slow cooker, place browned turkey and all ingredients except for the cilantro leaves and shredded cheese in the slow cooker. Cover and cook on low for 5 hours or until the vegetables are cooked. Garnish with cilantro and shredded cheese, if desired. If you prefer a spicier chili, you can increase the amount of chili powder and cumin, and use chili-style diced tomatoes instead of plain diced tomatoes.

Healthy Sloppy Joes
MAKES 4 SERVINGS, ABOUT 80 CENTS PER SERVING, INCLUDING BUNS

I like sloppy joes but don't like canned sauces that are overly sweet, even when they're free with a coupon. This is a healthy recipe that everyone in our family likes.

1 lb. lean ground beef
1 14.5-oz. can diced tomatoes, undrained
2 Tbsp. tomato paste
1 carrot, finely diced
½ cup frozen corn (optional)
½ tsp. salt
2 tsp. sugar
1 Tbsp. Worcestershire sauce
2 tsp. red-wine vinegar
sandwich buns, pasta, or rice, for serving

Brown and drain the ground beef. Add the remaining ingredients, bring to a boil, lower the heat, and simmer covered for 30 minutes until thickened. Serve over toasted sandwich buns, pasta, or rice.

Arroz con Pollo (Chicken with Rice)

MAKES 4 SERVINGS, ABOUT $5.00 TOTAL, OR $1.25 PER SERVING

½ tsp. minced fresh garlic

½ tsp. dried oregano

2 Tbsp. red-wine vinegar

4 boneless, skinless chicken breasts (about 1½–2 lbs.)

1 Tbsp. vegetable or olive oil

1 14.5-oz. can diced tomatoes, drained

½ cup chopped onion (½ small onion)

½ cup chopped green pepper (½ small pepper)

2 cups water

¾ cup long-grain white rice

1 tsp. salt

2 chicken bouillon cubes

8 green olives (optional)

1 Tbsp. chopped fresh cilantro leaves and stems (optional)

Mix together the garlic, oregano, and red-wine vinegar. Pour it over the chicken breasts in a dish to marinate, and refrigerate for 1 hour. After marinating, brown the chicken in the oil for 6–8 minutes, turning once, then remove to a plate. Add tomatoes, onion, and green pepper to the pan and cook on medium-high heat until vegetables soften, about 3–4 minutes. Add the water, rice, salt, and bouillon, and olives and cilantro (if using). Stir and bring to boil, then reduce heat to low. Add chicken back to the pan, cover, and cook 25–30 minutes or until the rice has absorbed the liquid and the chicken is cooked through.

Oven-Baked Crunchy Chicken

MAKES 4 SERVINGS, ABOUT $3.60, OR 90 CENTS PER SERVING

3 cups cornflakes

1 Tbsp. plus 1 tsp. sesame seeds

1 tsp. paprika

½ tsp. salt

½ tsp. black pepper

¼ cup skim milk

4 boneless, skinless chicken breasts (about 1½ lb.)

Preheat oven to 400 degrees. Spray an 8-inch square baking pan with nonstick spray. Place cornflakes in a large resealable bag and crush by hand or with a rolling pin. Add the sesame seeds, paprika, salt, and pepper to the bag, shake well, and set aside.

Pour the milk into a bowl and dip each piece of chicken in it, then place the chicken in the bag with the cornflake mixture and shake well. Repeat with each piece of chicken. Place the chicken pieces in the sprayed baking pan and bake for 20 minutes or until the chicken is cooked through.

My Favorite Tarragon Chicken Salad

MAKES ABOUT TWO POUNDS OF PREPARED CHICKEN SALAD AT A COST OF
$2.50 PER POUND

MAKES 8 HALF-CUP SERVINGS AT ABOUT 60 CENTS PER SERVING
(NOT INCLUDING COST OF BREAD)

A local restaurant serves the best chicken salad but their recipe is top secret. I've experimented in my kitchen to try to duplicate their recipe and this is very close. It's what I serve to friends when I have luncheons, and it's a family everyday favorite, too.

1.5- to 1.75-lb. package boneless chicken breasts

¾ cup light mayonnaise

¼ cup light sour cream

¼ tsp. salt

2 tsp. tarragon

1 stalk celery, diced

4 oz. red grapes, cut in half (1 cup whole grapes)

¼ cup toasted, chopped almonds or pecans

Poach or bake chicken breasts at 350 degrees for 25 minutes. Allow to cool until you can handle, and either shred chicken with a fork or pulse for just a couple of seconds in a food processor (I like the food processor result the best). Be very careful not to overprocess—you want the meat to be shredded, not creamed. Mix the mayonnaise, sour cream, salt, tarragon, and celery in a large bowl, then stir in chicken. Fold in grapes and nuts. Cover and refrigerate for at least an hour to chill. Stir before serving and add more mayonnaise if necessary. Serve one scoop on a lettuce leaf per person, or serve in a half pita bread, rolled in a tortilla wrap, or any kind of bun or bread.

Roasted Vegetable Pizza
MAKES 4 SERVINGS, TOTAL RECIPE COST $4.00 FOR 2 MEDIUM OR 1 EXTRA-LARGE PIZZA, OR $1.00 PER SERVING

FOR MARINADE:
¼ cup vegetable oil
2 Tbsp. balsamic vinegar
½ tsp. salt
½ tsp. minced fresh garlic
½ tsp. dried thyme

3–4 cups chopped fresh vegetables, such as zucchini, yellow squash, green or
     red peppers, broccoli, or onion, or a combination (see note below)
1 batch homemade pizza crust to make 2 medium pizzas (page 236) or
     prepared pizza crust of your choice
1 cup tomato sauce or pasta sauce
2 cups shredded mozzarella (or one 8-oz. package)

Preheat oven to 400 degrees. Mix marinade ingredients and pour over chopped vegetables.

Put marinated vegetables in a 9x13-inch baking pan and roast at 400 degrees until the vegetables are browned, about 20–30 minutes.

While vegetables are cooking, roll out two medium pizza crusts, place on baking sheets, and allow the dough to rise on the baking sheets until the vegetables are ready. Top each pizza crust with ½ cup of the tomato sauce or pasta sauce, and then top each pizza with half of the cooked vegetables to cover. Sprinkle 1 cup of shredded mozzarella on top of each pizza, and bake each pizza (one at a time) on the bottom rack of the oven at 400 degrees until the cheese is melted and slightly browned, about 15–20 minutes.

Note: I use whatever vegetables are the best price in the produce department that day. For a recent pizza, I went with one yellow squash at $1 per pound instead of zucchini at $1.79 per pound, and one green and one red pepper at 50 cents each instead of broccoli at $2.79 per bunch, along with one-quarter of a large yellow onion.

Pizza Variations
Using the same crust recipe, we like to make these pizzas as well. Any topping you like will do!

Cheese and Green Pepper Pizza
MAKES 2 MEDIUM OR ONE EXTRA-LARGE PIZZA, 4 SERVINGS $3.00 PER RECIPE, OR 75 CENTS PER SERVING

1 batch pizza crust dough (page 236)
1 cup pasta sauce
1 green pepper, diced
2 cups shredded mozzarella (or one 8-oz. package)

Preheat oven to 400 degrees. Recipe makes either one extra large or two medium pizzas. Roll out pizza crusts and let rise 5–10 minutes. Spread ½ cup of pasta sauce on each crust, sprinkle each crust with half of the green pepper, and then top with 1 cup of cheese per pizza. Bake at 400 degrees on the bottom rack of the oven until cheese is melted and slightly browned, about 15–20 minutes.

Grandma's Favorite Meat Loaf
MAKES 6 SERVINGS, $4.35, OR 73 CENTS PER SERVING

My mother's recipe is my kids' favorite and it's simple to make. We like to make sandwiches with the leftovers the next day.

    1½ pounds ground beef
    3 slices soft bread
    1 cup milk
    1 large egg, slightly beaten
    ¼ cup minced onion
    1¼ tsp. salt
    ¼ tsp. black pepper
    ¼ tsp. celery salt
    1 Tbsp. ketchup
    1 Tbsp. Worcestershire sauce
    1 Tbsp. horseradish (optional)
    ½ cup ketchup to use as topping (optional)

Preheat oven to 350 degrees. Combine all ingredients in a bowl, mixing well. Pat mixture into a 8x5-inch loaf pan and top with ½ cup of additional ketchup, if desired. Bake 1½ hours until meat reaches an internal temperature of 160 degrees. Allow to sit 10 minutes before serving.

Family's Favorite Lasagna
MAKES 10 LARGE SERVINGS, $12, OR $1.20 PER SERVING

    1½ lb. ground beef, browned and drained
    ½ cup minced fresh onion
    ½ tsp. garlic powder
    2 bay leaves
    ¼ tsp. oregano
    ½ tsp. dried basil
    1 tsp. salt

1 14.5-oz. can diced tomatoes with juice

2 6-oz. cans tomato paste

½ cup wine (cooking sherry)

3 cups cream-style cottage cheese (24 oz.)

2 large eggs, beaten

1 tsp. salt

½ tsp. black pepper

1 Tbsp. parsley flakes

½ cup grated Parmesan

6–8 lasagna noodles, cooked according to directions on the package

1 lb. mozzarella cheese, shredded (16-oz. package)

Preheat oven to 375 degrees. Combine the beef, onion, garlic powder, bay leaves, oregano, basil, salt, tomatoes, tomato paste, and wine in a large frying pan, and simmer on medium-low after bringing to a boil, approximately 45 minutes.

Mix the cottage cheese, eggs, salt, pepper, parsley, and Parmesan in a bowl.

Layer the following in a 9x13-inch pan: Spray the pan with cooking spray or grease with oil to prevent noodles from sticking. Layer half of the noodles, half of the cottage-cheese mixture, half of the beef sauce, and half of the mozzarella. Repeat the layers once more, finishing with the mozzarella cheese. Bake at 375 degrees for 30 minutes. Allow to sit for 15 minutes before serving.

Desserts

Graham-Cracker Crust
MAKES ONE 9-INCH PIECRUST, ABOUT 60 CENTS

This makes one 9-inch no-bake piecrust at a cost of about 60 cents. I use a resealable bag and a rolling pin to crush the crackers, or you could use a food processor or blender. This is a great crust for ice-cream pies. I use the least expensive store-brand graham crackers for these crusts. You could also substitute 1¼ cups vanilla wafers or cornflake crumbs for the graham-cracker crumbs to make a good crumb crust.

> 7 full graham crackers, crushed to make 1¼ cups crumbs
> ¼ cup sugar
> 6 Tbsp. margarine or butter, melted

Mix cracker crumbs and sugar together. Stir together to combine with melted margarine or butter, and pat into pie pan. Chill in the freezer for a few minutes before filling.

Ice-Cream Pie

Makes 2 pies, 6–8 servings each. Before toppings, the basic ice-cream pie costs about $1.60 to make when I find ice cream on sale for $2 per carton: about 27 cents per slice if you cut it into 6 slices, or 20 cents if you cut it into 8 slices.

I like to make ice-cream pies because everyone in our family enjoys them and they are the easiest special dessert to make. When ice cream hits a rock-bottom sale price, it's a good idea to buy an extra carton and make a couple of ice-cream pies for the freezer. One 48-ounce carton of ice cream will make two pies, although a half-gallon 56-ounce carton would fill the crusts a little more generously, if you can find a brand that sells a half-gallon carton. The basic ice-cream pie requires only a graham-cracker crust and half a carton of ice cream, softened. You can make your pie as elaborate as you'd like by adding ice-cream toppings, such as syrups, sprinkles, nuts, or whipped cream.

> 2 prepared graham-cracker crusts (page 251)
> 48- or 56-oz. carton ice cream (any variety)
> Chocolate syrup or any flavor ice-cream topping (optional)
> Colored or chocolate dessert sprinkles (optional)

Toasted chopped nuts (optional)

Whipped cream (optional)

Take the ice cream out of the freezer to soften for 5–10 minutes before making the pies. If desired, drizzle ice-cream syrup on the bottom of the prepared crust before adding the ice cream. Scoop half the carton of ice cream into the crust and spread it into the crust evenly as it softens. Drizzle chocolate syrup on the ice cream, and top with dessert sprinkles or nuts (if using). Put the pie in the freezer to set at least 15 minutes; cover with plastic wrap and foil if you will be storing the pie in the freezer for more than a day or two. Take the pie out of the freezer to soften for 5–10 minutes before slicing to serve. Top each piece with whipped cream if desired.

Family Favorite Chocolate-Chip Cookies

MAKES 4 DOZEN COOKIES, $3 PER BATCH, OR 6 CENTS PER COOKIE (WITHOUT NUTS)

Years ago my son's preschool teacher brought the most wonderful cookies to class on a day I was working in the classroom. Making cookies is a favorite hobby of mine, so I asked her for her recipe. Apparently she was known for her wonderful cookies and she politely responded, "Every Southern woman is entitled to one secret and that is mine." So I started experimenting in my kitchen to duplicate her wonderful cookies. I never got it exactly right, but this recipe was my best result and now people ask me for it when they taste the cookies. If I only get one secret, it's not going to be a cookie recipe, so here you go! They are a delicious bargain worth sharing.

1 cup butter-flavored shortening

1¼ cups white sugar

¼ cup dark corn syrup

2 large eggs

1 tsp. vanilla

2¾ cups all-purpose flour

1 tsp. baking soda

1 tsp. salt

1 12-ounce bag chocolate chips

1 cup chopped walnuts or pecans (optional)

Preheat oven to 375 degrees. Cream shortening, sugar, and corn syrup in a large bowl until light and fluffy. Blend in eggs and vanilla. Mix the flour, baking soda, and salt in a separate bowl, then mix the dry ingredients into the egg mixture. Blend in chocolate chips and nuts (if using). Drop the dough by tablespoon on an ungreased cookie sheet 2 inches apart (12 cookies per sheet). For cookies that are crisp on the outside and soft on the inside, bake 10–12 minutes, or until cookies are browning a bit but still look slightly underbaked. Allow to cool on cookie sheet to firm up for 2–3 minutes after taking out of the oven. Transfer to a wire rack to cool. You can experiment with the cooking time to get the type of cookies you prefer: Shorten the time for chewier cookies or increase it for crispier cookies.

A savings note: Admittedly, chocolate-chip cookies are one of the more expensive varieties of cookie to bake because of the cost of chocolate chips and nuts. Name-brand chocolate chips are usually better than store-brand chocolate chips, so for the very best cookies I buy name-brand chips. I save by buying large packages of nuts and name-brand chocolate chips at a wholesale club, where they cost roughly $1.40 for the equivalent of a 12-ounce bag of chocolate chips, much less than my supermarket's price of $2.89. However, when I can buy real chocolate bars free or practically free with coupons, I chop the bars to use for chocolate-chip cookies.

Fudge Pie

My friend Nanette shared this recipe with me and my family got hooked the first time I made it. It serves 8 to 12, depending on the size of slices you serve. The total cost of the pie is only about $1.25 if you make your own piecrust before the cost of optional whipped cream or ice cream.

This is an inexpensive dessert that uses basic pantry ingredients, but is elegant and delicious. Your dinner guests will rave, and they'll never guess that it took you less than 15 minutes to make.

    2 large eggs
    1 stick butter or margarine, melted
    1 cup sugar
    ¼ cup all-purpose flour
    ¼ cup unsweetened cocoa powder
    1 tsp. vanilla
    1 regular piecrust (recipe follows), unbaked
    Cool Whip or ice cream, for serving (optional)

Beat eggs slightly, and add melted butter or margarine. Add sugar, flour, cocoa, and vanilla, mix well, and pour into the unbaked piecrust. Bake at 350 degrees for about 30 minutes or until firm. Serve warm with Cool Whip or ice cream.

SINGLE PIECRUST:

When I get the urge to make this simple fudge pie for dessert, chances are pretty good that I don't have an unbaked pie shell on hand. Rather than make an extra trip to the store, I can use 33 cents' worth of ingredients I always have on hand and it takes less than 10 minutes—I timed it!

    1½ cups all-purpose flour
    ½ tsp. salt

½ cup butter-flavored shortening

3 Tbsp. water

Stir together flour and salt, then cut in shortening using a pastry blender or two knives until the texture resembles gravel. Stir in water until the dough forms a ball and knead for a few seconds until the dough is smooth. Roll the dough into a disk between two pieces of waxed paper. Take off one piece of waxed paper and put the dough in a round pie plate, then remove the second piece of waxed paper and shape the dough into the pan. Flute the edges of the crust with your fingers or a fork and trim off the extra dough with a knife.

Famous Coconut Cake

This is my friend's famous "secret" coconut cake. At the church bake sales, people buy this cake from her before the sale! It is delicious and very easy to make using coupon bargains!

1 box white cake mix (as well as any ingredients needed to prepare the cake
    per the package directions)

2 cups sugar

1 8-oz. container sour cream

12 oz. shredded dried coconut, plus more for decorating

1½ cups Cool Whip

Bake the cake mix according to the directions on the package for two round layers. Slice each layer in half horizontally, so the end result is four total layers.

Mix the sugar, sour cream, and coconut, reserving 1 cup of this icing mixture to use to top the cake. Spread the remaining icing over the first three layers of cake as you stack them.

Mix the Cool Whip with the reserved icing and spread on the top layer of the cake. Sprinkle some coconut on top. Keep refrigerated.

Layered Trifle Dessert

Another great way to use up those cake- and brownie-mix bargains is to make an elegant trifle dessert, which is very impressive and ideal for serving to company. A trifle is served in a flat-bottomed glass dish, like a large fruit-salad bowl or even a large square glass baking dish. An actual trifle dish is a large, round, flat-bottomed bowl with a glass standing base.

It's easy to make a trifle. It can be inexpensive if you improvise and create a trifle using bargain ingredients, but it can get pretty expensive if you go out and buy specific ingredients for one trifle recipe. Once you know what the four basic layers of a trifle are, it's easy to improvise:

- Baked cake squares (variations include brownies, ladyfingers, or angel food cake)
- Pudding (variations include using yogurt instead of pudding)
- Fresh fruit (variations include frozen fruit, canned pie filling, or even canned fruit)
- Nondairy whipped-cream topping (I use Cool Whip)

I saw a recipe for a fruit trifle that called for a large angel food cake, pudding, fresh raspberries, and Cool Whip. Instead of buying a $4 angel food cake at the store, I made a white cake in a 9x13-inch cake pan from a free (with coupons) cake mix, adding 3 egg whites at a cost of 30 cents for 3 eggs. Instead of paying $6 for two containers of raspberries, I used fresh strawberries in season at $1.50 per pint, and I used coupons to buy Cool Whip (50 cents a tub) and Jell-O instant vanilla pudding ($1.03 when prepared with 3 cups of milk). If I had followed the exact recipe and hadn't used coupons, the trifle would have cost $12 to make. By improvising, it cost about $4.83 to make 12 servings, a cost of about 38 cents per serving.

Twenty-one

From Saving to Giving: Helping Others with Cut Out Hunger

With a snip of your scissors or a click of your mouse, you can put food on a needy child's dinner plate tonight. It really is that simple. Using Strategic Shopping principles can benefit not just your family but also other families in your community. Once you've mastered ways of chopping your own grocery budget, it's easy to take the extra step and purchase pantry staples at huge discounts or even get them for free, and then donate them to help others. The less fortunate in your community will be grateful for your expertise and generosity.

In this chapter we're going to discuss:

- how my charitable shopping program, Cut Out Hunger, got started and how it works
- success stories from other CouponMom.com members who have put Cut Out Hunger to work to benefit their communities
- how to get your children on board and involved with your family's saving and giving

Attacking Need with Coupons:
How Cut Out Hunger Began

In the fall of 2000, I noticed an urgent appeal in our church bulletin. A local food pantry that aids needy families in our community was turning people away because its shelves were bare. The bulletin listed a number of items the pantry needed to begin fulfilling its mission again. With one glance I realized that most of these items could be purchased at a deep discount by using coupons and sales, and inspiration struck.

That week, my supermarket was running a super double coupon promotion, so I grabbed my coupons and hit the store. Shopping with coupons for people I knew I might never even meet, I filled a cart with $60 worth of food and paid just $15. This discovery was too good not to share, and I was eager to spread the word.

When I delivered the items to the food pantry, I decided to meet with the charity's director to share my coupon strategies with her. I noticed that the charity's waiting room was packed with clients waiting to meet with her, too. I was surprised to see so many people in my own backyard seeking emergency food support, and dismayed that the food pantry couldn't help them.

Strategic Shopping, I thought, could help solve this problem. Careful use of coupons combined with store promotions could allow anyone to stock up on pantry necessities for very little—in many cases, for free—and donate those items. After that day, I officially adopted the food pantry in my area as a "family member" and started shopping for the charity as part of my weekly shopping for my own family. After tracking my shopping for several weeks, I soon learned to spot the best bargains and free items that would make good donations. An idea was born, and I called it Cut Out Hunger.

I started teaching small groups of people the principles of Strategic Shopping to trim their own grocery bills while attacking the need in our community. The message was simple: Strategic Shopping allows people to save enough on their own food that they're able to afford to buy items to donate. And mastering Strategic Shopping often results in getting many items for free. I hoped that a charitable giving program that cost donors next to nothing—besides their time—would be successful.

In March 2001, a few months after I started my small-group teaching sessions, I launched the Cut Out Hunger website. It began with the best grocery deals across my state and eventually across the country. We changed the site's name in 2005 to CouponMom.com, but the concept has remained the same. By using the tips and strategies we discuss on CouponMom.com, it's possible to cut your grocery bill in half and feed needy people in your community as well. Helping others seems to be second nature to many coupon users, and a 2009 survey of CouponMom.com members found that 84 percent of respondents said they donated items they bought at bargain prices to charities, friends, or family members in need on a regular basis.

How Cut Out Hunger Works

If you already use coupons, it's easy to work the Cut Out Hunger approach into your regular shopping. Simply keep an eye out for the best nonperishable coupon deals, even on items your family doesn't typically use. Our family keeps a "charity box" in the garage to collect items for donation. Over the course of each month, we fill the box with a variety of items food pantries can always use, such as peanut butter, toothpaste, shampoo, pasta, cereal, and canned goods. By combining coupons, stocking up during sales, and taking advantage of all store savings programs, we're able to buy these items for pennies or less. But their impact in our community is priceless.

I recommend that you donate to agencies that serve people in your immediate area. You can participate in food drives at the schools or places of worship in your neighborhood or help with scout troops' programs and mail-carrier food drives. You can also take your food donations directly to a local food pantry, soup kitchen, or homeless shelter. It shouldn't be hard to find someone who needs a helping hand. Google the term "food pantry" and the name of your area to be directed to community shelters, soup kitchens, and food pantries like the one I found. Delivering food directly to the charity helps you make a personal connection. Volunteers will be thrilled to tell you exactly which items the organization needs. You may decide to become a volunteer yourself and donate your time as well as grocery items.

CouponMom.com can help you help others. The site lists the best grocery deals at dozens of stores across the country, and items that make good donations are denoted with the word "charity" beside them. These include items typically found on food-bank wish lists: nonperishable high-protein items such as peanut butter, canned tuna, meats, beans, and canned milk; fruit and vegetables; and rice, pasta, and pasta sauce. Charities also can always use personal hygiene items such as toothpaste, toothbrushes, shampoo, and deodorant. I'd be willing to bet that any food bank in the country consistently needs those items. Fortunately, they're products you can always buy with coupons!

So, where do you find enough coupons to save on your own groceries while helping others? That's never been a problem for me. If you're just getting started, it makes sense to collect more than one copy of the Sunday newspaper coupon circular. You can buy extra copies of the newspaper on Sundays; some stores will sell them at a discount on Sunday afternoons. Or you can put the word out that you need coupons for charity. Let your non-coupon-using neighbors and friends know what you're up to, and they'll probably be glad to offer their coupon circulars. When I first began Cut Out Hunger, I ended up with more donated coupon circulars than I could use. It was a fun way for my entire community to get involved, and not only was I able to buy plenty of items for charity each week, but I also doubled my family's grocery savings by using the extra coupons for our shopping as well.

Success Stories from the CouponMom.com Community

I love getting e-mails and reading the CouponMom.com Forum to learn about the creative, generous ways members help those in need with coupon bargains. Our members donate to food pantries, women's shelters, and humane societies (using coupons for free pet food). They also give to college students, family members who are struggling financially, and friends and neighbors going through hard times, and they send care packages to soldiers overseas.

Here are some inspirational success stories that CouponMom.com members have shared with me.

"My husband and I were going on vacation in July 2006, and I took Stephanie's first book, Greatest Secrets of the Coupon Mom, *with me. I've always loved couponing and had been doing it for many years. I read Stephanie's book through in one sitting, unable to put it down. I've also had a passion for feeding the hungry, and from her book, I found a way to tie together my two passions. I was thinking how wonderful it would be if I could get my congregation at Grace United Methodist Church in Gainesville to feed the poor 'for free' using some of Stephanie's techniques and her website. I presented it to my small group of ladies, and they were 100 percent behind me. We then started what has become a weekly flier."*

—Gail Wise of Gainesville, Florida

Gail e-mails about 450 people once a week with a list of products that her local food bank needs. She usually chooses an item offered with a "buy one, get one free" promotion and finds coupons on CouponMom.com to make the deal an even better buy for her fellow volunteers. Members of Gail's church purchase the items she suggests each week, along with others they're able to buy at bargain prices, and bring them to church each Sunday. Three shopping carts, on loan from a local Publix supermarket, are parked at the front of the sanctuary. Members place their donated items in the carts at the beginning of each service—Gail says everyone loves watching children add their items—and church members deliver the items to their local food bank each Tuesday. "Last year we donated over 11,000 pounds of food," Gail said. "Can you believe that? Over 5 tons of food!" Gail calls her program Stomp Out Hunger with Grace and is teaching other churches in her area how to start programs of their own. For her efforts, Gail received a much-deserved award at a community banquet in her area. Congratulations, Gail!

I could fill an entire book with the wonderful anecdotes I hear from CouponMom.com members. They inspire me and just make me happy. Here are a few more.

"A couple months ago, an apartment building burned to the ground. I rounded up 30 boxes of cereal, 25 toothbrushes and toothpastes, and about 20 razors, and brought them to the families directly the very next morning. My husband, a firefighter, was at the scene for over 24 hours. He came home, showered, and drove me back to the site so I could give the 'goody bags' to everyone in need."

—Lisa, a CouponMom.com member in Massachusetts

"I hadn't been sure about where to donate all this extra stuff I've been accumulating, so I finally did a Google search for my city name and 'where to donate.' It turns out my city published a flier with information on where to donate things, and there is a food bank in my city! I dropped off my first two bags of food and toiletries today. It felt so good! I said a little prayer asking the items to be a blessing to the recipients and also explained to my toddler daughter what we were doing. I can't wait to do this more with her as she grows!"

—Christine, A CouponMom.com member in California

"I contacted our church's social ministry board yesterday to see if they knew of families in our church who were in need. They definitely do and have received requests from those who have lost their jobs and aren't receiving unemployment yet. I like the idea of giving my donated goods to fellow members I see at church every week."

—NiftyThrifty, a CouponMom.com member in Michigan

Get Your Kids Involved

Summer vacation is a great time to get your children in on your saving and giving routine. They have time on their hands and community charities are often in greater need, as families whose children are served by free-lunch programs during the school year may need to find other ways to feed everyone. At the same time, food pantry donations often go down during the summer, since many people who give during the year may be away on vacations.

It is never too early to teach our children the reality of hunger in our communities and the important role they can play in helping to provide for families in need. One summer I taught my eleven-year-old son to buy food and personal-care items for our local charity. Not only did he learn the math and budgeting skills to stretch his weekly charity budget of $3, but with this method he also realized how easily a small amount of money can help others. Each week he bought a few items using the coupon system and put them in the family charity box, and then I took him to our local charity to let him donate the items to the food pantry volunteers personally. He was amazed at how many items he was able to buy—and donate. He learned budgeting skills while developing a charitable spirit. I can't think of a more enriching summer program for children.

Your kids are probably better at using the computer than you are anyway, so it's super-easy for them to use CouponMom.com to find great deals for donating. In fact, my son's third-grade teacher was the inspiration for the CouponMom.com No-Clip System. We were teaching nine-year-olds how to shop for charity items with coupons, and she immediately recognized that it would be too tedious and confusing for kids to have to cut out and organize a stack of coupons, to use only a few. It was her idea for me to start listing the dates certain coupons were printed so that the students needed only to keep track of the circulars. Then they would be able to search CouponMom.com and easily figure out where to find specific coupons they needed. As it turns out, that system works pretty well for adults, too!

Get started by having your child find the coupon circulars from the Sunday newspaper. Have him or her write that day's date on the cover of the circular. (This can be an exercise in perfecting penmanship as well!) Then have your child save circulars in a box or file. When you decide which items you'd like to donate, search CouponMom.com to discover which circulars contain the coupons you need. Then it's time to get out the scissors.

Teaching your child the Cut Out Hunger program can be a lesson in patience, too. If you wait until an item goes on sale and then use a coupon, it may be possible to get that item for nothing. Free is especially good when your budget is $3! Even if you don't use coupons, you can still find deals by shopping sales.

Cut Out Hunger and Drugstores

Both Walgreens and CVS/Pharmacy have promotions that give shoppers automatic rebates in the form of coupons for use on future purchases. CVS/Pharmacy calls these Extra Bucks, and Walgreens calls them Register Rewards. Both are generous programs and are much easier to use than mail-in rebates, especially for children. When my son began his charity shopping, I gave him one of my Extra Bucks rewards from a previous week, so his first order was free. Each week he bought Extra Bucks promotional items so he received more Extra Bucks rewards for the following week and did not have any out-of-pocket expenses at the register after his initial week. With a little planning, he was able to continue getting free items each week using this method of rolling the Extra Bucks to the next week. The free items included toothpaste, toothbrushes, deodorant, and shampoo, which charities always need. (The drugstore savings chapter gives full details on how these programs work.)

Scanning weekly advertising circulars for drugstores or your grocery store is a great way to spot great charity freebies. Look for sales and "buy one, get one free" offers from the newspaper. The weekly CVS/Pharmacy ad matches promotional items with their Extra Bucks rewards, making it easy to find good freebies for charity.

Over the years I've heard from many teachers, Scout leaders, Sunday School teachers, and youth-group organizers who have taught students to buy food for charity with coupons. These folks have taught everyone from four-year-olds in vacation Bible school to twenty-year-old college students how to save and give. The Cut Out Hunger concept works because there is very little cost, and people of every age appreciate the joy of donating food to charity.

Here's an example of the great stories I hear from CouponMom.com members:

> *"Your program inspired me to ask my daughter's Spanish club to collect coupons to buy inexpensive food for for the Community of Faith Food*

Pantry, which serves more than eighty families a week in Northern Virginia. The group of nine- to twelve-year-olds will be volunteering there later this summer, and the pastor in charge is grateful—not only for the extra food but for the kids' second-language skills, which will come in handy, since most of the families are Spanish-speaking."

—Kim, a CouponMom.com member in the
Washington, D.C., area

Use Coupons to Help Our Nation's Servicemen and Servicewomen

Troops, listen up. We're on a mission to help the good men and women serving our country overseas. I'm officially enlisting every one of you for Operation Expiration. Now drop and give me 20 . . . expired coupons!

Shoppers often complain that coupons expire before they can be used, but military personnel serving abroad can still use them. Grocery stores and commissaries at U.S. military bases overseas will accept grocery coupons up to 6 months past their expiration date. If you find yourself with expired grocery coupons, you can send them to one of the bases to help military families save money on groceries.

A few bases have contacted me to help publicize this program to readers. In response to their requests, we've created a special section on Coupon-Mom.com called Military Coupon Program. This section lists addresses for several overseas military bases. Simply mail any type of grocery coupons you'd like to send to one of the addresses (from the newspaper, mail, or printed online). You will pay domestic postal rates rather than international postal rates.

They suggest you send coupons for products in categories such as canned food, dairy, frozen food, personal-care items, household cleaners, baking mixes, cereals, beverages, and baby items, such as diapers. It's helpful if you sort the coupons by category in envelopes. Because it can take several weeks for your coupons to reach the person who's going to use them, send coupons that are not more than than three months past their expiration date. And of course it is fine to send non-expired coupons.

Cutting out and sorting coupons for the military families who are serving your family and others is also a great project for social groups, youth groups, scouting organizations, and school service programs. Students can collect coupon circulars in a box at school or their place of worship and have plenty of coupons to cut out. Again, this is a great lesson for our kids. It teaches them organizational skills while instilling an appreciation for servicemen and sevicewomen.

A Final Word

You don't have to be a wealthy philanthropist to make a real difference in your area. A nine-year-old with a $3 budget can get started today at meeting the needs of less fortunate families in your area. I think you'll find that the Strategic Shopping principles and the Cut Out Hunger program go nicely together, and that reaching out to help needy families in your community or military families serving abroad can be a wonderful bonding experience for your own family.

Acknowledgments

I am thankful to so many people who have helped get this book off the ground. A big thank-you to Nanette Noffsinger for her friendship and dedication in spreading the gospel of grocery coupons; to Janis Donnaud for sharing her vision and working diligently to make this book a reality; to William Shinker, Lucia Watson, Megan Newman, Miriam Rich, Lisa Johnson, Lindsay Gordon, and the entire team at Avery who took on the project; to Jennifer Brett for her creative flair and unflappable ability to work under pressure; to Lisa McMains and Julie Butterfield for their research assistance; and to Gary Seacrest for helping sort out the details.

Thank you to the entire team at CouponMom.com, who kept the operation running smoothly while I worked on the book. Thank you to the thousands of CouponMom.com members who donate food to charity to help feed the hungry; God bless you. Thanks most of all to my husband, Dave, and sons, David and Chris, for their understanding and patience, and for keeping their sense of humor throughout it all.

Resources

The following websites, books, articles, and studies have been used in researching this book.

WEBSITES

Grocery Stores and Other Retailers

www.aldi.com
www.save-a-lot.com
www.andersonsmarket.com
www.wholefoodsmarket.com
www.traderjoes.com
www.samsclub.com
www.costco.com
www.bjs.com
www.walmart.com
www.target.com
www.kmart.com

Farmers' Markets and USDA Information

The following is a directory of independent discount and salvage grocery stores.
http://www.andersonsmarket.info/directory
http://www.ams.usda.gov/ USDA Agricultural Marketing Service, Farmers market directory
www.pickyourown.org

Savings and How-to Guides

Thrifty fun tips: http://www.thriftyfun.com/tf21851078.tip.html
www.makeyourownyogurt.com
Member input on wholesale club deals: www.moneysavingmom.com
Organic Trade Association: www.ota.com
Go Organic website with coupon book: www.organicearthday.org
Certified Natural Organic website: www.naturallygrown.org
Erin Huffstetler, Frugal Living Guide: frugalliving.about.com
www.hillbillyhousewife.com/tomatojuice.htm
Measurements: www.yankeegrocery.com/ygfoodequiv.html
www.asknumbers.com/PoundsToGrams.aspx
www.omega3faq.com/omega-3-recommendations.php
Food substitutions: www.standeyo.com/News_Files/Food/ingred_subs.html

Bakery Outlet Directories

Interstate Bakeries Corporation, 740 outlets in the United States: www.bakeryoutlets
    .com/storelocator.asp
Weston Bakeries Corporation: www.gwbakeries.com/outlet.cfm
Bimbo Bakeries Corporation: www.bimbobakeriesusa.com/our_brands/outlet_stores.html

Dollar Stores

www.99only.com/index.htm (California, Nevada, Arizona, Texas)
www.dollartree.com/custserv/locate_store.cmd (thousands of stores in 48 states)

Discount Stores

www.familydollar.com
www.dollargeneral.com
www.aldi.com
www.save-a-lot.com
www.bottomdollar.com

Other Resources

www.clarkhoward.com
www.ultimatecheapskate.com
www.msn.com
www.amazon.com
www.commissaries.com
www.upromise.com

BOOKS

The Colorado Cache Cookbook, Junior League of Denver, 1978
Eat Healthy for $50 a Week, by Rhonda Barfield, Kensington, 1996
Fix-It and Forget-It Lightly, by Phyllis Pellman Good, Good Books 2004
20-Minute Menus, by Marian Burros, Simon and Schuster 1989
Good Food Gourmet by Jane Brody, Bantam, 1992
Better Homes and Gardens New Cook Book, Bantam 1981
Mindless Eating: Why We Eat More Than We Think, by Brian Wansink, Bantam, 2006

ARTICLES

Melinda Fulmer. "Dollar Stores: Where the Deals Are." MSN Money. http://articles.moneycentral.msn.com/SmartSpending/FindDealsOnline/dollar-stores-where-the-deals-are.aspx?ucpg=2.

Crossroads Resource Center report on USDA census data on farmers' markets. "Direct Farm Sales Rising Dramatically, New Agriculture Census Data Show." http://www.crcworks.org/press/direct090214.pdf.

Market basket cost comparison of Aldi to supermarkets and discount stores. "Aldi Hammers Low Prices with Grocery Price Comp Study." *Progressive Grocer.* http://www.progressivegrocer.com/progressivegrocer/content_display/supermarket-industry-news/e3i8ec34ef6f7ad9c7420545b0e44760920.

Dolson, Laura. "How to Make Cheap Steak Taste Good." About.com (May 2008). http://lowcarbdiets.about.com/od/cooking/a/goodcheapsteaks.htm?p=1.

Donvan, John, and Charles Herman. "Costco: a Bulk Buyer's Playground." ABCnews.com (April 2008). http://abcnews.go.com/Business/IndustryInfo/story?id=4726747&page=1.

Stewart, Martha. "Why Organic Milk Has Longer Shelf Life." *OC Register.* http://www.ocregister.com/life/milk-jewelry-pasteurized-1850484-silver-organic.

"National Center Works to Extend Shelf Life of Milk." http://www.ncfst.iit.edu/Media/maesl.html.

Banks, Drusilla. "Food Freshness: The Date on the Label." http://urbanext.illinois.edu/thriftyliving/tl-foodfreshness.html.

Millman, China. "'Flexitarians' Outpace Vegetarians." *Pittsburgh Post-Gazette* (Feb. 3, 2009). www.mailtribune.com/apps/pbcs.dll/article?AID=/20090203/LIFE/902030305.

Rosenthal, Elizabeth. "As More Eat Meat, a Bid to Cut Emissions." *New York Times* (Dec. 4, 2008). www.nytimes.com/2008/12/04/science/earth/04meat.html?scp=1&sq=as%20more%20eat%20meat%20a%20bid%20to%20cut%20emissions&st=cse.

Rainforest Action Network. "Facts About Beef." http://ran.org/new/kidscorner/about_rainforests/factsheets/facts_about_beef/.

Black, Ben. "Bottled Water Demand May Be Declining." Worldwatch Institute (Sept. 8, 2008). http://www.worldwatch.org/node/5878.

Abelson, Jenn. "Wal-Mart Drives for More Mass. Grocery Business." *Boston Globe* (Feb.

10, 2009). http://www.boston.com/business/articles/2009/02/10/wal_mart_drives_for_more_mass_grocery_business/.

"Survey: More Customers Turn to Coupons." *Supermarket News* (Feb. 13, 2009). http://supermarketnews.com/news/survey_coupons_0213/.

Organic food trends: Source: The Hartman Group, The Many Faces of Organic 2008, Summer 2008.

Jones, Sandra M. "High-end Beauty on a Budget." *Los Angeles Times* (June 13, 2009).

From Frugalliving.about.com; Erin Huffstetler, Frugal Living Guide. http://frugalliving.about.com/

"Understanding the USDA Beef Grading System." The BBQ Report (March 2, 2006). www.bbqreport.com/archives/barbecue/2006/03/02/understanding-the-usda-beef-grading-system.

Industry Websites

"Supermarket Facts: Industry Overview 2008." Food Marketing Institute. http://www.fmi.org/facts_figs/?fuseaction=superfact.

Studies on Shopper Behavior

Jones, Timothy. University of Arizona food waste study. http://couponing.about.com/od/groceryzone/a/food_waste.htm?nl=1.

Khandelwal, Manjima. "Body Language: A Study of Shopper Modality." Nielsen. http://en-us.nielsen.com/etc/medialib/nielsen_dotcom/en_us/documents/pdf/consumer_insight.Par.71594.File.pdf.

"Not on the List? The Truth about Impulse Purchases." Knowledge@Wharton (Jan. 7, 2009). http://knowledge.wharton.upenn.edu/article.cfm?articleid=2132.

Williams, Diane. "The Arbitron Retail Media Study, Volume 1: The Impact of Retail Audio Broadcasting in Grocery and Drugstores." http://www.arbitron.com/downloads/RetailMediaStudy.pdf.

"With U.S. Consumers Watching Their Wallets More Than Ever, Tuning into Shoppers' Mindsets Key to Warding Off Brand Switching." Nielsen (Oct. 16, 2008). http://en-us.nielsen.com/main/news/news_releases/2008/october/nielsen_with_u_s.

Organic Food Research

Naughton, Keith. "Natural Response: As Prices of Organic Foods Rise, Plain Old Fruits and Vegetables Suddenly Look Better." *Newsweek* (May 12, 2008). www.newsweek.com/id/135377.

"Organic Labeling and Marketing Information." United States Department of Agriculture Agricultural Marketing Service (October 2002; updated April 2008). www.ams.usda.gov/AMSv1.0/getfile?dDocName=STELDEV3004446.

Bittman, Mark. "Eating Food That's Better for You, Organic or Not." *New York Times* (March 22, 2009). www.nytimes.com/2009/03/22/weekinreview/22bittman.html? scp=1&sq=eating%20food%20that's%20better%20for%20you,%20organic %20or%20not&st=cse.

Knitter, Sally. "How to Get Chlorine out of Drinking Water Easily." eHow. www.ehow .com/how_4574610_chlorine-out-drinking-water-easily.html.

Natural Sources

Hoback, Jane. "FDA Refuses to Define Natural." *Natural Foods Merchandiser* (Jan. 22, 2008). http://naturalfoodsmerchandiser.com/tabId/109/itemId/2873/FDA-refuses-to-define-natural.aspx.

Houchins, Jeannie. "Is There a Definition for Natural Foods?" Institute of Food Technologists press release (June 30, 2008). www.am-fe.ift.org/cms/?pid=1000744.

Certified Naturally Grown Sources

www.naturallygrown.org

Maiser, Jennifer. "10 Steps to Becoming a Locavore." *PBS Now* (week of November 2, 2007). www.pbs.org/now/shows/344/locavore.html.

Appendix 1. Selected Organic and Natural Food Companies with Printable Coupons

Company Name	Website URL	E-mail sign up required to print coupons?
After the Fall	www.atfjuices.com	No
Alexia Foods	www.alexiafoods.com	Yes
Apple & Eve	www.appleandeve.com	Yes
Back to Nature	www.backtonaturefoods.com	Print $5.00 money-back guarantee form
Batter Blaster	www.batterblaster.com	No
Blue Diamond	www.bluediamond.com	No
Borden	www.bordenorganic.com	No
Brown Cow	www.browncowfarm.com	Yes
Cedar's	www.cedarsfoods.com	No
Coleman Natural Foods	www.colemannatural.com	
Country Choice	www.countrychoicenaturals.com	Yes
Delallo	www.delallo.com	No
Dogswell	www.dogswell.com	No
Dreamfields Foods	www.dreamfieldsfoods.com	Yes
Earth's Best	www.earthsbest.com	Yes

Earthbound Farm	www.ebfarm.com	Yes
Enjoy Life	www.enjoylifefoods.com	No
First Juice	www.firstjuice.com	Yes
Halo	www.halopets.com	Yes
Hansen Beverage Company	www.drinkjuniorjuice.com	No
Health eSavers	www.healthesavers.com	Yes
Hill's Pet Nutrition	www.hillspet.com	Yes
Homemade Baby	www.homemadebaby.com	Yes
Horizon Organic	www.horizonorganic.com	Yes
Ian's Natural Foods	www.iansnaturalfoods.com	Yes
Knudsen & Sons, Inc.	www.knudsenjuices.com	Yes
Laura's Lean Beef	www.laurasleanbeef.com	Yes
Litehouse	www.litehousefoods.com	Yes
Mambo Sprouts	www.mambosprouts.com	No
Mrs. Meyer's	www.mrsmeyers.com	Yes
Nature's Oasis	www.naturesoasismarket.com	Yes
Northland	www.northlandjuices.com	Yes
Oikos	www.oikosorganic.com	Yes
The Organic Cow	www.theorganiccow.com	No
Organic Prairie	www.organicprairie.coop	No
Organic Valley	www.organicvalley.coop	Yes
PJ Madison's	www.pjmadisons.com	Yes
Rice Select	www.riceselect.com	No
Santa Cruz Natural	www.scojuice.com	Yes
Seeds of Change	www.seedsofchangefoods.com	No
Seventh Generation	www.seventhgeneration.com	No
Silver Spring Foods	http://silverspringgardens.com	Yes

Simply Organic	www.simplyorganicfoods.com	No
Smart Chicken	www.smartchicken.com	Yes
Soy Dream	www.tastethedream.com	Yes
Stonyfield Farm	www.stonyfield.com	Yes
Tribe	www.tribehummus.com	No
Wild Harvest	www.wildharvestorganic.com	No

Appendix 2. Organic and Natural Food Companies That Mail Free Coupons in Response to E-mail Requests

Alexia	www.alexiafoods.com
Amy's	www.amyskitchen.com
Apple & Eve	www.appleandeve.com
Arrowhead Mills	www.arrowheadmills.com
Born Free/Radlo Foods	www.radlo.com
Clif	www.clifbar.com
Coleman	www.colemannatural.com
Country Choice	www.countrychoicenaturals.com
Earth's Best	www.earthsbest.com
Earthbound Farm	www.ebfarm.com
Eggland's Best	www.egglandsbest.com
Ians	www.iansnaturalfoods.com
Kashi	www.kashi.com
Lakewood	www.lakewoodjuices.com
Lundberg	www.lundberg.com
Mrs. Meyer's	www.mrsmeyers.com
Rachel's	www.rachelsdairy.com
R. W. Knudsen Family	www.knudsenjuices.com

Rudi's Organic Bakery	www.rudisbakery.com
Santa Cruz Organics	www.scojuice.com
Soy Dream	www.tastethedream.com
Stonyfield Farm	www.stonyfield.com
Sue Bee Honey	www.suebee.com
Traditional Medicinals	www.traditionalmedicinals.com
Vans International Foods	www.vansfoods.com
Yogi	www.yogiproducts.com

Appendix 3. Companies That Mail Coupons in Response to an E-mail Request via Their Website

Please note: Coupon availability and specific offers can vary based on each company's supplies.

Company Name	Company or Brand URL
Amy's Kitchen	www.amyskitchen.com
Bar S	www.bar-s.com
Barber Foods	www.barberfoods.com
Bayer/Flintstones Vitamins	www.flintstonesvitamins.com
Birds Eye Foods	www.birdseyefoods.com
Carl Buddig & Company	www.buddig.com
Chiquita/Fresh Express	wwwfreshexpress.com
Citrus World/Florida's Natural	www.floridasnatural.com
Colgate-Palmolive	www.colgate.com/app/Colgate/US/HomePage.cvsp
The Dannon Company	www.dannon.com
Dean Foods/Garelick Farms	www.garelickfarms.com http://www.deanfoods.com/brands.aspx
Frito-Lay/Tostitos	www.tostitos.com
General Mills/Yoplait	http://yoplait.com/

George Weston Bakeries (Bimbo and Boboli)	www.boboli.com
Grand Brands/True Lemon	http://www.truelemon.com/
The Hain Celestial Group	www.celestialseasonings.com
The Hain Celestial Group/ Terra Chips	http://www.terrachips.com/
H. J. Heinz Company	www.heinz.com
H. J. Heinz Company/Lea & Perrins	www.leaperrins.com
Interstate Bakeries Corporation/Wonder	http://www.wonderbread.com/#/home
Jasper Wyman & Son	http://www.wymans.com/
Johnson & Johnson	www.jnj.com/connect
Johnson & Johnson/Viactiv	http://www.viactiv.com/index.jhtml
Ken's Foods/Sweet Baby Ray's	http://www.sweetbabyrays.com/
Kimberly Clark/Kotex	www.kotex.com/na/default.aspx
Martin's Famous Pastry Shoppe	www.martinspotatorolls.com/pages/about.asp
McCormick & Company	www.mccormick.com
Mt. Olive Pickle Company	http://www.mtolivepickles.com/
Ocean Spray Cranberries	http://oceanspray.com/
Nestlé/Edy's	www.edys.com
Nestlé/Purina	http://catchow.com/
P&G	http://pgpromotions.archway.com
P&G/Cheer	http://www.cheer.com. Click on Promotions link.
P&G/Febreze	www.newfebreze.com/coupon/MailRequest.php
Pepperidge Farm	http://www.pepperidgefarm.com/
Perdue	http://www.perdue.com/
Pillsbury/Smucker's	http://www.smuckers.com/

Reckitt Benckiser/ Electrasol	http://electrasol.com/
S. C. Johnson & Son/Glade	www.glade.com
S. C. Johnson & Son/Pledge	http://www.pledge.com/
S.C. Johnson & Son/Saran	http://www.saranbrands.com/
Tetley	http://www.tetleyusa.com/
Turkey Hill Dairy	http://turkeyhill.com/
Tyson Foods	http://www.tyson.com/
Unilever/Ragú	http://www.ragu.com/
Zatarain's	http://zatarains.com/

Index